W9-CNQ-706

Project EXCEPTIONAL

Exceptional Children: Education in Preschool Techniques
for Inclusion, Opportunity-Building, Nurturing, and Learning

A Guide for Training and Recruiting
Child Care Providers to Serve
Young Children with Disabilities

Volume 1

Edited by Anne Kuschner, Linda Cranor, and Linda Brekken

Publishing Information

Project EXCEPTIONAL: A Guide for Training and Recruiting Child Care Providers to Serve Young Children with Disabilities, Volume 1, was prepared under the direction of the Child Development Division, California Department of Education.

This publication was edited by Ralph Hanson, working in cooperation with Eva Vasquez, Child Development Consultant; Linda Cranor, Project EXCEPTIONAL Coordinator; and Anne Kuschner, Project EXCEP-TIONAL Director. It was designed and prepared for photo-offset production by the staff of the Bureau of Publications, with the cover and interior design created and prepared by Cheryl McDonald and Juan Sanchez. Typesetting was done by Anna Boyd, Jamie Contreras, Jeannette Huff, and Carey Johnson.

It was published by the Department of Education, 721 Capitol Mall, Sacramento, California (mailing address: P.O. Box 944272, Sacramento, CA 94244-2720). It was printed by the Office of State Printing and distributed under the provisions of the Library Distribution Act and *Government Code* Section 11096.

© 1996 by the California Department of Education
All rights reserved

ISBN 0-8011-1256-7

Ordering Information

Copies of this publication are available for $18.50 each, plus sales tax for California residents, from the Bureau of Publications, Sales Unit, California Department of Education, P.O. Box 271, Sacramento, CA 95812-0271; fax (916) 323-0823. See page 197 for complete information on payment, including credit card purchases.

A partial list of other educational resources available from the Department appears on page 196. In addition, the *Educational Resources Catalog,* and a 1996 supplement to the catalog, describing publications, videos, and other instructional media available from the Department can be obtained without charge by writing to the address given above or by calling the Sales Unit at (916) 445-1260.

Notice

The materials presented in this document are designed to provide accurate and authoritative information on the topics covered. They are made available with the understanding that neither the California Department of Education, the Napa County Office of Education, nor the authors are rendering medical, legal, or other professional advice. Because new laws and regulations are forthcoming and research continues, trainers should ensure that the information they present is always current.

Contents

Bea Gold, M.A.

This topic includes a historical perspective of the disability rights movement from an era of state institutional care to community-based services. It highlights the significance of equal opportunities for persons with disabilities and their families. The critical need for child care options for children with exceptional care needs is discussed, as well as the ways in which *everyone benefits* when children with disabilities are included in local child care settings.

Gina Guarneri, M.A.

The focus of this material is *ability awareness and respect for diversity.* Hand in hand with looking at how myths affect one's perceptions, attitudes, and actions, the importance of knowing one's feelings and values about disabilities is discussed. An underlying theme is the significance of the development by children of feelings of positive self-worth and the important role caregivers play in viewing children in the context of their "wholeness."

Barbara Coccodrilli Carlson; Linda Swenson Cranor; and Anne Kuschner, M.A.

Highlighted in this topic are the special issues that families of young children with disabilities face when looking for child care. The similarity in needs of families with and without children who have disabilities is a primary theme. Emphasis is placed on the uniqueness of individual family members and the diversity of families in general. The normal emotional reactions parents may experience on learning of their child's disability are reviewed. The caregiver's role in providing services to families is examined.

Beth Hannaman, M.A.; and Kristin Zink, M.A., M.S.

Key concepts of developmentally appropriate integrated care are presented and discussed. Also examined is the role of the caregiver in the creation of an environment that enhances the optimal development of all children. The primary focus of this material is on observation, play, and social interaction. The benefits and challenges of *including children with disabilities* in community care are emphasized throughout.

Preface

The goal of Project EXCEPTIONAL is to increase the quality and quantity of child care options for children with disabilities throughout California.

Project EXCEPTIONAL was developed by the Napa County Office of Education, with funding from the Child Development Division of the California Department of Education. The project was originally funded under Senate Bill 2194, sponsored by State Senator Becky Morgan. Additional funding for the continuing product development and training efforts of Project EXCEPTIONAL has been awarded to the California Institute on Human Services at Sonoma State University through a grant by the federal Office of Special Education and Rehabilitation Services (OSERS), Washington, D.C.

The primary focus of the project has been to develop for California's child care and development field a replicable statewide training model for the inclusion of young children with disabilities, birth through five years of age, in community child care settings.

An additional task was to conduct three statewide Training of Trainers workshops to familiarize participants with both the content and the model. Participants were representative of interagency, community-based teams. Each of these teams has in turn developed community action plans for implementing training for child care and development staff at the local level. Trainings conducted by the community teams have far exceeded the anticipated outcomes of the trainers workshops. The enthusiastic replication of these trainings across the state continues to validate the tremendous need of child care and development staff for information about the care of young children with disabilities.

The *Project EXCEPTIONAL* publication consists of two volumes. Volume 1 contains nine monographs written for the purpose of training and recruiting child care and development staff to work with young children with disabilities and their families. Volume 2 is a collection of training activities which have been aligned with each of the major content areas in Volume 1. Included in Volume 2 is the section titled "Successful Staff Development: Tips and Techniques for Training."

All children benefit when young children with disabilities are included in family and community child care settings staffed by trained and sensitive caregivers. The Department hopes that the use of this guide will help make that ideal a reality.

JANE IRVINE HENDERSON
Deputy Superintendent
Child, Youth, and Family Services Branch

JANET POOLE
Administrator
Professional Development Unit
Child Development Division

EVA VASQUEZ
Child Development Consultant
Professional Development Unit
Child Development Division

Acknowledgments

This body of work (Volumes 1 and 2) represents the efforts of a dedicated group of parents and professionals from throughout California. It is with sincere gratitude and admiration that we acknowledge these individuals for their contributions.

Administrative Support

Ed Henderson, Superintendent; **Tony Apolloni,** Assistant Superintendent; and **Erwin Bollinger,** Director of Special Education, Napa County Office of Education

Advisory Committee

- **Kathy Alverado,** Alverado Family Child Care, Calimesa
- **Maurine Ballard-Rosa,** California State University, Sacramento
- **Linda Brekken,** Personnel Development for Infant Preschool Programs, California Department of Education
- **Barbara Coccodrilli Carlson,** Child Care Law Center, San Francisco
- **Joya Chatterjee,** Santa Clara Unified School District
- **Gary Deluhery,** Bayshore Child Care Services, Daly City
- **Yolanda Garcia,** Santa Clara Office of Education
- **Bea Gold,** Child Advocate, Los Angeles
- **Claire Gover,** Solano Family Children's Council, Fairfield
- **Sara Jimenez-McSweyn,** Children's Institute International, Los Angeles
- **Deborah Johnson,** School of Mental Health, Los Angeles Unified School District
- **Marie Kanne Poulsen,** University Affiliated Program, Children's Hospital, Los Angeles
- **Betsy Qualls,** Special Education Division, California Department of Education
- **Amanda Shipman,** Drew Child Development Corporation, Los Angeles
- **Kate Warren,** BANANAS, Inc., Child Care Resource and Referral Agency, Oakland
- **Norman Yee,** Wu Yee Resource and Referral Center, San Francisco

Consultants

Linda Brekken, Debbie Duplantis, Ginger Gregory, Dillon Henry, Keeta Lewis, Paulette Litz, Lynne Vaughan, and Helen Walka

Document Setup and Technical Editing

Daniel Kent, Josephina Kent, Mary Laughton, Marney McKinley, and Dorothy Pitts

Photographer

Jenette Raymond

Photo Sites

ASI Children's Center, California State University, Sacramento; Community Resources for Children, Napa; First Step Children's Center, Oakland; the home of Jim and Claire Gover, Vallejo; the home of Karl and Patty Schweiger, Napa; Napa County Office of Education, Early Childhood Special Education and Child Development Programs; Napa Valley Child Care; Napa Valley Head Start; Play and Learn Family Day Care, Fairfield

Secretarial Assistance

Diane Howell, DeLora Slattery, and Kelly Tate

Technical Computer Assistance

Lynne Vaughan

Trainers

Ann Carr, Gary Deluhery, Yolanda Garcia, Whit Hayslip, Kathy Heftman, Dillon Henry, Deborah Johnson, Nora Snowden, and Mary Ann Walker

Reviewers

Gina Guarneri, Sharon Hawley, Whit Hayslip, Kathy Heftman, Kim Thomas-Dozier, Nancy Lim-Yee, Mary Ann Walker, and project advisers

Writers

- Barbara Coccodrilli Carlson
- Ann B. Carr
- Abby J. Cohen
- Bea Gold
- Gina Guarneri
- Beth Hannaman
- Kathy Heftman
- Keeta Lewis
- Eleanor W. Lynch
- Marie Kanne Poulsen
- Karla Snorf
- Nora Snowden
- Kate Warren
- Kristin Zink

Special thanks go to **Robert Cervantes,** former Director of the Child Development Division, for his dedicated leadership in the field of early childhood development and his commitment to support exemplary practices in California; and to **Mary Smithberger** and **Eva Vasquez,** Child Development Consultants, for their support of this project and work on behalf of all young children and their families.

Note: The titles and locations of the persons included in this list were current at the time this document was developed.

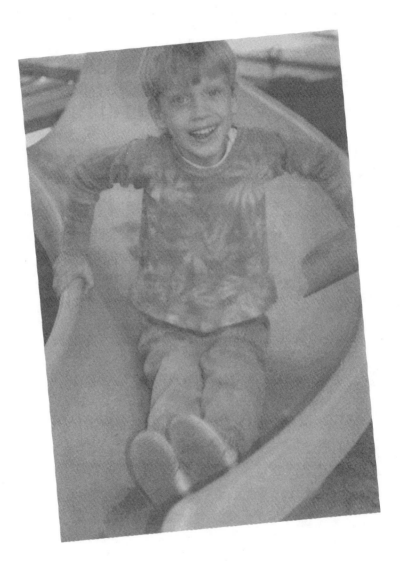

The photographs in this publication show children who have a range of disabilities or are at risk for becoming disabled. They document solitary moments as well as social ones with families and friends at home, in preschool, and in the community.

Gratitude is extended to the families that have offered their support to this project by allowing us to include these photographs of their children.

Introduction

Until one is committed, there is hesitancy,
The chance to draw back, always ineffectiveness
Concerning all acts of initiative and creation.
There is one elementary truth,
the ignorance of which kills countless ideas
and splendid plans.
That the moment one definitely commits oneself
then Providence moves, too.
All sorts of things occur to help one,
that never would otherwise have occurred.
A whole stream of events issues from the decision,
Raising on one's favor all manner
of unforeseen incidents and meetings and
material assistance
which no one could have dreamt would have
come their way.

— Johann Wolfgang von Goethe

eeting the goals of Project EXCEPTIONAL has involved the individual commitment of many people willing to come together in a collaborative statewide effort. Their purpose was to create a product that would influence how the concept of community is viewed to include and value the uniqueness and diversity of each of its members. For this purpose to be accomplished, it has been critical to understand issues and needs that affect families and child care and development staff. It has been equally important to learn what is working well at local levels and to encourage opportunities for those experiences to be shared with others.

All materials developed through Project EXCEPTIONAL should reflect the integrity of what each contributor believes to be important—not only in the

care of children with disabilities but in the care of all children. Equally important has been the task of developing materials that reflect sensitivity, an understanding of families of children with disabilities, and the growing need for child care that is affordable and accessible. The purpose of the project is to highlight the critical need for child care and development staff to include children with disabilities in their care and to consider the importance of the community in training and in the development of materials. The greatest influence on creating child care options for families of children with disabilities is the identification of local resources and people that together can achieve a common goal.

All aspects of this project have been guided by a set of belief statements developed by staff, advisers, and writers. The statements that follow represent the perspectives of families, child care and development staff, and persons specializing in early childhood education and special education.

Belief Statements

- When children with disabilities are included in community child care settings, everyone benefits: all children, all families, all professionals, and all communities.

- All children have a right to grow up, play, and live in their own communities. They have a right to feel included, welcomed, and accepted in every aspect of their lives.

- Child care professionals are in favorable positions to bring young children together. They have an opportunity to influence significantly the lives of individual children as well as tomorrow's generations of adult decision makers.

- Child care is a need every family has. Families who have children with disabilities often have additional or greater needs because their options are often limited or nonexistent.

- Child care agencies act responsibly when they demonstrate the willingness to collaborate on local levels and provide services that address family need and support family focus.

- Every professional who works in community services should understand the nature of discrimination and its effects on the lives of those with limited access.

- At the heart of successful child care placements is willingness to assist families, build relationships with those families, and trust their capabilities as quality caregivers.

- Children accept diversity more easily when they are young. Each of us is responsible for providing greater access and inclusion in our communities for children with disabilities and their families.

Supporting Change

Project EXCEPTIONAL deals with the process of change: in how we view children; how parents are able to meet their own needs and the needs of their children; how legislation assists individuals with disabilities in their efforts to be included in their communities and everyday life experiences; and how professionals see their roles. Under any circumstance change is a complicated process—whether it involves an individual, a group of individuals, or large systems. We must pay close attention to those whose lives may be influenced by change. Change implies a willingness to be flexible and accommodate a variety of opinions and needs. It occurs when all of those involved have ownership in the process and a common vision about the ultimate outcome. Finally, success is ensured when it is recognized that change is not static but is a process of moving forward and at times taking divergent paths.

Every individual can become a change agent. Social change begins with a single step or action that makes a difference in the life of another. Full inclusion of individuals with disabilities in all aspects of community life must be viewed within the context of social change.

Foundations Underlying Project EXCEPTIONAL

Project EXCEPTIONAL consists of two volumes. Volume 1 contains nine monographs written for the training and recruitment of child care and development staff who work with young children with disabilities and their families. Volume 2 is a collection of descriptions of training activities aligned with each of the nine major content areas in Volume 1. Included in Volume 2 is the chapter titled "Successful Staff Development: Tips and Techniques for Training."

Belief statements have been incorporated throughout Volumes 1 and 2. In addition, project staff and writers agreed on the following foundations as a guide for writing the training monographs and training procedures:

1. **Fundamentals.** Materials are intended to be introductory. Typically, individuals in the field of child care have a range of skills and training experiences. These materials are written for trainers who will be working with groups of caregivers who have limited or no experience caring for children with disabilities.

2. **Adaptability.** Materials used in training sessions can easily be adapted to the specific levels of experience or needs of the users. For example, a community college instructor may want to align the material with coursework in early childhood education. Another trainer may want to use materials from selected content areas in providing community workshops for family child care providers and center staff.

3. **Key concepts.** Key concepts have been incorporated in each specific training area. They are focused on group training because this publication is not intended to be a specific how-to training manual that can address every anticipated area of need. However, references and additional resources are included to provide trainers with more information.

4. **Focus on the whole child.** Critical to the use of the materials is that the child be viewed within the context of family,

culture, and community. Children are viewed as children first—before their disability is considered.

5. **Enhancement of child development knowledge and skills.** Materials have been developed to enhance what child care and development staff already understand about caring for young children and to build on that existing knowledge and experience. Resistance to new challenges often stems from lack of information. By sharing information, identifying available resources, and providing ongoing training and support, child care and development staff will further develop their skills.

6. **Collaboration and teaming.** Through the development of strategies that support people working together, the concepts of teaming and collaboration are built into the core areas of training. The successful placement of children with disabilities into community child care settings is often dependent on the ability of families and professionals to develop a workable program together.

7. **Development of confidence and competence.** A philosophical underpinning of effective care is that for children, families, and providers alike, confidence and competence are fostered when individual strengths are identified, recognized, and enhanced.

8. **Respect for individuality and diversity.** Fundamental to the development of the project materials is the belief that all services should be directed in accordance with the concerns, priorities, and needs of individual children and families. All children need to be understood in relation to age, gender, personality, culture, and family makeup. Knowing children on an individual basis is the

key to providing successful child care experiences for all children. It would be unreasonable to expect anyone to learn all there is to know about each area of disability.

9. **Benefits for everyone.** To be effective change agents and to support providers in their work, trainers must communicate that when children with disabilities are included in child care settings, everyone benefits. In this way, professionals become active in changing stereotypes and broadening understanding of human diversity and the uniqueness of the individual.

Design of Project Training Materials

Project EXCEPTIONAL offers several innovative approaches to training.

First, it emphasizes the role of the family as a unit in natural community settings and highlights the importance of including parents in the planning and conduct of trainings.

Second, it provides a curriculum that emphasizes interdisciplinary approaches and the training of community teams in the benefits of cooperative program planning and implementation.

Third, it uses a training-of-trainers model but predicates that training on the attendance of a community team composed minimally of child care and development staff, parents or parent advocates, and early childhood education and special education professionals. This requirement sets the stage for interagency cooperation at the local level.

The nine monographs in Volume 1 are designed as resources for trainers and may also be used as references for child care and development staff. These materials can be used in a sequence of training sessions or in individual topic-specific workshops. The information is presented at an introductory level to assist trainers in presenting concepts that may be unfamiliar to child care and development staff. Key points are identified at the end of each narrative as a means of highlighting significant concepts.

Volume 2 includes training activities that correspond to the nine core areas in Volume 1. Activities designed to facilitate the interactive learning of participants have been created to enhance the collaborative learning process of trainers and participants. Each activity is planned to allow the participants to complete an experiential learning cycle.[1] Experiential learning occurs when a person engages in some activity *(experiencing)*, shares reactions to that activity with other participants *(publishing)*, abstracts some useful insight that could be used outside the activity setting *(generalizing)*, and puts that insight to work by determining how it could be used in actual situations *(applying)*.

Many of the training activities can be used with different content, and a variety of activities are provided so that trainers can select the most suitable activity for a particular group. Trainers should feel free to modify activities to meet the needs of participants. The activity format is designed to assist trainers in selecting appropriate activities and in planning, implementing, and evaluating each activity.

Targeted Audiences

Project EXCEPTIONAL materials were developed as a guide for training and recruiting child care providers to serve young children with disabilities.

Materials have been designed for use by community college and university instructors and by community trainers who conduct workshops for the following audiences:

- Child care and development staff

- Family day care providers

- Resource and referral staff

- Parents of young children with disabilities

- High school classes, including those in vocational programs

- Paraprofessionals in early childhood education and special education programs

- Specialists and personnel in special education who have limited experience working with community child development programs or family day care homes

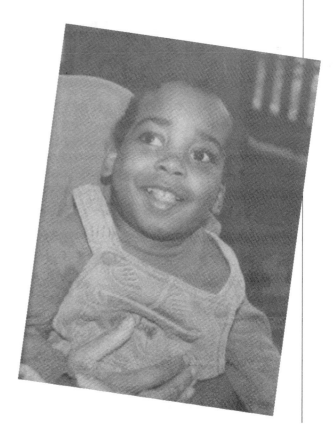

---

1. J. W. Pfeiffer. *The Encyclopedia of Team Development Activities*. San Diego: University Associates, Inc., 1991.

Community Commitment

A basic premise of Project EXCEPTIONAL is that all communities include child care providers who, given support and training, are willing to care for children with disabilities. In addition, there is the belief that the needed expertise and training can be found in all communities. However, in spite of numerous individual efforts, a number of significant barriers remain to obtaining child care for families in California. Lacking is an awareness of how critical the need is. In addition, only limited efforts are being made to coordinate the recruitment and training of child care providers. This project has evolved in recognition of the need. Training sessions throughout California have reinforced the importance of offering opportunities for community teams to come together. As a result of quality training and opportunities for statewide networking, many more individuals have begun to share a vision for including young children with disabilities in local child care and development settings.

What its children become, that will the community become.

— Suzanne LaFollette

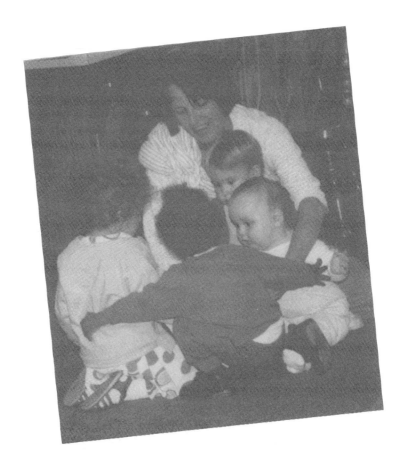

Chapter 1

Who Will Care for Our Children?

A Historical Perspective of Services for Young Children with Disabilities

By Bea Gold, M.A.

Introduction

ndividuals with disabilities have come a long way in their quest for equal opportunities, access to participation in their communities, and recognition as contributing members of society. The inclusion of citizens with varying needs in our communities and schools has been brought about through the dedicated work of people with disabilities, their families, and advocates representing many fields and disciplines. The disability rights movement is a people's movement that values and respects

There is always one moment in childhood when the door opens and lets the future in.

— Graham Greene

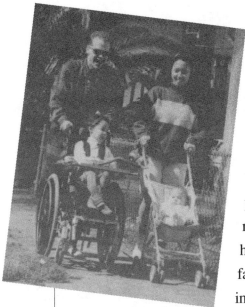

the uniqueness that each individual brings to the family, community, and society.

The disability rights movement has been guided by the belief that visions become realities when people are supported in fulfilling their dreams. As a result of this movement, a greater understanding of the needs, desires, and hopes of individuals with disabilities of all ages and their families has evolved. This understanding has led not only to an increase in community-based services but also to a greater emphasis on the development of services that are driven by the needs of families. These services include those that support families and enable them to build on their own strengths. As a result, advocacy efforts on behalf of young children with exceptional needs and their families have led to a focus on the inclusion in community child care settings of a growing number of these children. Caregivers providing these services strengthen these efforts by ensuring that community options in child care are available to *all* children and their families.

The purpose of this chapter is to promote an understanding of the critical need in California to increase options in child care for young children with disabilities. To do so requires an understanding of the disability rights movement in the United States and its effects on children, families, child care, and child development. This chapter is intended as a resource for child care and development staff and for administrators and others who provide leadership and training in child care and child development.

Highlighted in this chapter are issues related to the changing demographics of the American family, the needs of families who have children with disabilities, the child care system, and the coordination of community services. A historical overview of the advances in the rights of individuals with disabilities is provided, including legislation and court rulings that have paralleled the achievements of the civil rights movement.

ABOUT THE AUTHOR

Bea Gold is a child development specialist who recently retired as the founding director of Child and Family Services. CFS is an agency concentrating on child care, Head Start, and programs for infants and preschool children with disabilities and their families. She serves on the editorial panel of the National Association for the Education of Young Children, represents the California First Chance Consortium on the Child Development Coalition, and works as an advocate for exceptional children. She entered the field of early childhood special education in 1963 and is fortunate to have been able to observe firsthand the significant changes in laws and services that affect the lives of young children with disabilities and their families.

Our Changing Society

In my visits with disabled people around the world, I have learned that we all share the same dream—of being valued members of society with an equal chance of success.

— Judy Heumann

A number of evident changes in our society have resulted from the efforts of those seeking to carve out a new world. The language we use to describe individuals with disabilities has changed, public and private services and buildings are more accessible, and people of diverse strengths and needs are living and working side by side in our communities.

The belief that individuals with disabilities are people first and people with disabilities second shapes the language that we use and sends powerful messages. When referring to a child with exceptional needs, it is most appropriate to refer to "children with disabilities" or "a child who has a hearing impairment" rather than say "handicapped children." This language emphasizes that *children with disabilities are children first,* with the same needs as all children. Other options for referring to children with disabilities that may be less stigmatizing include children with varying abilities or who are differently able. It is important to see the whole child, including strengths as well as special needs. This concept of people first is reflected in the terminology of recent legislation—the Americans with Disabilities Act (ADA) and the Individuals with Disabilities Education Act (IDEA). A discussion of these laws is presented later in this chapter. Suggestions for thinking about our language are also included in Appendix 1-A.

The visibility of individuals with disabilities is increasing not only in daily life but in the media as well. Such films as *The Scent of a Woman, Rain Man, My Left Foot, Born on the Fourth of July, Forrest Gump, Man Without a Face, Philadelphia*, and *Nell* feature people with varying disabling conditions, needs, and abilities. So do such television series as *Life Goes On, Reasonable Doubts, Sesame Street*, and *Mr.*

Rogers's Neighborhood. In addition, advertisements are including children who are differently able. This media visibility helps to portray individuals with disabilities as having many abilities. It parallels our changing communities and the increasing number of children and adults with exceptional needs seen in our restaurants, churches, schools, parks, and in all other aspects of daily life.

Access to public buildings and services has increased the number of opportunities that individuals with varying abilities have to participate within their own communities. For example, public transportation systems are now designed to accommodate all needs; elevators not only have Braille on the control panel but also have a voice system that tells what floor one is on; and telecommunication devices allow the deaf or hard of hearing to communicate by telephone. Curb cuts and restroom facilities for individuals with exceptional needs are now taken for granted and appreciated by many people who have strollers for their young children or are on crutches.

The Needs of Families

Dramatic changes in the structure of American families have occurred during the past three decades. Because we are so mobile, many parents can no longer rely on nearby relatives to provide advice, emotional support, and assistance in caring for children. Families are very different from the *Ozzie and Harriet* television images of the early 1960s. Families of the 1990s include single-parent households, teenage parents, grandparents, and adoptive and foster families.

Risk factors for families of young children have increased across all social and economic levels. Examples of risk factors include poverty, environmental hazards, low birth weight resulting from inadequate prenatal care, and birth to a parent who is substance-addicted. These risk factors, in combination with advances in medical technology, have resulted in a greater survival rate for more children with handicapping conditions or other medical complications. The growing number of families of young children who may need early intervention services, including child care, are reflected in these trends. It is estimated conservatively that children with disabilities make up 10 percent of the school-age population. We see more families raising children with disabilities who will require extensive medical and educational support.

In the past, families were often advised to institutionalize their children with exceptional needs. Today, however, many families choose to raise their children at home. Supporting children in their own communities benefits children, their families, and local communities on many different levels. Nonetheless the economic realities of providing for a child with a handicapping condition result in increased cost to the family. Expenses often include costs for health and medical care, therapy services, transportation, special equipment, education, and diet. In extreme cases medical and nonmedical expenses directly attributable to the child's exceptional needs, estimated to average 12 percent of family income, can move a middle-class family into the category of the working poor. To meet these expenses, many parents of children with disabilities must earn additional income. And yet mothers of children with disabilities work an average of 100 hours per year less than parents of children without disabilities and earn an estimated 20 percent less because of their children's need for exceptional care.

Families of children with disabilities also face limited choices of child care, perhaps keeping the parents or guardians from becoming active members of California's workforce. And when they cannot find adequate child care, the families often experience additional problems and frustrations. The solution to this lack of options is to provide quality child care programs that include children with disabilities and are readily available and affordable. There is widespread support for parental choice in selecting child care and for the inclusion of young children with disabilities in community child care settings. What is needed is a statewide coordinated effort to address the issues of recruitment, availability, affordability, and training.

The Child Care Issue: Lack of Options

I am the single parent of a five-and-a-half-year-old severely handicapped daughter. . . . There is no such thing as day care available to my daughter. It does not matter who pays for it or what the cost is; it simply does not exist. I went through two licensed and four unlicensed day care homes (for six children and under) and one roommate. All but one told me on a Friday afternoon that they could no longer watch my daughter for whatever reason. . . .

— A mother's testimony before Congress

The 1990 U.S. Census disclosed that there are more than nine million children under the age of five in day care. The number of children in child care centers has almost doubled since 1977, and the number of working mothers with children under the age of three has, it is estimated, doubled since 1970. Children with disabilities are among this number—if their parents are able to find care. Little need exists to discuss the necessity for most mothers to work to maintain even a modest lifestyle. When a family has a child with a disability, the financial need can be even greater; but the parents may have fewer options for the care of their child.

A study of California's care services for children with disabilities (Berkeley Planning Associates 1988) showed that families were unable to find care by trained providers; and, even if found, parents were unable to afford the care. (See Appendix 1-B for the summary of the study.) The study also states that child care providers were interested in offering care to children with exceptional care needs; and if they received training, support, and appropriate compensation, they would be willing to serve these children. In 1988 an estimated 159,000 California children with exceptional needs, one-fourth of whom were below the age of five, had working mothers. In addition, more than 80,000 mothers of children with exceptional needs required child care. On the basis of estimates of population growth, child care needs, and the incidence of disability,

30,000 to 35,000 families of infants and preschoolers with disabilities were in need of child care in the early 1990s.

Meeting the Challenge in California

The Federal Child Care and Development Block Grant legislation of 1990 requires that states describe how they will serve children with disabilities and provides a mechanism for this purpose by which funds for training and support can be made available to child care providers. In 1992 California enacted legislation similar to the mandates of the federal Head Start preschool program requiring that children with disabilities make up 10 percent of the population served in child care and development programs.

Learning about the unique needs of young children with disabilities and their families and finding specialized services in the community may present challenges to child care providers. Providers need training, ongoing support, and technical assistance in addition to access to resources so that they can expand their skills and knowledge in this new area. When these supports are in place, caregivers report positive experiences in meeting the caregiving needs of children with disabilities. They report that these experiences have helped them consider the needs of all children.

As providers begin to work with and get to know children with disabilities and their families, they often say things such as the following:

- "He is more like the other children than different."

- "It works both ways; the children learn from each other."

- "I didn't know what to expect, but she's a great kid."

- "He learned to drink from a cup here first, and I loved it."

- "Her mother would have had to go on welfare if we didn't take the child."

- "We use every resource in the community to make it work, but it *does* work!"

California has supported with public funds a great variety of child care arrangements. The Child Development Division of the Department of Education contracts with both public and private nonprofit agencies to provide center-based care and family care homes. The Alternative Payment Program supports parental choice by allowing the parent to select from licensed child or exempt care in either the provider's or family's home. (Providers may be exempt from licensing if they serve children from only one family other than their own.)

Approximately 90 child care resource and referral agencies located throughout California assist parents in locating licensed care.

Although these additional supports and funds are often available, families and child care providers are not always aware of these resources. For example, if a program has a current contract with the California Department of Education, the law provides an adjusted reimbursement rate for children with exceptional needs at 1.2 times the regular rate. Children with severe handicapping conditions are reimbursed at 1.5 times the regular rate. However, as indicated in a statewide survey conducted by the Berkeley Planning Associates in 1988, less than 1 percent of the total enrollment of children in state-subsidized programs is billed at the higher rate allowed for children with disabilities. As attention is focused on increasing child care options for children with disabilities, all available financial and support resources must be used to the maximum to make this goal a reality. Additional information on adjusted reimbursement rates for children with exceptional needs is provided in chapter 9, titled "Nuts and Bolts: Administrative Issues in Serving Children with Exceptional Care Needs and Their Families."

Child care and development staff will need training and support if changes are to occur in the quantity and quality of services available to young children with disabilities. Families need to be able to select the best setting for their child, feel safe with their choice, and be able to trust their child care providers. Unless providers from a variety of programs are exposed to concepts about children with exceptional needs and are willing to attempt to include them in their programs, the term *parental choice* will be meaningless.

Coordination of Community Resources

When community-based child care works well for a child with disabilities, it often owes its success to a collaborative effort involving all agencies or programs connected with the family. Families often rely on numerous agencies and services to meet the ongoing needs of their children. How well these services work for the child and the family depends largely on the willingness of all to communicate and coordinate their roles, responsibilities, and goals for the child. In addition, families are helped when agencies work together to reduce stress in securing services and when the time required for managing transportation or coordination of services is minimized. These outcomes are realized when child care providers are regarded as critical members of a team in providing services to young children with disabilities and their families and the child care environment is viewed and used as an appropriate placement for these children.

Historical Perspective

When the architects of our republic wrote the magnificent words of the Constitution and the Declaration of Independence, they were signing a promissory note to which every American was to fall heir. This note was the promise that all men . . . would be guaranteed the unalienable rights of life, liberty, and the pursuit of happiness.

— Martin Luther King Jr.

As the rights of individuals with disabilities have been guaranteed, services for young children and their families have increasingly become a priority at the federal, state, and local levels. At the heart of this movement is the value we as Americans place on our children as our future and our belief that *every* child deserves equal opportunities to play, grow, and develop side by side with family and friends.

For the past 50 years, advocacy groups have been attempting to get federal legislation passed guaranteeing the rights of persons with disabilities. The U.S. Congress has passed laws and the U.S. Supreme Court has handed down major rulings to ensure the right of the individual to equal access to facilities, equal educational opportunities provided in integrated settings, and admission to jobs based on ability to do the work regardless of race, color, creed, national origin, ancestry, sex, marital status, disability, religious or political affiliation, age, or sexual orientation. Efforts continue to ensure that civil rights gains will not be lost. Advocates for individuals with disabilities have worked alongside other civil rights groups to ensure that citizens with disabilities are not denied those rights guaranteed by the Bill of Rights. *Americans enjoy more rights today than ever before, gained through the efforts of those who were willing to fight for what they believed were the rights of all Americans.* A review of the historical perspective will help us understand the changes that have occurred and their impact on young children with disabilities, their family members, and the child care community.

Key Federal Legislation and Court Decisions

The following federal legislation or policy decisions have had a major impact on civil rights for individuals with disabilities and the expansion of services to infants and preschoolers with exceptional needs and their families. (A historical time line of these issues is included in Appendix 1-C.)

- ***Brown*** v. ***Board of Education.*** In 1954 *Brown* v. *Board of Education of Topeka, Kansas,* came before the U.S. Supreme Court, which ruled that "separate educational facilities are inherently unequal." Although the case had to do with segregation of African-American children, the impact has been felt by all, including children with disabilities. Throughout the years the civil rights movement has been a model for advocates who deal with legal issues raised by citizens with disabilities in their pursuit of civil rights.

- **Head Start preschool program.** In 1965 Congress funded the Head Start preschool program as a part of the War on Poverty. In 1972 Congress passed legislation that required Head Start to reserve 10 percent of the program's enrollment for children with handicapping conditions.

- **Handicapped Children's Early Education Program.** As interest grew at the federal level in new theories of early childhood development that stress the importance of the first five years of life, programs were developed to apply these theoretical principles to young children with disabilities and their families. In 1968 the Handicapped Children's Early Education Program was established through federal legislation to create more and better services for young children with disabilities and their families. Young children were served in many different community settings, and parents were involved as partners in their child's education. Before 1968 very few programs were offered for young children with exceptional needs. Programs were usually offered at special centers or institutions and segregated by disability. Children who were blind or deaf or had orthopedic conditions were served categorically with other children with the same diagnosis.

- **Disability awareness and rights.** In the 1960s and 1970s several events increased acceptance of individuals with disabilities. In the early '60s President John F. Kennedy established the National Commission on Mental Retardation. Its creation brought national publicity to issues facing families with members who were developmentally disabled. Also in the '60s and '70s, Vietnam veterans spoke out for the rights of others with physical disabilities.

- **Section 504 of the Rehabilitation Act.** Section 504 of the Rehabilitation Act of 1973 (Public Law 93-112) requires accessibility to public facilities for individuals with disabilities. As a result, curbs in many places have been modified to allow wheelchairs to cross streets; special parking places have been provided so that people with exceptional needs are able to park close to the facility they need to enter; Braille indicators have been provided on elevators; toilet facilities have been made accessible for wheelchairs; and, more recently, sound systems have been installed at traffic lights to inform people with visual loss as to when it is safe to cross the street. *These changes promote equal access so that all people have the opportunity to lead full lives.*

- **The Education for the Handicapped Act.** In 1975 PL 94-142, the Education for the Handicapped Act (EHA), was enacted. This law requires states to ensure that children with disabilities receive a "free appropriate public education" with their nonhandicapped peers in the least restrictive environment (LRE) to the greatest extent possible. States were also encouraged to serve children with disabilities under the age of five. California established a mandate for preschoolers with "intensive needs" in 1980. Despite the emphasis on services in the least restrictive environment, there is no universal, "regular," publicly funded preschool program; and thus in some communities it has been difficult to provide special education programs in typical settings. During the reauthorization process in 1990, the EHA was renamed the Individuals with Disabilities Education Act (IDEA).

- **PL 99-457, the amendments to the Education for the Handicapped Act.** A significant feature of this revision, enacted in 1986, was the addition of services for infants and preschoolers and their families. The Handicapped Infant and Toddler Program (Part H) establishes incentives for states to plan for coordinated, comprehensive, multidisciplinary services to infants and toddlers with disabilities and their families over a five-year period. The program emphasizes family-focused services and interagency collaboration. The Preschool Handicapped Program (Section 619 of Part B) allowed states to phase in services for preschoolers with disabilities and their families over five years. The full mandate began on July 1, 1991. Both sections of this legislation emphasize the provision of services in natural environments.

- **The Americans with Disabilities Act.** The Americans with Disabilities Act (ADA) of 1990 is the most recent landmark civil rights protection bill that guarantees equal opportunities in employment, public accommodations, transportation, state and local governmental services, and telecommunications. *Under ADA day care providers may not refuse to serve persons who meet the definition of "disabled" or deny them the opportunity to participate in or benefit from the services offered* (Child Care Law Center, 1991).

- **Individuals with Disabilities Education Act (IDEA).** PL 101-476, the Individuals with Disabilities Education Act (IDEA), formerly known as the Education for the Handicapped Act, was enacted in 1990. In addition to expanding and otherwise changing the provisions for various services, this law also made a significant shift in terminology from "handicapped child" to "a child with a disability." The reauthorization of this legislation adds assistive technology, the use of computers, and other adaptive equipment as an early intervention service. Technology for individuals with disabilities has resulted in the development of competent, self-sufficient individuals. For example, children who just a few years ago were unable to make their needs known today have computerized devices that can help them talk, walk, or act in other positive and independent ways.

- **Federal Child Care and Development Block Grant.** The Federal Child Care and Development Block Grant of 1990 focuses on the quantity and quality of child care, parental choice, affordability of care, consumer education, the parents' complaint process, and provider training. This child care grant provides priority funding for low-income families and special-needs children. It also provides funds for improvement in the quality of child care programs. Each state has developed a plan for the use of these federal funds. California has included in the state plan the requirement that operators of child care and development programs (those receiving state and/or federal funds) include children with disabilities as 10 percent of their population. California has also developed planning councils in each county to address local needs, including how to serve children with special needs and how training for child care providers will be addressed.

Key California Legislation and Policy

- **Lanterman Developmental Disabilities Services Act.** In 1969 the Legislature passed into law the Lanterman Developmental Disabilities Services Act, which established a statewide program through 21 regional centers to provide services to people with mental retardation, cerebral palsy, epilepsy, and autism in community-based programs. The Lanterman Act was set up to help support people with developmental disabilities so that they would be able to live in their own communities. The Act provides community-based services to prevent or minimize institutionalization and dislocation from family and community. Emphasis is placed on providing services that enable people with developmental disabilities to maximize their potential capabilities for independent, productive lives in their home communities. The Act also provides a commitment to prevent and minimize disabilities through early intervention and prevention services.

- **Assembly Bill 1674.** In California AB 1674 (Rosenthal) was enacted in 1984 to provide opportunities for children with disabilities to be served in regular child care and child development programs; however, the bill provided only minimal funding, which has not increased since. This program serves approximately 100 children in ten mainstream programs and is funded through the California Department of Education, Child Development Division.

- **Preschool special education program.** In 1987 California implemented the preschool portion of PL 99-457, the amendments to the Education for the Handicapped Act, through AB 2666 (Hannigan). The intent of the legislation was to provide early education for children with disabilities in order to reduce family stress, reduce the later need for special education, and save costs for society. Prior to AB 2666 California provided special education services to preschoolers with "intensive needs" only. This law requires California to provide special education services also to preschool children with less intensive needs.

The funding model and program standards for this program encourage serving preschoolers with disabilities in natural environments. Consequently, many models for providing special education services in child care and development programs have been implemented. This program requires planning and continuing coordination between early childhood and special education staff.

- **California Early Intervention Program.** Part H of PL 99-457 has been implemented in California through the California Early Intervention Program, with the Department of Developmental Services as the lead agency, to plan for services to *infants* who are identified as disabled or at risk of becoming disabled. Major emphasis has been placed on state and local planning and coordination of services. At the state level the Interagency Coordinating Council—made up of parents, service providers, and agency representatives appointed by the Governor—has worked to advise the lead agency on policies to implement this program. Locally, 26 local planning areas have been established to facilitate interagency planning and coordination. Community-level needs assessments have

repeatedly identified *child care for young children with disabilities* as one of the most significant priorities to address. Several projects have been funded to explore providing child care for this population and to train child care providers. One great lesson learned from early intervention programs is the importance of networking to develop interagency services for young children. Thus, new ways of providing services have helped to make services more available in child care settings.

- **SB 2194 (Morgan).** This legislation, enacted in 1990, provided funds for staff development for child care centers and family day care providers who work with children who have exceptional care needs.

Summary

Don't think that a small group can't change the world. Indeed, that's the only way it can happen.

— Margaret Mead

Over the past three decades services to individuals with disabilities have changed significantly. Advocacy on the part of families and professionals who believe that children should have the right to live and be educated in their homes and communities has laid the foundation for our current service systems. Out of these beliefs have come the most recent gains in the disability rights movement that ensure the quality of life for individuals of all ages with disabilities. Services beginning at birth have been expanded with emphasis on serving the young child within the context of family life. This approach has meant serving young children where they typically are—in their home or in a child care setting.

Child care providers are in a unique position to provide important services for young children with disabilities, their families, society, and themselves. When children with disabilities are included with their same-age playmates, they have the opportunity to learn from each other. The child with a disability has the opportunity to learn through age-appropriate experiences, and the child without special needs can learn to help, accept, and appreciate differences in others. Equally important, children with disabilities are given real-life opportunities to be with and make friends.

For families of children with disabilities, leaving their children with caregivers is often quite stressful, unless they are confident that the care providers accept and respect their children and will be able to handle their exceptional caregiving needs. Addressing the concerns of families and

their economic needs for employment is a critical service that allows families to function in positive ways and enables parents to contribute and participate in their community and society. Providing options in child care for children with disabilities gives parents choices and increased opportunities to pursue their own life goals: going to school, having a job, enjoying time with friends and family, or pursuing personal interests.

Society benefits on many levels as child care providers create environments in which children of diverse abilities and needs are cared for. Perhaps of greatest importance is the early fostering of acceptance among individuals who are different. Given adequate training and support, the experiences of including children with disabilities and their families in child care programs enhance professional growth, improve the quality of services for all children, and benefit everyone involved.

The social and legislative changes outlined in this chapter are only one part of the picture. One cannot legislate how other human beings are perceived and treated. The greatest barriers to changes in interpersonal behavior are attitudes. What supports the disability movement and sustains it is the change in our society's attitudes toward diversity and the understanding that all individuals are entitled to full participation in life.

Through the dedicated work of providers caring for young children with disabilities, the stereotypes and barriers that have traditionally kept these children segregated are beginning to break down. Efforts to increase the number of child care and development staff who will use their influence creating options in child care for children with disabilities are essential if we are to continue to move forward.

To address the question, Who will care for our children? families, child care providers, and other helping professionals must come forth with a shared voice on behalf of *all children.*

KEY POINTS

1. Over the past 30 years, the changing demographics of the American family, our child care system, and the needs of families who have children with disabilities have led to a focus on including young children with disabilities in child care.

2. The language that we use sends powerful messages. It is preferable to say "children with disabilities" or "children who have a particular condition" and to emphasize that children with disabilities are children first, with the same needs as all children.

3. Such risk factors as prematurity, poverty, and environmental hazards, in combination with advances in medical technology that allow more children with disabling conditions and other risk factors to survive, have increased the number of families of young children who may need early intervention services, including child care.

4. A study of California's child care services for children with disabilities (Berkeley Planning Associates 1988) showed that families were not able to find care with trained providers; and, even if they found the care, they could not afford it. On the basis of estimated population growth, child care needs, and incidences of disability, approximately 30,000 to 35,000 families of infants and preschoolers with disabilities are in need of child care in California.

5. Providers serving children with disabilities in their family day care homes or centers become a part of the many other community agencies or programs that provide services, such as special education services and speech or physical therapy, that the family must rely on to meet their child's special needs.

6. As the rights of individuals with disabilities have developed, services for young children and their families have become an increasing priority at the federal, state, and local levels. At the heart of this movement is the value we as Americans place on our children as our future and our belief that every child deserves equal opportunities to play, grow, and develop side by side with family and friends.

7. Federal legislation and policy decisions have had a major impact on civil rights for individuals with disabilities and the expansion of services to infants and preschoolers with disabilities and their families.

8. The Americans with Disabilities Act of 1990 is the most recent civil rights protection bill that guarantees equal opportunities in employment, public accommodations, transportation, state and local governmental services, and telecommunications. *Under the ADA day care providers may not refuse to serve persons who meet the definition of "disabled" or deny them the opportunity to participate in or benefit from the services offered.*

9. Services have been expanded to individuals with disabilities from birth on with an emphasis on serving the young child in the context of family life. This approach has meant serving young

children where they typically are—in their homes or in a child care setting. These changes require additional training for professionals in a variety of disciplines and service delivery systems and particularly for child care and child development professionals.

10. For the benefit of our society, interpersonally and economically, child care providers are creating environments in which children with and without disabilities are included together as they grow and develop into caring and accepting human beings. For the child care provider with adequate training and support, the inclusion of children with varying abilities and their families in their programs enhances professional growth and improves the quality of services for all children in their care.

Selected References and Resources

"Americans with Disabilities Act of 1990," *Legal Update* (Winter, 1990).

Banana's Child Care Provider's Guide for Identifying and Caring for Children with Special Needs. Oakland: Banana's, Inc., Child Care Information and Referral and Parent Support, 1988.

Berkeley Planning Associates. *Child Care and Development Needs in California Families of Children with Disabilities.* Sacramento: California Department of Education, 1988.

Calder, J., and K. Henry. *Building a Special Needs Component into Your Child Care Resource and Referral Service.* Oakland: Banana's, Inc., Child Care Information and Referral and Parent Support, 1983.

California Special Education Programs: A Composite of Laws. Sacramento: California Department of Education (issued annually).

Child Care for Children with Exceptional Needs. Sacramento: Child Development Advisory Committee, 1989.

Child Care Needs of Exceptional Children. Sacramento: Governor's Advisory Committee on Child Development Programs, 1983.

Early Childhood Services: A National Challenge. New York: Ford Foundation, 1989.

Gold, B. *Just a Kid Like Me* (Video). Los Angeles: Child and Family Services.

Gold, B. *Just a Little Extra* (Video). Los Angeles: Child and Family Services.

Hymes, J. L., Jr. *Early Childhood Education, Twenty Years in Review: A Look at 1971–1990.* Washington, D.C.: National Association for the Education of Young Children, 1990.

"Mainstreaming Young Children with Exceptional Needs," *On the Capitol Doorstep* (August, 1989).

Resource Guide for Early Childhood Special Educators. Sacramento: Special Education Resource Network, 1984.

Suarez, T. M.; J. L. Hurth; and S. Prestridge. "Innovation in Services for Young Children with Handicaps and Their Families: An Analysis of the Handicapped Children's Early Education Programs Funded from 1982 to 1986," *Journal of the Division for Early Childhood,* 1988, Vol. 12, No. 3, 224–237.

Winget, P. "New State Emphasis on Prevention, Service Coordination," *The Special Edge* (April-May, 1991).

Appendix 1-A

It's the 'Person First'—Then the Disability.

If you saw a person in a wheelchair unable to get up the stairs into a building, would you say "there is a handicapped person unable to find a ramp"? Or would you say "there is a person with a disability who is handicapped by an inaccessible building"?

What is the proper way to speak to or about someone who has a disability?

Consider how you would introduce someone (Jane Doe) who doesn't have a disability. You would give her name, where she lives, what she does, or what she is interested in. She likes swimming or eating Mexican food or watching Robert Redford movies.

Why say it differently for a person *with* disabilities? Every person is made up of many characteristics, mental as well as physical, and few want to be identified only by their ability to play tennis or by their love for fried onions or by the mole that's on their face. Those are just parts of us.

In speaking or writing, remember that children or adults with disabilities are like everyone else—except they happen to have a disability. Following are a few tips for improving your use of language as it relates to disabilities and handicaps:

What do you see first?
- *The wheelchair?*
- *The physical problem?*
- *The person?*

1. Speak of the person first, then the disability.

2. Emphasize abilities, not limitations.

3. Do not label people as part of a disability group—don't say "the disabled"; say "people with disabilities."

4. Don't give excessive praise or attention to a person with a disability; don't patronize them.

5. Choice and independence are important; let the person do or speak for himself or herself as much as possible; if addressing an adult, say "Bill" instead of "Billy."

6. A disability is a functional limitation that interferes with a person's ability to walk, hear, talk, learn, and so forth. Use the term *handicap* to describe a situation or barrier imposed by society, the environment, or oneself.

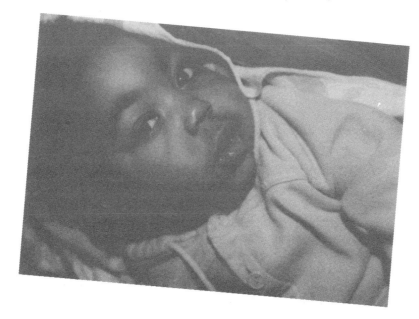

Say	Instead of
child with a disability	disabled or handicapped child
person with cerebral palsy	palsied or C.P. or spastic
person who has . . .	afflicted, suffers from, victim of
without speech, nonverbal	mute or dumb
developmental delay	slow
emotional disorder, or mental illness	crazy or insane
deaf or hearing impaired and communicates by signing	deaf and dumb
uses a wheelchair	confined to a wheelchair
person with retardation	retarded
person with epilepsy	epileptic
with Down syndrome	mongoloid
has a learning disability	is learning disabled
nondisabled	normal, healthy
has a physical disability	crippled
congenital disability	birth defect
condition	disease (unless it is a disease)
seizures	fits
cleft lip	harelip
mobility impaired	lame
medically involved or has chronic illness	sickly
paralyzed	invalid or paralytic
has hemiplegia (paralysis of one side of the body)	hemiplegic
has quadriplegia (paralysis of both arms and legs)	quadriplegic
has paraplegia (loss of function in lower body only)	paraplegic
of short stature	dwarf or midget

What else can you do? If you see or hear reporters use incorrect terminology (even to save space in a headline or time on the air), call them up or send them this list of terms so that they can be aware of the appropriate words to use. Tell them it matters to you and to people with disabilities.

Appendix 1-B

Executive Summary

Children with disabilities or exceptional needs are currently underrepresented in both state-supported and privately funded child care facilities in California. For many families access to child care is limited, and lengthy waiting lists are common. And the family whose child requires any kind of special attention often will face even greater barriers.

Faced with the endemic problems of low pay and high staff turnover in the child care field, already burdened providers may see any child with an exceptional need as undesirable or unmanageable. At the very least providers may be uninformed about disabilities. Those child care providers who are willing to accept children with disabilities will usually need additional staff training and more staff time per child. In addition, stipulations in insurance policies, particular licensing regulations, and inaccessible facilities often limit their capacity to serve these children.

The complexities of arranging care for a child with disabilities can have profound effects on day-to-day life and lifestyle choices for family members. Lack of appropriate child care for an exceptional-needs child can prevent a parent from seeking employment. If employed, many parents experience severe career limitations as a result of unsettled or unsatisfactory child care arrangements. A family with no relief from the demands of caring for an exceptional-needs child can be at risk of extreme emotional stress, isolation, and even child neglect and abuse.

These are some of the findings of a year-long study by Berkeley Planning Associates (see Selected References, page 20) on the child care and development needs of families that include children who have disabilities. This research was done for the Child Development Division of the California Department of Education at the request of the Legislature. Although these issues have been addressed at federal, state, and local levels in a variety of forums, this study is California's first comprehensive statewide needs assessment on this special population. The main purposes of the study were to:

- Describe the population of children with disabilities in California and estimate the extent of their need for child care and developmental services.

- Describe the special services and improved access to services needed by different segments of the population and identify effective service models.

- Develop recommendations for improving services.

Information for this report was gathered from a large-scale survey of parents with exceptional-needs children in four regions of California; from interviews with parents, service providers, and state and local agency representatives; and from reviews of the secondary data available from state agencies and national studies. The surveyed families were selected from the client and enrollment lists maintained by regional centers (Department of Developmental Services), California Children Services (Department of Health Services), and special education classes in public schools.

Findings of the Study

The major topics for discussion are current needs and patterns of use, barriers to finding and receiving child care, and innovative program models.

Current needs and patterns of use

1. *Number of children with exceptional needs.* Because there is no centralized statewide collection of information on all children with disabilities, it is not possible to produce an exact count of the population. However, two different types of projections have produced similar estimates. In 1985 there was an estimated total of between 221,000 and 242,000 children with the kinds of exceptional needs that would affect their child care conditions or requirements. This number was predicted to grow by an additional 33,000 by the year 1990. A large proportion of these

children will need some form of child care as infants, preschoolers, or school-age children. Given the extent of employment participation by mothers, it is estimated that:

    a. A total of 159,000 exceptional-needs children have mothers who are employed. About one-quarter of these children are five years of age or younger.

    b. At least 80,000 of the employed mothers of exceptional-needs children need child care at any given time.

These are conservative estimates in which all the disabilities are not identified and all the reasons for which child care is needed are not accounted for.

2. *Available child care services.* There are two state-supported child care programs that target children with disabilities: a program for severely disabled children in six sites serving children with severe disabilities in segregated, specialized settings; and a mainstreaming program at ten sites providing child care and development services to exceptional-needs children at integrated child care settings. The two programs serve only about 300 children. In other state-subsidized programs less than 1 percent of the total enrollment is billed at the higher rate allowed for children with disabilities. Thus, the current level of direct state support covers fewer than 1,000 of the exceptional-needs children who require child care services.

3. *Current use of child care.* The overwhelming majority of survey respondents (84 percent) used some kind of child care, much of it informal or unlicensed or both. Large numbers of surveyed families relied on relatives and child care providers who were untrained in serving people with disabilities. Responses revealed a patchwork of services to cover needs. The most common pattern of care was a combination of part-time arrangements. Many parents expressed a need for more hours of care than are currently available to them.

Two-thirds of all the child care used by these families was located in homes—either their own or that of a family day care provider, friend, or relative. Most of the in-home care that was paid for by the government was identified as respite care. Respite programs are clearly not the same as regular child care in intent or in practice. Respite is, as the name implies, temporary relief from the stresses of caring for a person with disabilities. Its high proportion here is a testimony to the relative lack of other forms of child care support available.

Barriers to finding and receiving child care

1. *Limited alternatives available.* According to results from the mail survey, parents of exceptional-needs children do not have enough alternatives when looking for child care. Some 37 percent of the parents responding indicated that they were "forced to take whatever they could find" in the way of child care services. If reflective of all exceptional-needs families, these responses suggest that the families of as many as 90,000 children with disabilities in California lack adequate child care alternatives.

2. *High cost of child care.* Presented with a list of possible difficulties encountered in trying to obtain appropriate care, 42 percent of the surveyed parents indicated that care was too expensive. When parents were asked to identify their top choices for state action to improve child care for their children with disabilities, an *increase in subsidies* was ranked number one.

Problems with the cost of child care were not limited to low-income families. The expense of raising a child with disabilities puts many middle-class families into the category of the working poor. Of those responding to the survey, those in the income category of $25,000–$35,000 per year represented the lowest proportion of all respondents indicating adequate alternatives for child care (only 3 percent). One employed professional parent estimated spending $10,000 per year on child care for one child. Many mothers told of promising careers or higher-paying jobs that were lost because of inadequate child care. Similar findings based on client experiences were recounted by many child care providers and referral agency staff.

3. *Need for training of child care providers.* Both child care providers and parents interviewed for the study emphasized the need for training and education to improve the quality and increase the availability of child care. Similarly, 37 percent of parents surveyed noted that there had been a lack of qualified providers available for their exceptional-needs children. *Improved provider training* was the second highest recommendation for state action. Among a list of possible reasons for a provider's refusal to accept their child, parents most frequently reported that the "caregiver has no prior experience with disabilities or exceptional needs." Although there are several local efforts under way to make this training available to providers, there is no coordinated training being initiated from the state level; nor is training occurring in every local service area.

4. *Importance of appropriate program design.* Study findings revealed that there is great potential for and interest in the integration of children with disabilities into child care and development programs that serve children without disabilities. Mainstreaming was a high priority for parents surveyed and interviewed as well as for providers and experts in child development. Some respondents argued that *all* children with disabilities could be served in mainstream settings, given enough resources to provide the high staff-to-child ratios and specialized services and equipment needed for some children.

Most of the providers and other professionals contacted for the study acknowledged the need for a continuum of care, from specialized settings for children needing particular kinds of assistance (e.g., those who are severely medically involved or have severe emotional disabilities) to age-appropriate mainstream programs. The gap in child care services for school-age children was emphasized by many respondents.

5. *Specialized program needs.* Even within the exceptional-needs population, some conditions present special challenges. In particular, several problems were found to be especially acute for subgroups of that population:

   a. Insurance and licensing are particularly problematic for providers who wish to serve children who are medically fragile or have chronic illnesses.

   b. Staffing and training requirements are extraordinary for programs serving those with severe emotional disabilities.

   c. Lack of accessibility to child care settings and specialized support services may present particular barriers for families living in rural areas.

   d. Some adolescents and young adults, especially those with developmental disabilities, need after-school programs that provide supervision and appropriate activities, even though they are past the age of typical enrollees in most child care programs.

Innovative program models

A wide assortment of service models have been developed at the local level in California to address the child care and developmental needs of children

with disabilities. These efforts range from general-
ized provider training and support to specific direct
services: for example, therapy in a preschool
setting, specialized child care for medically fragile
children, and integrated after-school programs.
Many of these models are demonstration projects
with limited, temporary funding; and all are limited
to specific local areas.

Recommendations for Action

There are a number of actions that can be taken
by state and local agencies to increase the amount
and improve the quality of child care and development services available to exceptional-needs
children. These actions cannot, however, be accom-
plished without an additional commitment of
resources. The following recommendations are
offered with the understanding that all entail some
cost and that an attempt to implement any of them
without additional resources would be likely to
result in an offsetting decrease in service in another
area—an outcome that is not the intent of the
preparers of this report.

Provider training and support

1. With increased funding to the Child Development Division (CDD), establishment of an
   exceptional-needs unit to provide technical
   assistance and act as a state-level liaison to
   other agencies

2. Increased funding to the child care resource
   and referral programs to create (or continue)
   support for the exceptional-needs program

3. Funding for interagency training agreements
   by which the existing expertise of state
   agencies can be used for provider training and
   support

4. Inclusion of a special education component in
   early childhood education programs that are
   directed toward licensing and credentialing
   care providers.

Integration of child care into comprehensive service plans

1. Explicit consideration of child care arrangements as part of case management performed

by all state agencies serving exceptional-
needs families

2. Nomination of child care representatives to
   state and local interagency task forces dealing
   with early intervention services

Cost and reimbursement strategies

Funding to conduct a detailed analysis of provider reimbursement and parent eligibility features
of CDD programs, followed by revision of the CDD
fee and reimbursement schedules as they pertain to
exceptional needs

Specialized service needs

1. Monitoring of insurance availability (by
   CDD's exceptional needs unit) for providers
   serving children with disabilities, especially
   those children who are chronically ill or
   medically fragile

2. Establishment of a pilot program in the
   Department of Social Services (DSS) to
   license day care providers to serve children
   with chronic illness, conditioned on nursing
   assessment, training, and consultation

3. Establishment of a revolving loan fund or the
   modification of an existing revolving loan
   fund administered by CDD for the physical
   site modifications needed to accommodate
   children with disabilities

4. Creation of an interagency mechanism for the
   funding of pilot projects designed to develop
   alternative service models for groups with
   unusual program requirements. This mechanism would include the CDD, the Department
   of Health Services, the Department of Developmental Services, the Department of Social
   Services, and the Department of Mental
   Health.

5. Establishment of a credential and permit
   waiver process through the cooperation of
   CDD, DSS, and the Commission on Teacher
   Credentialing to enable persons with specialized educational backgrounds to serve as
   child care providers without a credential in
   early childhood education

6. Self-review of relevant state agency policies to facilitate the provision of and reimbursement for therapeutic services in day care settings

Respite care

Development of an interagency statewide plan under which respite services would include children with all types of disabilities as well as those at risk of abuse or neglect

Accessibility

Required annual reporting of service to exceptional-needs children by all CDD providers for the next four years as a way of assessing the effectiveness of other measures and of determining the necessity for stronger action at a later date

Appendix 1-C

Historical Time Line

State events

1969. The Lanterman Act was passed into law to help support people with developmental disabilities and enable them to live in their own communities. The Act funds community-based services that seek to avoid or minimize the institutionalization of those people and their dislocation from other family members.

1982. Special education preschool services are mandated for children with "intensive needs."

1984. AB 1674 (Rosenthal) funds ten projects to provide services to children with disabilities in child care programs.

1987. California decides to participate in and accept infant and preschool funds from PL 99-457.

AB 2666 (Hannigan) establishes program standards and expanded eligibility for preschool special education services.

The California Early Intervention Program is established to implement PL 99-457. The Governor appoints the Department of Developmental Services as the lead agency and appoints members to the Interagency Coordinating Council.

1990. SB 2194 (Morgan) provides funds for training child care and development staff to serve children with disabilities.

Federal events

1954. *Brown* v. *Board of Education.* This landmark U.S. Supreme Court decision declares that "separate educational facilities are inherently unequal."

1965. The Head Start preschool program is funded.

1972. The Head Start preschool program requires that local programs include children with disabilities at 10 percent of enrollment.

1973. Section 504 of the Rehabilitation Act is passed, guaranteeing civil rights for people with disabilities.

1975. PL 94-142, the Education for the Handicapped Act (EHA), is passed, guaranteeing a free appropriate public education for children with disabilities.

1986. PL 99-457 amends the EHA and adds the Infant/Toddler Program and the Preschool Program.

1990. PL 101-476. The EHA is amended to become the Individuals with Disabilities Education Act (IDEA).

Federal child care and development block grant legislation is passed.

The Americans with Disabilities Act guarantees equal opportunities in employment, public accommodations, transportation, state and local governmental services, child care, and telecommunications.

Chapter 2

More Alike Than Different

By Gina Guarneri, M.A.

Introduction

Children with disabilities and their families often face the lifelong challenge of adapting to the limitations caused by disability. A child may learn to walk with a cane, to read braille, to paint with a paintbrush in the mouth, or to communicate in sign language. In each of these instances the child experiences success by adapting to the disability. For children with disabilities to be successful, they must be given the same opportunities to play and learn that are provided to all

I am not my disability. My disability is part of who I am.

— Millicent Rogers

29

other children. They must have opportunities to participate in activities with other children and adults in the family, school, neighborhood, and community. Similarly, families need to be supported in the care of their children and to be informed of available services. Child care options should give these families greater access to the communities in which they live.

Often, children with disabilities are denied opportunities for equal participation. Commonly held beliefs about disability frequently limit opportunities and choices for children. For example, some people believe that young children with physical disabilities need to be protected from active friends and therefore should not join play groups; others believe that children with certain disabilities are incapable of learning and that adults should do everything for those children. In addition, some children might be considered too severely disabled to benefit from participating in typical childhood experiences. These beliefs result in the young child being denied the experiences needed to make friends and learn. The basis for this limitation is often misinformation and fear of the unknown.

All children, regardless of circumstance, are more alike than different. They all need safe, nurturing environments that will foster optimal growth and development. They all need to develop positive self-esteem and to be valued for their personal uniqueness and abilities. This chapter will examine certain attitudes and beliefs about disabilities and the influence of these attitudes on young children. The argument will be made that child care providers can and should create an environment of acceptance for all children, and that, through this acceptance, the development of all children will be enhanced. Suggestions for encouraging children and families to be accepting of all children are included.

ABOUT THE AUTHOR

Gina Guarneri is the mother of two young children who were cared for by a wonderful family day care provider during the first three years of their lives. She is a special education teacher by training. Her career has centered on providing services to infants and preschoolers with disabilities and their families by first serving as a teacher and coordinator of an infant program and then providing in-service training to other professionals. A major focus of her professional career has been the examination of the relationship between professionals and families in view of the different cultural and family influences brought to the relationship.

Stereotypes

Are the following statements true or false?

- The use of wheelchairs is confining. People who use wheelchairs are wheelchair bound.

- All people with hearing loss can read lips.

- People with disabilities are more comfortable with other individuals who have disabilities.

- People with disabilities are brave and courageous.

- People who are blind acquire a sixth sense.

The preceding statements are *false*. They are common misconceptions or stereotypes (see page 33). Stereotypes often result in people being treated differently from others. For example, if we believe that people with disabilities are more comfortable with other people with disabilities, we will not invite them to work, live, and play with us. This lack of opportunity may, in fact, result in the person with disability being denied a happy, productive life.

Stereotypes are beliefs about a group of people. They limit perceptions of what an individual can do. They may be statements or actions that say, "We do not like or value you." They deny individual differences, abilities, and personalities. Negative stereotypes are usually based on fear of the unknown, a lack of information, misinformation, or a lack of experience.

Development of stereotypes

Stereotypes are passed on from adults to children and from child to child. Often, stereotypes are learned when we are young. We may have heard our parents say, "Poor Stephanie, her daughter Annie is retarded. She will never learn to walk or talk." Or we may have seen older children calling a boy with glasses "four eyes." Or when we saw a man in a wheelchair and asked "What's that?" we were told, "Don't stare!" and were quickly moved away without being given an answer to our question. This nonanswer left us confused, gave us no information about the wheelchair, and implied that we had said

something wrong, although we were not sure what it was.

Many of us did not know people with disabilities when we were young. When we were young and saw a person with a disability, we may have been afraid of "catching" it. We may have been afraid because we knew the person was different but did not understand why. We did not know about disabilities; consequently, when we heard false statements, we did not know that what was said was untrue.

We also learn stereotypes through the mass media, such as television and movies. If movies portray people with disabilities as scary, bad, or helpless, we will believe that people with disabilities can be only scary, bad, or helpless.

Cultural and religious beliefs about disability may also produce stereotypes. For example, some families may believe that a child was born with a disability as punishment for the bad behavior of one or both

parents. *Case in point:* A family believed that their daughter was born with a cleft palate (a hole in the palate of the mouth) because the father had engaged in an extramarital affair. Although he denied having had an affair, his wife and parents asked him to leave home. Fortunately, a counselor from a similar culture, who understood the belief, was able to explain the cause of cleft palate to the family and assisted in the father's moving home. Other beliefs include families who view their child with a disability as a "gift from God," or see a disability as resulting from an act of negligence on the part of the mother: she did not drink enough milk or drank too much milk, or was lazy or too active during the pregnancy.

Cultural and religious beliefs may, however, help the family understand the disability and bring hope that things will get better. Lighting candles in church, participating in healing ceremonies, and using herbal medicines and acupuncture are examples of practices based on such beliefs. Child care providers must respect the cultural and religious practices of families. Sometimes, we will not agree with the practice and will need to ask ourselves whether the belief is harmful. If it is not (and most, if not all, are not), then we need to respect the family and their beliefs.

Effects of stereotypes on behavior

Stereotypes influence how we act toward each other. If we believe that a person who is deaf will be able to hear if we yell, we will yell at all those who are deaf. (Yelling does not help someone who is deaf hear us. Talking naturally while looking directly at the person will help the person to communicate.) If we believe that all children with disabilities are incapable of doing things for themselves, we will do everything for them.

Stereotypes are perpetuated in everyday sayings. An example is the saying, "Like the blind leading the blind" when people do not know what they are doing. We are saying that blind people cannot be trusted to help themselves—that they are helpless and ignorant.

Without being aware of what we are doing, we teach our beliefs and attitudes about disability and differences to the children we take care of. Children learn by observing adults and other children. Often, the young child's primary teachers are family members and child care providers. The words we use, the way we treat children, the books we read to children, and the television shows we watch with them offer the message that all people are valued or that some people are valued more than others.

It is critical for care providers to think about how we talk to and act toward all children. Do we value some children more than others? Do we treat some children differently from others? Do we allow all children to feed and dress themselves if possible? It may be difficult to recognize stereotypes in ourselves because, if we *believe* something, we think everyone believes the same thing. It is important to talk about our beliefs with others, challenge others and ourselves about our beliefs, and be willing to change our beliefs if necessary. The activities provided in this chapter will assist you in thinking about your own attitudes and beliefs.

The following statements are the explanations of the myths and misconceptions contained in the statements on pages 30 and 31.

Myth	Fact
Wheelchair use is confining; people who use wheelchairs are wheelchair bound.	A wheelchair, like a bicycle or a car, is a device that allows someone to get around.
All persons with hearing disabilities can read lips.	Not all people with hearing disabilities are able to read lips, and lipreading skill varies greatly among people who use it.
People with disabilities are more comfortable with others who have disabilities.	People with disabilities are demanding the right to work, go to school, and play with the nondisabled. For years people with disabilities have been placed in separate schools and institutions. This has reinforced the myth that people with disabilities would "rather be with their own kind."
People with disabilities are brave and courageous.	Adjusting to a disability requires adapting to a lifestyle, not bravery and courage.
People who are blind acquire a sixth sense.	Although people who are blind develop their remaining senses more fully, they do not have a sixth sense.

Development of Self-Esteem

The most important lesson learned of all (in my childhood) was that I don't have to be perfect to be loved. That no one does.

— Alice Walker

Self-esteem involves the development of positive self-regard. It is the desire to like ourselves and to have others like us. The development of self-esteem begins in infancy and continues throughout our lives. When a mother smiles to an infant who is cooing, dad tells a toddler she is beautiful, and brother says "thank you" to a preschooler, the child learns, "I make people happy. They like me. And, as a result, I like myself." When an infant is able to crawl to the ball, a toddler is able to pull up his pants, and a preschooler is able to write her name,

the child feels good and develops self-esteem. "Figuring out who I am and who you are and how I feel about me and you are central, absorbing tasks for three-, four-, and five-year-olds" (Derman-Sparks 1989, p. 31). Children who feel good about themselves and know others appreciate them have high self-esteem. Conversely children who do not like themselves and think others do not like them have low self-esteem.

Young children must develop positive self-esteem. They learn about themselves and their world by interacting with other children and adults. To have the courage to explore and take chances ("If I try to walk, I might fall"), the child must have self-confidence, which in turn leads to success and a sense of self-esteem. Helping children value themselves is a significant role that providers play. Beginning in infancy, children need to be offered choices, given opportunities to meet their own challenges, and afforded empathy for their feelings.

Young children are good observers; they notice how we treat them, other children, and their families. If we talk positively to children, they will feel good about themselves. On the other hand, if we talk negatively, they will feel badly about themselves. For instance, if Anita, a very active child, hears the care provider say, "That Anita! She never sits still! I always have to tell her to sit down! She never sits long enough to finish anything!" Anita may begin to believe that she is bad and develop low self-esteem.

Young children learn by doing—through practice and by trial and error. Disabilities should not limit our expectations for children. What children learn and how they learn it may vary depending on the extent of their disabilities. A boy learning to put on his shirt will get his arms stuck, put it on backwards and upside down, and try to fit his head into the sleeve. By trying to put his shirt on many times, he learns to do it. If we believe that Juan, who has limited use of his arms, cannot learn to put his shirt on, we will always do it for him and Juan will not

learn how to dress himself. He will see that all the other children dress themselves and he cannot. Juan will start to feel like a failure and may develop low self-esteem. It is imperative that the child care provider establishes an environment that encourages exploration, successful interactions, and respect for all children. The point is not that Juan learns to put on a shirt "like" the rest of the children. He may not be able to do so because of limitations imposed by his physical disability. It is important to ensure that Juan has equal opportunities to learn to put on his shirt and that special adaptations or the need for some assistance does not take away from his growing sense of competence and confidence.

Young children's perceptions of disabilities

Research (Conant and Budoff 1983, Eggers 1983, Weinberg 1978) has shown that children begin to recognize disabilities as being different from a very early age. Two-year-olds are developing their sense of self as individuals separate from and interconnected to others. A beginning awareness of different physical abilities is part of this process (Derman-Sparks 1989). Three- to five-year-olds recognize obvious disabilities (blindness, deafness, orthopedic differences) but do not recognize mental retardation (Conant and Budoff 1983). In a study by Weinberg (1978), children were shown drawings of a child sitting in a wheelchair and the same child in a preschool chair. The children were asked the difference between the pictures. The three-year-olds did not recognize the wheelchair as different, but the four- and five-year-olds pointed out the wheelchair and were able to explain its use (i.e., "The boy can't walk").

As preschoolers are learning about differences, they will begin to develop their beliefs about disability. In Weinberg's study the children were asked to choose who they would rather play with—the child in the wheelchair or the child in the preschool chair. The three- and four-year-olds chose the child in the wheelchair as often as the child in the preschool chair. But, the five-year-olds consistently chose the child in the preschool chair. Because the preschool years are a critical time in the development of the child's sense of self and others, caregivers should teach children to be accepting of all children and adults. Preschoolers should be taught about disabilities so that they do not become misinformed, fearful, or negative. Derman-Sparks (1989) and Eggers (1983) have shown that disability awareness training in the preschool years will help children to be accepting of all other children regardless of ability.

Strategies to Create an Accepting, Inclusive Climate

The most effective way to help children accept a child with a disability is to create an atmosphere of acceptance of all children. We must treat all children equally, talk positively about all children, and help them develop nonbiased feelings. Following are strategies to help create a positive, accepting environment.

Acknowledge differences

Young children observe differences. Point out differences to children. By pointing out differences, we are saying, "We all do things differently, and that's okay." For example, during block play say, "Mia is making a tall tower with her blocks, Mark is making a long line, and Monica is scattering her blocks all around." During snack time you might point out that Joaquin is using a special spoon to help him eat his yogurt.

Model appropriate behavior

Children learn by imitation. They do what we do. Reflect on the words you use and how you treat children. Do you allow all of the children to feed themselves, even though it would be easier and quicker to feed Linda? Do you praise all of the children for their artwork? Even Tiffany, who still scribbles?

State the rules for treating others respectfully

An important goal of the toddler and preschooler is to learn how to treat others. State the rules clearly and do not allow them to be broken. "We do not call people names. That is not allowed here." Help children to see how their behavior affects others. "How do you think Michael felt when you told him he could not play? How would you feel if the other children told you to leave?"

Educate children

Toddlers learn by doing and by interacting with objects through all their senses. By their preschool years children are able to learn through discussion. Talk about a disability and how it impacts a person's life. Ask the children questions. For example, after reading a story about a child who is deaf, ask the children, "How could your mommy tell you it is time for dinner if you were not able to hear?"

If a child with a special need is going to be enrolled in your program, tell the children. Explain the disability. If possible, have the child or a family member demonstrate special equipment to the class. For example, during circle time, the child or the parent or both could show the other children how the wheelchair, crutches, or hearing aid work.

Answer children's questions honestly, simply, and clearly

Children will notice disabilities and ask questions. Give them the answers to their questions and be honest. Young children are always asking why. If you do not know the answer, say "I do not know." More suggestions on answering children's questions are given in following sections of this chapter.

Reassure children

Children may wonder whether they will "catch" the disability. Explain as well as you can the cause of the disability: "Robert was born with a short arm." Reassure the children that they will not catch it: "You were born with two long arms."

Allow children to explore through play

Children learn through play. Help children learn about disabilities through play.

After seeing a child in a wheelchair, children may want to play "wheelchair." Push the children around the room in a chair. If the parent and child who own the wheelchair say it is all right to do so, allow the children to climb onto and out of the chair and push each other. Make a "hearing aid" out of cardboard for the children to wear on their ear. Caution: Children must learn that articles of special equipment are not toys. Ask family members before allowing children to try out the equipment. Teach the children to respect the equipment, being careful not to discourage their interactions or their natural curiosity to explore, learn, and become more comfortable with something new.

Read children's books

The children's books in your center or home should be selected carefully. They should include stories about children with disabilities and stories that are not about the disability but do include pictures of children or adults with disabilities. A suggested list of children's books is included in Appendix 2-B. Strategies to evaluate children's books for bias are included in Appendix 2-C.

Involve children in adapting the classroom or activity for the child

Preschoolers love to solve problems. If a child is not able to participate in an activity because of his or her special need, ask the other children how to make the situation easier for that child. Include the child with the disability in the discussion. *Example:* "I noticed that Mei (who is blind) keeps walking into the bikes on the playground. How can we help her to know where the bikes are?"

Allow other children to participate in a new way also. One teacher discovered that a child with a physical challenge could paint best when lying on his stomach with a wedge underneath him. Soon all of the children were painting in this way.

Answering children's questions about others

Preschoolers, especially four- and five-year-olds, will ask questions about differences they see. We should answer their questions honestly, simply, and clearly. Sometimes they will not ask a question but by their behavior will tell the care provider what is bothering them. The care provider should then help the children express themselves. *Example:* Malcolm, who has a tracheostomy, a surgical opening to his windpipe, joined a preschool class. Jessie stared at the tracheostomy, not saying anything. The care provider said, "I notice you're looking at Malcolm's tracheostomy. Do you want to know what it is?" Jessie shook her head yes. The care provider said, "It's a tracheostomy. Malcolm can't breathe through his nose and mouth as you do. The tracheostomy helps him to breathe."

We should think about how to answer questions before they are asked. The following sample situations are adapted from *Explaining Special Needs: Preschool Children in Integrated Settings* by the San Diego County Office of Education:

Child	Adult
"Why does she have those things on her legs?"	"Those are braces; they support her legs and help her walk."
"She's a baby because she wears diapers."	"No, she's not a baby. She can't feel when she has to go the bathroom, so she needs a diaper."
"That's only a toy on his ear."	"It's not a toy. It's called a hearing aid and helps him to hear."
"Why does he take so long sweeping? He goes so slow."	"His muscles don't work as well as yours. It takes him longer, but he gets the job done."
"I can climb up these stairs really fast—faster than him."	"Yes you can. Some people go fast and some go slow. That's okay."

Helping children answer others' questions about themselves

Children will be answering questions about their handicaps throughout their lives. They need the support of the care provider to learn how to answer these questions. Following are suggestions developed by Louise Derman-Sparks and the Anti-Bias Curriculum Task Force. Caregivers should:

- Find out how the child's parents are explaining the specific disability to the child and to others.

- Help children find words to answer questions. Discuss with them what they wish other children to know. Some children may need or want to practice what they will say privately to the teacher first.

- Find out what they want you to tell other children. The words and manner of your response will model ways in which they will respond to questions.

- Teach the children that they have the right to choose whether to answer another child's question, say they do not want to answer, or say they would rather the questioner ask the teacher.

- Show support for children's feelings about having to answer questions about their disabilities. "I know it's hard sometimes when other children ask about why you wear a brace and that sometimes you wish they wouldn't ask so many questions. When you feel tired, sad, or angry about it, let me know, and we can talk about it."

Helping all families accept all children

Families of nondisabled children in your program may have questions about the children with disabilities. A common concern of parents is that their nondisabled child will imitate inappropriate behavior. Assure parents that although children learn through imitation, imitating another child's negative behavior is likely to be a short-lived response and that they will imitate positive behaviors as well. Such responses are the child's way of learning about the disability. Strategies that caregivers can use to reassure parents and help them understand include:

- Answering all questions honestly and clearly while respecting confidentiality.

- Asking the family members of the child with a disability how they would like you to explain the disability.

- Modeling appropriate behavior. As do children, adults also learn by observing

others. Use positive, nonbiased language when talking to children and parents.

- Providing family members with written resources about specific disabilities.

- Telling parents when they visit your day care facility before enrollment that you take care of children with disabilities. Explain how an integrated program benefits all the children. Include a statement in the program description that children with varying abilities attend your program.

Common questions about serving children with disabilities

I don't know how to care for a child with disabilities. Can I handle the responsibility? Most child care providers are very capable of caring for children with disabilities. The skills required are typically the same skills needed to care for any child. The primary ingredients in providing quality care to children with special needs are the desire, a willingness to be flexible, and an openness to learn from children, families, and specialists.

Do all children with mental retardation require intensive, individual care? The abilities of children vary. The same is true of children with mental retardation. Some will be able to participate in all activities with only minor changes required. Others will need varying levels of adult assistance at times throughout the day.

Will I need to protect the child with disabilities from being hurt during play with the other children? All children need protection from harm. Children with disabilities do not need protection from trying new things, interacting with other children, or failure. Children with exceptional needs need to learn to be independent. They need to experience the same fun, successes, and failures that all children experience.

Will I have to change my whole routine to accommodate a child with a disability? Children with disabilities enjoy and learn from the same activities as all children. They like to paint, play with blocks, and play outside. Depending on the severity of the condition, some or all activities may need to be changed to make them easier for the child. A small number of these children (1 percent of the total population) will be totally dependent on adults for assistance in activities.

How can I learn more about disabilities? Educate yourself. Conferences, workshops, and educational journals provide information on disability. Read a book or rent a videotape. Many books and motion pictures provide personal accounts of living with a disability. Recommended journals, books, and motion pictures are listed in Appendix 2-D, and toll-free telephone numbers of organizations that provide information on disabilities are listed in Appendix 2-E. The local child care resource and referral program may also have books or videos of interest.

Where can I go for help? A number of individuals may be willing to provide information, assistance, and support. Parents and other family members are the best resource for information about their own children. Most parents would gladly spend time teaching care providers and other children about their child's special needs. Ask the parents what professionals are providing early intervention services to their child. Special education teachers, therapists, and public health nurses are usually available to offer information and suggestions. Most doctors will explain the child's disability to care providers. Some child care resource, referral, and respite agencies offer

training on providing child care for children with disabilities.

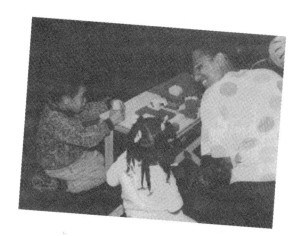

Summary

The attitudes and beliefs of child care and development professionals have a significant impact on how children with disabilities and their families are accepted by other children and families. Children are more alike than different. During the first five years of their lives, they are more receptive to differences. This is a critical time for turning the tide of stereotyping and discrimination into a climate of inclusion and the appreciation of diversity.

A major task for the toddlers and preschoolers is to learn about themselves and others. During these early years the foundations for self-esteem and attitudes toward others are built. The inclusion of children with disabilities in child care programs provides wonderful opportunities for young children to learn from each other and develop acceptance of all children. Child care providers are responsible for creating an environment that is positive, challenging, and accepting.

Perhaps in the future the efforts of families and professionals who strive for opportunities of inclusion for young children will result in increased numbers of persons with disabilities who are living and working successfully in their own communities. This vision can be realized when people have the knowledge, experience, and attitudes that promote equal opportunities for *all* children.

As we think of the future and envision what we want for our children—happiness, friends, love, productive and fulfilling work—we can see children with disabilities achieving the same things. These are the goals and outcomes that many families have strongly advocated and endorsed over the years. However, unless they are shared by the larger community, the limits will always be there in other people's perceptions and attitudes. We are building a foundation for the realization of those goals by providing the initial experiences that will enable children to keep moving ahead and pushing the limits of their potential.

Let us work toward that dream.

KEY POINTS

1. Our attitudes and values about disability influence how we treat people with disabilities.

2. Negative attitudes or stereotypes result from lack of information, misinformation, fear of the unknown, and lack of experience.

3. The toddler and preschool years are critical in the development of the child's self-esteem. Positive interactions with family and friends will result in positive self-esteem. Conversely, negative remarks and interactions may result in low self-esteem.

4. Research shows that at about the age of three, children begin to notice differences in people, and children as young as five may begin to exclude children with disabilities. Research also shows that talking about differences and stressing the acceptance of all will result in children accepting and valuing all children.

5. The child care provider can establish an atmosphere of acceptance of all children and families.

6. The child care provider has many resources to assist in meeting the special needs of children.

References

Awareness Is the First Step Towards Change: Tips for Disability Awareness. National Easter Seal Society, n.d.

Brandon, Nathaniel. "The Psychology of Self-Esteem," in *How to Talk So Kids Will Listen and Listen So Kids Will Talk.* New York: Avon Books, 1980.

Conant, S., and M. Budoff. 1983. "Patterns of Awareness in Children's Understanding of Disabilities," *Mental Retardation,* Vol. 21, 119–25.

Derman-Sparks, L., and the Anti-Bias Curriculum Task Force. 1989. *Anti-Bias Curriculum: Tools for Empowering Young Children.* Washington, D.C.: National Association for the Education of Young Children.

Eggers, N. 1983. "Influencing Preschoolers' Awareness and Feelings Regarding Depicted Physical Disabilities," *Early Child Development and Care,* Vol. 12, 119–26.

Explaining Special Needs: Preschool Children in Integrated Settings. San Diego County Office of Education, n.d.

Weinberg. N. 1978. "Preschool Children's Perceptions of Orthopedic Disability," *Rehabilitation Counseling Bulletin,* Vol. 21, 183–89.

Appendix 2-A

Myths About Disability

Everybody's fighting some kind of stereotype. People with disabilities are no exception. The difference is that the barriers we face begin with people's attitudes about us. And these attitudes are often rooted in misinformation and misunderstandings about who we are and how we became disabled.

The First Step campaign of the National Easter Seal Society sets out to change some of the misconceptions that get in our way—when we are looking for a job, trying to get around in our communities, and working to become accepted for who we are.

Awareness is the first step toward change.

Some myths and facts about people with disabilities:

Myth 1 People with disabilities are brave and courageous.

Fact Adjusting to a disability actually requires adapting to lifestyle, not bravery and courage.

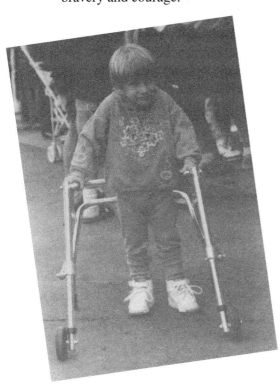

Myth 2 All persons who use wheelchairs are chronically ill or sickly.

Fact The association between wheelchair use and illness has probably evolved because hospitals use wheelchairs to transport sick people. A person may use a wheelchair for a variety of reasons, none of which may have anything to do with lingering illness.

Myth 3 Wheelchair use is confining; users of wheelchairs are "wheelchair-bound."

Fact A wheelchair, like a bicycle or an automobile, is a personal assertive device that enables someone to get around.

Myth 4 All persons with hearing disabilities can read lips.

Fact Lipreading skill varies greatly among people who use it and is never wholly reliable.

Myth 5 People who are blind acquire a sixth sense.

Fact Although most people who are blind develop their remaining senses more fully, they do not have a sixth sense.

Myth 6 People with disabilities are more comfortable "with their own kind."

Fact Years of grouping people with disabilities in separate schools and institutions has reinforced this misconception. Today, more and more people are taking advantage of new opportunities to join the mainstream of our society.

Myth 7 Nondisabled people are obligated to "take care of" their fellow citizens with disabilities.

Fact   People may offer assistance to whomever they choose, but most disabled persons prefer to be responsible for themselves.

Myth 8   Curious children should never be allowed to ask people about their disabilities.

Fact   Many children have a natural, uninhibited curiosity and ask questions that some adults might find embarrassing. But scolding children for asking questions may make them think there is something "bad" about having a disability. Most people with disabilities won't mind answering a child's question.

Myth 9   The lives of people with disabilities are totally different from those of nondisabled people.

Fact   People with disabilities go to school, get married, work, have families, do laundry, grocery shop, laugh, cry, pay taxes, get angry, have prejudices, vote, plan, and dream like everyone else.

Myth 10   It's all right for nondisabled people to park in accessible parking spaces for a short time.

Fact   Because accessible parking spaces are designed and situated to meet the needs of persons who have disabilities, these spaces should only be used by people who need them.

Myth 11   Most people with disabilities are unable to have sexual relationships.

Fact   Any person can have a sexual relationship by adapting the sexual activity. People with disabilities can have children naturally as well as adopt them. People with disabilities, like other people, are sexual beings.

Myth 12   People with disabilities always need help.

Fact   Many people with disabilities are quite independent and capable of giving help. But if you want to help someone with a disability, ask first if they need it.

Myth 13   There's nothing one person can do to help eliminate the barriers confronting people with disabilities.

Fact   Everyone can contribute to change. You can help remove barriers by:

- Understanding the need for accessible parking and leaving it for those who need it
- Encouraging the participation of people with disabilities in community activities by making sure that meeting and event sites are accessible
- Understanding children's curiosity about disabilities and people who have them
- Advocating a barrier-free environment
- Speaking up when negative words or phrases are used in connection with disability
- Writing producers and editors a note of support when they portray people with disabilities as they do others in the media
- Accepting people with disabilities as individual human beings with the same needs and feelings you might have
- Hiring qualified disabled persons whenever possible

Source: The First Step Campaign, National Easter Seal Society.

Appendix 2-B

Books for Children

These books are available at local bookstores or libraries.

Bahan, Ben, and Joe Dannis. *Signs for Me: Basic Sign Vocabulary for Children.* San Diego: Drawn Sign Press, 1990.

This is a book of sign language for children.

Boesel, Kathryn, and Allison Boesel. *Trouble with School: A Family Story About Learning Disabilities.* Bethesda, Md.: Woodbine House, 1993.

This book follows Allison and her mother as each tells her side of the story of the diagnosis of Allison's disability and the adjustment to her learning needs.

Brown, Tricia, and Fran Ortiz. *Someone Special, Just Like You.* New York: Henry Holt, 1984.

This is a book of photographs of children with disabilities who are doing things all preschoolers like—dancing, painting, climbing, looking, listening, and more

Foldin, Mickey. *Signing for Kids: The Fun Way for Anyone to Learn American Sign Language.* New York: Perigree Books, Berkley Publishing Group, 1991.

This user-friendly sign language book includes illustrations and explanations for each sign.

Hubbard, Ethan. *Straight to the Heart: Children of the World.* Chelsea, Vt.: Craftsbury Common Books, 1992.

Black and white photographs of children and families from different parts of the world fill this book. The author's profits support children's relief societies around the world.

Jasmine, Cairo. *Our Brother Has Down's Syndrome.* Buffalo: Annick Press, 1985.

In this book, two sisters talk about their brother Jai, who has Down syndrome.

Kates, Bobbi Jane. *We're Different; We're the Same.* New York: Random House, 1992.

This is a Sesame Street book featuring the muppets. Colorful pictures and simple words illustrate how we are all different (we have different skin, eyes) and the same (our skin keeps us warm; we see with our eyes). Although this book is not specifically about disabilities, it celebrates the differences and sameness in people. The pictures include a child and an adult in a wheelchair.

MacLachlan, Patricia. *Through Grandpa's Eyes.* New York: Harper Trophy, 1980.

A boy, John, tells us in this book about a day with his grandpa. John's grandpa is blind, and John experiences the day as his grandpa does—through touch, smell, and hearing. This is a story not only about blindness but also about the special relationship between a boy and his grandfather.

Martin, Bill Jr., and John Archambault. *Knots on a Counting Rope.* New York: Henry Holt, 1987.

A grandfather tells his grandson the story of the boy's birth. The story gives the boy hope and encouragement to live with his blindness.

O'Shaughnessy, Ellen. *Somebody Called Me Retard Today . . . and My Heart Felt Sad.* New York: Walker & Co., 1992.

Simple language and beautiful paintings tell the story of the talents and strengths of a girl and the sadness she feels when another child calls her "retard."

Peterson, Jeanne. *I Have a Sister; My Sister Is Deaf.* New York: Harper & Row, 1977.

A child tells a story about her sister, who is deaf.

Prall, Jo. *My Sister's Special.* Chicago: Children's Press, 1988.

A boy talks about his sister, who is disabled.

Rabe, Bernice. *Where's Chimpy?* Morton Grove, Ill.: Albert Whitman & Co., 1988.

In this book, Misty and her dad hunt for Misty's monkey, Chimpy. The story is told through photographs of Misty, who has Down syndrome, and her dad.

Raffi. *One Light, One Sun.* New York: Crown Publishers, 1990.

Members of different families are pictured going about their day. One family member is a boy who uses a wheelchair.

Rosenburg, Maxine. *My Friend Leslie: The Story of a Handicapped Child.* New York: Lothrop, Lee and Shepard Books, 1983.

Karen tells the story in this book of her friend Leslie, a student in her kindergarten class who has multiple disabilities.

Russo, Marisabina. *Alex Is My Friend.* New York: Greenwillow Books, 1992.

A boy talks about his friend Alex, who is shorter than he, cannot run fast, and is in a wheelchair. But they are still best friends.

Smith, Lane. *Glasses: Who Needs Them?* New York: Viking Press, 1991.

This book provides humorous answers to a boy's concerns that wearing glasses will make him look like a "dork."

Yashima, Taro. *Crow Boy.* New York: Viking Press, 1983.

In this story, children make fun of a boy who is different until they learn that he has a special talent.

Zelonky, Jay. *I Can't Always Hear You.* Austin, Tex.: Raintree Steck-Vaughn, 1980.

Kim, a girl with a hearing impairment, begins going to her neighborhood school. She finds that she isn't as different as she had feared, because everyone she meets has individual differences too.

Appendix 2-C

Ten Quick Ways to Analyze Children's Books for Bias Against People with Disabilities

1. **Check the illustrations**
   a. *Look for stereotypes.* A stereotype is an oversimplified generalization about a particular group that usually carries derogatory implications. Look for illustrations that demean or ridicule people because of their disability.
   b. *Who is doing what?* Do the illustrations show the person with a disability in subservient and passive roles or in leadership and action roles?

2. **Check the story line**
   a. *Standard for success.* Does the person with a disability have to "overcome" the disability before becoming successful? Or is the person a success while maintaining the strengths and limitations the disability presents?
   b. *Resolution of problems.* How are problems presented, conceived, and resolved in the story? Is the person with a disability considered to be "the problem?" Is the problem faced by the person with a disability solved by the intervention of a nondisabled person? Or is the person with the disability involved in the solution?

3. **Look at the lifestyles.** Are people with disabilities and their settings depicted in ways that contrast unfavorably with the unstated norm of the nondisabled? If their lifestyle is depicted as "different," are negative judgments implied?

4. **Weigh the relationships between people.** Do the nondisabled people in the story possess the power, take the leadership, and make the important decisions?

5. **Note the heroes.** For many years, books showed only "safe" minority heroes—those who avoided serious conflict with the establishment. When a hero with a disability is depicted in a book, is the person recognized for the same qualities that have made nondisabled heroes famous or because what he or she has done has benefited the nondisabled people? Whose interest is the person with the disability serving? The interests of people with disabilities?

6. **Consider the effects on a child's self-image.** Are norms presented that would limit a child's aspirations or self-concept? Or are children with disabilities given the message that anyone can achieve greatness?

7. **Consider the author's or illustrator's background.** Analyze the biographical material on the jacket flap or the back of the book. If the story is about a person with a disability, what qualifies the author to talk about the subject?

8. **Check on the author's perspective.** No author can be entirely objective. All authors write from cultural and personal contexts. Read the book carefully to determine whether the author's perspective substantially weakens or strengthens the value of the written work.

9. **Watch for loaded words.** A word is loaded when it has offensive overtones. Examples of loaded adjectives are *weak* and *lazy.*

10. **Look at the copyright date.** Before the 1970s, children's books did not even remotely reflect a pluralistic society. Copyright dates can be clues to how likely books are to be overtly negative about people with disabilities or to include people with disabilities in the story. However, a recent copyright date is no guarantee of a book's relevance or sensitivity.

Adapted from Louise Derman-Sparks and the Anti-Bias Curriculum Task Force, *Anti-Bias Curriculum: Tools for Empowering Young Children.* Washington, D.C.: National Association for the Education of Young Children, 1989.

Appendix 2-D

Resources for Adults to Learn About Living with Disabilities

Books

These books are available at local bookstores.

Berger, Larry; Dahlia Lithwick; and Steven Campers. *Voices from the Hole in the Wall Gang: I Will Sing Life.* New York: Little, Brown, 1992.

Seven children talk about their experiences with chronic illness or disability in this book, which includes poetry written by the children.

Bernstein, Joanne E., and Bryna J. Fireside. *Special Parents, Special Children.* Morton Grove, Ill.: Albert Whitman & Co., 1991.

Members of four families in which one or both parents have disabilities talk about family life.

Carrillo, Anna Cupolo; Katherine Corbett; and Victoria Lewis. *No More Stares.* Berkeley, Calif.: Disabilities Rights and Education Defense Fund, 1982.

In this book, women with disabilities tell about their life experiences through photographs, poetry, and stories.

Dorris, Michael. *The Broken Cord: A Family's Ongoing Struggle with Fetal Alcohol Syndrome.* New York: Harper and Row, 1989.

The author tells the story of his family's experiences in raising their adopted son, a child with physical and behavioral disabilities due to prenatal exposure to alcohol. This book was awarded the 1989 National Book Critics award for nonfiction.

Edwards, J., and D. Dawson. *My Friend David: A Source Book About Down's Syndrome and a Personal Story About Friendship.* Portland, Oreg.: EDNICK Communications, 1982.

This book is written by David, a man with Down syndrome, and his teacher, Jean. It tells the story of their friendship and provides information about Down syndrome.

Featherstone, Helen. *A Difference in the Family.* New York: Penguin Books, 1980.

This book draws on interviews with parents and professionals and the author's personal experience to discuss the emotional adjustment families go through when they learn of a child's disability. Suggestions for professionals to provide support are included.

Greenfield, Josh. *A Child Called Noah; A Place for Noah; A Client Called Noah.* New York: Harcourt Brace Jovanovich, 1988.

This series of books tells the story of a family in which a son has developmental delays.

Help Children Help Themselves and Others. Washington, D.C.: The Children's Foundation, n.d.

This publication is a good resource for operators of family day care and children's programs. It stresses the importance of examining personal attitudes and applying antibias concepts in day care. Suggestions are offered for activities that parents and providers can carry out with children and that employ antibias, multicultural approaches. The handbook serves as a guide to equity materials and contains an annotated bibliography of children's literature and adult resources. It is available from Children's Foundation, 725 Fifteenth Street, SW, Suite 505, Washington, DC 20005, telephone (202) 347-3300.

Kaufman, S. Z. *Retarded Isn't Stupid, Mom!* Baltimore: Paul H. Brookes Publishing Co., 1988.

A mother tells the story of her daughter's life and struggle for independence. Her daughter is mentally retarded.

Kupfer, Fern. *Before and After Zachariah*. Chicago: Academy Chicago Publishers, 1982.

The author tells her family's story about their son, Zachariah, and their decision to have Zach cared for in a residential facility.

Other resources

Biography: Examples of biographies of people with disabilities include *My Left Foot* and stories about Helen Keller and President Franklin D. Roosevelt.

Television Program: *Life Goes On* is about a family with an adult son who has Down syndrome and an adolescent who is HIV positive.

Videos: Popular motion pictures now available for rental on videotape include *My Left Foot, Coming Home, Born on the Fourth of July, Children of a Lesser God, The Scent of a Woman, Forrest Gump, Man Without a Face, Philadelphia,* and *Nell.*

Resources for Teachers and Day Care Providers

The following resources provide information on how to include children with disabilities in day care and preschool programs. Most of the resources are available from local resources and referral projects.

Derman-Sparks, L., and the Anti-Bias Curriculum Task Force. *Anti-Bias Curriculum: Tools for Empowering Young Children*. Washington, D.C.: National Association for the Education of Young Children, 1989.

The antibias curriculum is structured to provide education and day care for young children in a nonbiased, nondiscriminatory manner.

Mainstreaming Preschoolers. Washington, D.C.: Project Head Start; Head Start Bureau; Administration for Children, Youth, and Families; U.S. Department of Health and Human Services, n.d.

This series of eight manuals written for Head Start staff provides strategies for including children with disabilities in preschool programs and information on health impairments, visual impairments, speech and language disabilities, emotional disturbances, orthopedic disabilities, hearing impairments, learning disabilities, and mental retardation.

National Association for the Education of Young Children, 1834 Connecticut Avenue N.W., Washington, DC 20009-5786, telephone (800) 424-2460.

An organization for early childhood educators and child care providers, the association provides useful, inexpensive resources on a variety of topics.

Teaching Young Children to Resist Bias: What Parents Can Do. Washington, D.C.: National Association for the Education of Young Children, n.d.

This brochure provides practical tips for parents and information helpful to child care providers.

York, Stacey. *Roots and Wings: Affirming Culture in Early Childhood Programs*. Mt. Rainier, Md.: Gryphon House, 1991.

This practical resource provides information and suggestions for children's activities in programs that are receptive of all children.

Appendix 2-E

Where to Call for Help

Following is a list of toll-free telephone numbers of disability-related nonprofit organizations and agencies. The numbers can be dialed from anywhere in the country.

- Access Board, U.S. Architectural and Transportation Compliance Board—800-USA-ABLE
- ADA Helpline at the Equal Employment Opportunity Commission—800-669-EEOC
- Alzheimer's Association—800-272-3900
- American Cancer Society—800-ACS-2345
- American Council of the Blind—800-424-8666
- American Diabetes Association—800-232-3472
- American Foundation for the Blind—800-232-5463
- American Kidney Fund Information—800-638-8299
- American Liver Foundation—800-223-0179
- American Parkinson's Disease Association—800-223-2732
- Amyotrophic Lateral Sclerosis (ALS) Association—800-782-4747
- Arthritis Foundation—800-382-7800
- Asthma and Allergy Foundation of America—800-727-8462
- Better Hearing Institute—800-327-9355
- Cancer Information Service—800-4-CANCER
- Captioned Films for the Deaf—800-237-6213, Voice/TDD
- Children's Craniofacial Association—800-535-3643
- Children's Hospice International—800-242-4453
- Cleft Palate Foundation—800-24-CLEFT
- Cornella de Lange Syndrome Foundation—800-223-8355
- Council of Citizens with Low Vision—800-733-2258
- Courage Center Stroke Network—800-553-6321
- Crohn's and Colitis Foundation of America—800-343-3637
- Cystic Fibrosis Foundation—800-344-4823
- Drug Abuse Hotline—800-662-HELP
- Endometriosis Association—800-993-ENDO
- Epilepsy Foundation of America—800-332-1000
- Hear Now–National Hearing Aid Bank—800-648-HEAR, Voice/TDD
- Higher Education and Training for People with Handicaps—800-54-HEATH
- Huntington's Disease Society—800-345-4372
- Job Accommodation Network—800-526-7234
- Job Opportunities for the Blind—800-638-7518
- Juvenile Diabetes Association—800-223-1138
- Library of Congress Handicapped Hotline—800-424-8567
- Lupus Foundation Information Line—800-558-0121
- Multiple Sclerosis 24-Hour Information Line—800-624-8236
- Myasthenia Gravis Foundation—800-541-5454
- National Adoption Center for Special Needs and Physically Disabled Children—800-TO-ADOPT
- National AIDS hotlines: English—800-342-AIDS; Spanish—800-344-SIDA; Deaf—800-AIDS-TTY
- National Alliance for the Mentally Ill—800-950-NAMI
- National Captioning Institute—800-533-WORD, Voice/TDD
- National Center for Youth with Disabilities—800-333-6293
- National Down Syndrome Congress—800-232-NDSC

- National Down Syndrome Society—800-221-4602
- National Easter Seal Society—800-221-6827
- National Head Injury Foundation Family Helpline—800-444-NHIF
- National Health Information Center—800-336-4797
- National Hearing Aid Society Helpline—800-521-5247
- National Hospice Organization Helpline—800-658-8898
- National Information Center for Children and Youth with Disabilities—800-999-5599
- National Information Clearinghouse for Infants with Disabilities—800-922-9234
- National Kidney Foundation—800-622-9010
- National Neurofibromatosis Foundation—800-323-7938
- National Ogranization of Rare Disorders—800-999-6673
- National Organization on Disability—800-248-ABLE
- National Rehabilitation Information Center—800-34-NARIC
- National Reye's Syndrome Foundation—800-233-7393

- National Spasmodic Torticollis Association—800-487-8385
- National Spinal Cord Injury Association—800-962-6929
- National Spinal Cord Injury Hotline—800-526-3456
- National Tuberous Sclerosis Association—800-225-NTSA
- Orton Dyslexia Society—800-222-3123
- Retinitis Pigmentosa Foundation—800-638-2300
- Short Stature Foundation Helpline—800-24-DWARF
- Simon Foundation for Incontinence—800-23-SIMON
- Spina Bifida Association—800-621-3141
- Stuttering Foundation of America—800-992-9392
- Tourette's Syndrome Association—800-237-0717
- United Cerebral Palsy—800-872-1827
- United Leukodystrophy Foundation—800-728-5483
- United Ostomy Association—800-826-0826

Chapter 3

Living with Disability: The Family Perspective

By Barbara Coccodrilli Carlson; Linda Swenson Cranor; and Anne Kuschner, M.A.

Introduction

In the very best of worlds, the birth of a child is marked by a sense of awe, wonder, and joy. With few exceptions, people of every religion, race, and culture celebrate this remarkable event. When a baby enters this world, we are reminded of who we are, where we come from, and the possibilities we hope will unfold for this young child. The experience of birth is one of the most intimate events of our lives.

It is within this context of the universality of parenthood and its joys and sorrows that we consider

A parent is always a person first. He or she cannot be separated from parenthood, of course, but an individual is also much more than just a parent. Having a child is merely one part of a complicated role as a person. The parent is also a son or daughter, a husband or wife, a worker, a citizen, a consumer, and many other things.

— Leo Buscaglia

the impact on a family when an unexpected life event occurs, such as the birth of a child with a disability or the diagnosis of such a disability. This chapter will discuss the range of responses that we as human beings experience when something happens in our lives that is unplanned and is of such significance. It will build a framework from which to understand families that have a child with a disability. We know that all families are unique and that no single book or resource will prepare us for all we might need to know. However, by considering how families are more alike than different in the ways they cope and function, we will better serve all children and their families.

ABOUT THE AUTHORS

Barbara Coccodrilli Carlson is director of the early childhood program for the Miriam and Peter Haas Fund. She formerly coordinated the Integrated Early Childhood Programs Project for the New York State Council on Children and Families. She is an attorney and has worked as both an early childhood special education teacher and a "generic" child care teacher. She is the proud parent of two young children, one having special needs. At the time this chapter was written, Barbara was a staff attorney at the Child Care Law Center in San Francisco. Barbara has served on the executive committees of the High Risk Infant Interagency Council of San Francisco, the Epilepsy Society of San Francisco, and the Developmental Disabilities Council of San Francisco.

Linda Swenson Cranor is the mother of two sons, Shattuc and Sylas. Shattuc was born with severe multiple disabilities. Linda has an undergraduate degree in social work. She began her career working with Vietnam veterans at Letterman Hospital in San Francisco while employed by the American National Red Cross. She has worked in the field of early childhood staff development for the past ten years. Her professional focus has been to bring the family perspective to early childhood and special education professionals. Linda's primary area of interest is in supporting family options and promoting equal opportunities for children with disabilities and their families in order to enable them to enjoy fully inclusive lifestyles.

Anne Kuschner is working at the California Institute on Human Services through Sonoma State University. She has worked in the field of early childhood special education for the past 20 years as educator, field consultant, and trainer. At the time this chapter was written, Anne was the early childhood special education administrator for the Napa County Office of Education. Her areas of professional interest include family-professional relationships, program development, supervision, assessment, and infant mental health issues. Anne's family includes her husband, two children, and an assortment of animals.

The purpose of this chapter is to lay the foundation for understanding the effects that a disability may have on families and to set the stage for providers by asking, What does it mean to this family to have a child whose disability may significantly alter the ways in which family members had hoped to live, to parent, and to grow old? The chapter will also enable child care professionals to understand more clearly the needs and circumstances of families that seek child care for young children with disabilities—and the ways in which these needs and circumstances affect child care. The following factors are affecting the nature of care: the changing nature of the family and the accompanying need for child care; the parallel between a family's response to disability and a response to any significant loss or life event; the effects these responses can have on family functions; the family's need and capacity to access resources such as child care; and finally, the ways in which these factors affect care providers and the family-caregiver relationship.

The Need for Quality Care

The challenge of obtaining quality, affordable child care is faced by many parents at some point. All parents want the very best for their children—options and choices and equal access to work. They also want assurances that their choices will foster optimal development for their children.

We are experiencing significant changes nationwide in the reasons for the need for child care. These changes are accentuated by a changing definition of family, which now takes into account a variety of situations and arrangements. Families seeking child care may include two-parent families, single-parent families, blended families, or families in which children are cared for and raised by members of an extended family. Families include adoptive parents and foster parents as well as parents from diverse cultural, linguistic, and economic backgrounds. As the *who* needing child care has changed, so has the *why*. The nature of need reflects the economic health of our society and an era of diminishing human service resources. Typically, the need for child care is an economic necessity rather than a choice for many families. Families of children with disabilities are reflective of all families seeking care. It is important, however, to understand some of the unique challenges they face and the scope of their needs.

In 1988 a study was completed by Berkeley Planning Associates titled *Child Care and Development Needs in California Families of Children with Disabilities*. The study included a statewide survey of 1,200 parents and providers as well as a review of data on child care needs. Contained in the report were the following conclusions:

- By 1990 the need to care for an estimated 275,000 children with exceptional needs would affect conditions or requirements for child care.
- On the basis of employment patterns in 1988, 72 percent, or 197,850, of these children would need child care.
- At least 25 percent of the children with disabilities in need of child care would be age five or under.
- State support of child care for children of any age with disabilities covers fewer than 1,000 children.

Given these conditions, 84 percent of the 500 surveyed families using child care had turned to providers who were "untrained in serving children with disabilities" and the "most common pattern of care (was) a combination of part-time arrangements." In addition, 37 percent of respondents indicated that they were "forced to take whatever they could find" to meet their child care needs, a figure that suggests that as many as 90,000 children with disabilities lack adequate child care alternatives.

What makes families of children with disabilities deserving of special attention is their limited choice and lack of options. The implications for the child care field are clear: We must recruit, train, and support providers to care for young children with disabilities.

Understanding Significant Losses

When our myths, dreams, and ideals are shattered, our world topples.

— Kathleen Casey Thiesen

Many families with a child who has a disability commonly report the sense of personal loss experienced after the birth or diagnosis. In the telling of their stories, parents often relate that the child they had planned for or perhaps dreamed of before and during the pregnancy has been taken away. By understanding and learning how individuals or families cope with loss and grief, we will more realistically understand the impact this event may have on a family's ability to continue in its normal routines, meet basic needs, and obtain needed resources.

There are no rules for grieving and no patterns for how or when we should grieve. An event such as the death of a significant other, the onset of a terminal illness, or the birth of a child with a disability generally sets into motion reactions that are not only normal but also serve important functions. These reactions are useful, realistic expressions of a range of feelings that mobilize our internal strengths and external resources to cope with loss. Much has been written on the process of grieving and significant losses (Kubler-Ross 1969, Moses 1983, Trout 1983). *What is important for providers to understand is that these feelings are within a range of normal, healthful responses to the reality of having a child with disabilities.* Typical feelings include:

1. Denial: Denying the existence, permanence, or impact of the disability
2. Anxiety: Searching, questioning, being immobilized, or feeling overwhelmed
3. Guilt: Feeling responsible and having a sense of "I caused this to happen"; fearing the disability is a punishment; and questioning, "Why me?"
4. Anger: Acting out and experiencing a sense of violation and displaced feelings of anger
5. Depression: Feeling a sense of loss and great sadness, experiencing an inability to act, and lapsing into a state of low self-esteem

6. Adjustment: Developing the capacity to accept one's child for who he or she is

Parents of older children have said that this is a time of reevaluating what is meaningful in life, shifting values, and living through a process of readjusting their life's expectations.

Families will be experiencing some or all of these feelings at different times depending on when they recognize that their child has a disability. Biological or adoptive parents who have a child with an obvious disability are likely to go through this process shortly after the child arrives. Other parents may not realize that their child has any sort of special need until that need surfaces as a result of medical problems or delays in development. Many families begin an emotional roller-coaster ride at the time the first diagnosis is made. Foster parents and adoptive parents who know about the child's disability before accepting the child into their family may have chosen the child specifically because of the child's special need. Although they may not experience feelings of guilt or denial, they will certainly be subject to much of the same frustration and stress as other families in similar circumstances.

Regardless of when families learn of their child's disability, each family member's response is unique and the expression of grief will follow its own personal course.

Grieving is important because it provides the space and time that protect us from dealing with an event that may be too difficult to face. It allows us time to seek information and support. When we experience a loss or a traumatic life event, we often feel an accompanying sense of loss of control. The world seems chaotic, not neat and orderly. Going through the daily routines takes an enormous amount of energy. It is a time of great vulnerability—when responses and reactions are often triggered unexpectedly and may be perceived as extreme.

As the child grows older, this process of loss may feel as though it will last forever. Each birthday, each major developmental milestone not met, each friendship not made, each friend or relative whose child grows with no complications, and each major life transition can cause a recurrence of the original feelings. *Living with disability is a continuing process of growth and reevaluation.*

Finally, it is important to know that the degree to which a disability affects a family depends on an array of circumstances, including:

1. A family's or an individual's personal beliefs about disability, parenting, and values
2. The nature of the disability
3. The degree of severity of the handicapping condition and the level of difficulty experienced in caring for the child
4. The age of the child when diagnosed and the age of the parents
5. The coping abilities of individual family members and the family unit
6. Additional family stress, such as economic strain, health problems, needs of siblings, or job insecurity
7. The degree to which family supports are in place and helpful
8. The sex and birth order of the child
9. The number, ages, and sex of siblings
10. The additional stresses faced by families that have emigrated to this country, such as those caused by adjustments to a new culture and dealing with language barriers

Although knowing about these feelings is valuable, it is important to understand that analyzing parents in regard to their grieving process serves no purpose. Professionals can fall into a pattern of judging parental responses, and this practice can interfere with understanding the family perspective. This material is being presented so that child care and development staff can understand what it may be like for families of children with disabilities, allowing them to "walk in their shoes." It is not intended as a tool for analyzing family responses.

Understanding Families

To understand the unusual circumstances of families with members who have exceptional needs, we must begin with what is important to all families. One context from which to view families is to ask, "What is the purpose of family?" Simply stated, it is to meet the basic needs of individual members and the family unit as a whole. How it works will vary depending on the makeup of the family, the roles and responsibilities of members, the family's economic situation, its values, and its cultural background. The task of meeting these basic needs is no different for families that have a child with a disability. These functions and needs must be met before families can devote time and energy to other concerns.

In discussing the concept of family systems, Ann Turnbull (1983) describes the following eight functions performed by family members:

1. *Economic.* Generating income and making family financial decisions

2. *Physical.* Providing health care and fulfilling physical requirements for the home, such as maintenance, food, and clothing

3. *Rest and recuperation.* Providing individual and family recreation and the enjoyment of hobbies

4. *Self-definition.* Establishing self-identity, self-image, and a sense of belonging

5. *Affection.* Nurturing and loving, expressing emotion and intimacy

6. *Guidance.* Solving problems, giving feedback and advice, and shaping values and beliefs

7. *Education.* Encouraging schoolwork, homework, continuing education, and cultural appreciation

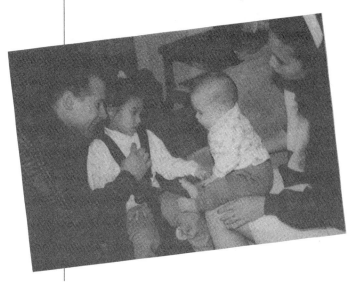

8. *Vocational.* Choosing a career, developing a work ethic, and supporting career interests

These family functions may be viewed from two additional perspectives. The first is the effect that the child's disability may have on the family's ability to meet day-to-day needs. Second is the adverse effect that a lack of child care may have on the family's ability to meet basic needs. A family unable to meet basic needs will most likely have difficulty in mobilizing the support, resources, time, or energy required to meet the extra demands of a child with a disability. Because families have different levels of flexibility and adaptation, how they cope with stressful life events, as a unit and as individuals, will be unique.

Another consideration is that a family's sense of well-being is often a reflection of the support systems available to them, including informal and formal networks of people or groups. Informal support is provided through the immediate family, extended family, friends, church members, or anyone intimately connected to the family. Formal support systems are agencies outside the family's intimate circle, such as human services, school programs, or health-related services. Cobb (1983) states that social supports enable people to feel that they are cared for and loved, are esteemed and valued, and are part of a network of mutual communication and obligation.

All families work toward meeting their basic needs. A family's ability to meet these needs within any of the eight areas described above by Turnbull (1983) is related to the availability of formal and informal support systems. When these systems are perceived as unavailable, inconsistent, or inadequate, the whole family is affected.

The birth or diagnosis of a child with a disability is often accompanied by the loss of a family's support systems. Support commonly expected from the extended family, such as child care, often does not exist. For example, as a reaction to loss and sorrow, grandparents may withdraw from interaction with the new child. Child care providers can offer support to families in place of the support of extended family members, and many families are likely to reach out in this way. However, it is important to acknowledge that professional boundaries exist between caregivers and parents. Although support can be offered on many levels, providers' roles will vary significantly from those of individuals in most informal support systems.

Close circles of friends, particularly friends with children of the same age as the child with the disability, often become less available. A family's circumstances may make old friends feel uncomfortable, guilty, or unable to share common child-rearing experiences. Families tend to make new friends among parents with children who have similar needs. Providers need to be aware of this tendency because it may influence a family's ability to make friends with other families with children in care. Families may benefit from referrals to parent organizations that focus on support for families of children with disabilities.

Families may be subject to a whole set of accommodations. For example, mothers may view themselves as unable to return to work or school because of the extensive level of care needed by their children. Parenting the child with a disability may become their career. This is particularly important for providers to remember because it may account for hesitancy or uneasiness on the part of the family to have the child cared for outside the home. Some two-parent families may make the choice for one parent to work in a reduced capacity—either part-time or at

a lower level of responsibility—to accommodate the child's medical and other agency appointments, frequent illnesses, or hospitalizations. The meeting of this family need may affect the parent's sense of self-esteem.

In addition to compromising the parent's ability to work, the child's disability may require frequent or highly specialized medical interventions, seriously affecting the economic well-being of the family. Insurance coverage, if available, often does not meet the cost of care in its entirety. One parent reported that the cost of her son's wheelchair was excessively high because a van had to be purchased and customized and a lift had to be installed to bring the child and chair into the van. Expenses such as these can leave a family financially devastated and most certainly stressed.

Often, families must make accommodations in other areas in which the parents of nondisabled children are unaffected. The capacity to enjoy leisure activities may be affected by the lack of accessibility or the severity of the child's handicap. Issues of division of labor in the care of the child with the disability may create stresses and affect the ability of the parents to meet the needs of other children in the family.

Accessing Services

One of the most difficult challenges parents of children with exceptional needs face is learning to secure services for their child. We are usually prepared for the birth of a child who develops typically, and we have a sense of familiarity with the tasks that will ensure such a child's passage through life. However, when a child is born or is diagnosed with a disability, parents may be unprepared for what that child's passage through life will involve.

Families may have to reach outside their intimate circle of support to find help within formal structures. Initially, the difficulty is simply in getting information, learning what is needed, and making decisions. This can be an overwhelming task when parents are coping with their grief, and they may feel inadequate or ill prepared. What was anticipated as a joyful time in their life may become a time of personal intrusion and increased anxiety about their capabilities to care for their own child. For this reason child care providers need to bring great sensitivity to their interactions with parents. The act of their asking for help and the realization that they are dependent on others to help care for their child may set family members apart in very painful ways.

Types of services needed

Children with disabilities may need a range of services and support from a variety of systems, each of which is generally governed by its own rules and regulations and has its own vocabulary. Each agency or service has a face, a form, and a telephone number. The highway of services may take a parent years to travel successfully. Typical of the types of services that families may need are the following:

- *Health services.* Children may have chronic or acute needs requiring highly specialized interventions. For some families finding health services that accept MediCal patients may consume a major amount of time. For example, MediCal dental care for children is very difficult to obtain. And families must sometimes drive as far as 60 miles to a dental office where this care is available.

- *Therapy.* Children who require therapy—such as physical, occupational, or speech and language therapy—and who are

eligible for services can often be seen only on a workday. As a result parents may have to take time off work or find alternate means of transportation.

- *Early intervention/early childhood special education programs.* Securing adequate educational services may involve participation in assessments, school meetings, and parent education activities and a host of other responsibilities and obligations.

Other agencies that may be involved with families include regional centers for developmental disabilities; public health departments; social service agencies; agencies that provide financial assistance and housing assistance; or specialized services agencies, such as the Blind Babies Foundation.

What it takes

Obtaining needed services for a young child with a disability is one of the most difficult, stressful, and frustrating experiences reported by parents. A family's access to support may depend on the availability of professionals who can speak their language; understand their culture, needs, and concerns; and help them work within the system. In addition, there may be gaps in services, waiting lists, processing delays, or cutbacks in services or personnel that make the search for help even more difficult. The list of ways to "fall through the cracks" is endless—a significant factor because available and accessible support services are what help families the most.

The challenges faced by families seeking services are significant. As families seek child care, providers may see the stress-related effects in a variety of ways:

- *Emotional impact.* Meeting new people, trying to understand what is needed to activate a service, being involved with a number of service agencies—all serve as constant reminders that their child is not "normal" or that their family is perceived as "different," perhaps "inadequate," or "not whole." Telling their personal story over and over to different professionals, filling out the required forms, and reiterating what is "wrong" require an enormous amount of emotional energy at a time when there is little left to give.

- *Physical impact.* Expending time and energy to meet the needs of a child with a disability, often in addition to the demands of the family and workplace, is exhausting. It can leave parents feeling enormously stretched and stressed and contributes to a sense of inadequacy because one cannot do it all.

- *Effects on the family system.* What is required to meet the needs of one family member most likely will significantly affect the quality and quantity of time available for other members. The needs of the child with the disability may overshadow the equally legitimate needs of other family members. Parents may find themselves constantly making choices between time for the child with exceptional needs, the siblings, and themselves.

Finding child care

Finding quality child care for infants and young children can be a trying experience for any family. For the parent of a young child with a disability, this difficult task brings numerous fears and concerns.

Like parents of all children, parents of children with disabilities will need to look for care that meets as many of their needs as possible. All parents look for a provider who:

1. Speaks the same language and understands the family's values
2. Lives close to their home or workplace
3. Offers rates that the family can afford
4. Has available space
5. Offers care during hours that are convenient
6. Provides a safe and healthful environment
7. Offers a program that encourages developmentally appropriate learning
8. Creates an emotional match with the family.

In addition to these considerations, parents of children with disabilities may have other concerns that contribute to the stress of securing child care. Parents will ask themselves:

1. Will there be anyone who will want to care for my child?
2. Will there be providers who know how to meet my child's exceptional care needs?
3. Will the provider want to charge more for my child, and how much will that be?

4. Will my child be treated differently or be excluded from the activities of other children?

5. Will the provider resent my child because of his or her disability?

6. How will the parents of other children react?

7. How will the other children treat my child? Will they be friends or will they tease?

8. Will my child be safe?

9. How will my child get to the infant program or the weekly therapy session? Can I juggle it all?

10. What if I cannot find care—what if no one will take my child?

Sadly and all too often, parents of children with disabilities are significantly limited in their options for child care. The choice of care at times comes down to who will not refuse the child. At a time when parents are already feeling a sense of loss of control over their lives, the lack of child care options and choice is deeply felt.

Considerations for Child Care and Development Staff

Influences on family-caregiver relationships

The purpose of this section is to help providers understand how a family's capacity to cope may influence the parent-provider relationship.

- *Lack of options.* Every county in California has a publicly funded child care resource and referral agency, but not every agency provides special referrals for children with disabilities or exceptional-care needs. When providers do indicate a willingness to accept children with disabilities, they are sometimes unable to accommodate the child for an extended period of time. For that reason many families change caregivers frequently.

- *One more system.* Parents may feel frustrated by the need to deal with one more set of rules; fill out one more set of forms; and answer one more series of personal questions about themselves, their child, and their family—and they may take out their frustration on the provider.

- *Inconsistent attendance.* Children's attendance is often inconsistent because of frequent illness, medical appointments, or special education programming. Already worried about finding any kind of child care for children with disabilities, the families of these children find the search for a program or provider willing to cope with inconsistent attendance to be one more obstacle confronting them.

- *Financial stress.* Child care providers may be affected by family stress resulting from financial problems. Typical expenses for families may include payments for health or therapy services, purchases of special equipment, assessment or evaluation fees, costs of transportation to appointments, and so on. Levels of financial assistance to families of young children with disabilities is often determined on income eligibility. Therefore, even parents who are middle-income wage earners may be significantly affected by these additional expenses, especially if the parents are not eligible for financial assistance.

Very often, the additional responsibility of parenting a child with exceptional needs affects the parents' ability to hold on to existing jobs. Finding positions that are flexible enough to accommodate the parents' need to be available for necessary appointments and planned or unexpected medical procedures or operations is very difficult. Lastly, families experience continuing stress in attempting to find and maintain child care placements that allow them to continue working and secure needed health care benefits for their child and the other members of the family.

- *Parental responses.* For many different and legitimate reasons, parents may seem withdrawn or depressed or may avoid being involved in typical parental activities. Providers may wonder whether they have done something wrong when the parents may simply be doing the best that they can at the moment.

Strategies for support

The following suggestions are offered to support providers who accept and include children with disabilities in their care programs. These suggestions have been shared by parents of children with disabilities and those who have provided care services for the children of these parents. This list is likely to grow in the years to come as others share their experiences.

- *Think of the child within the context of his or her family. Above all, embrace the belief that this little boy or girl is a child first.*

  1. Note and share the positive things about the child's day.
  2. Focus on the contributions a child makes while considering individual needs.
  3. Share the gains, even the smallest of steps.

- *Support, teach, and empower the family. But don't try to replace it. Learn from the parents how to help and care for their child. Remember to ask, "How is it for you?"*

  1. Ask such open-ended questions as, "Tell me about a typical day for Miko" or "In what ways do you consider Tom to have special-care needs?" when first meeting a parent.
  2. Ask for assistance from parents in solving specific problems.
  3. Share your observations, concerns, or feelings routinely and honestly.
  4. Understand that a parent may feel additional guilt or sadness when a child is left in care.

- *Assist parents in meeting other parents. Provide opportunities for families to come together in ways that foster enjoyable social interactions.*

  1. Introduce parents to one another. Most parents appreciate receiving a list of families with names of children and

phone numbers of other parents who have given written permission to be included on such a list.

2. Share specific interactions that occur between children during the day. Providers may want to post photos of children playing together in different activities.

3. Share your enthusiasm for providing special needs care.

4. Have information available on family support and local resources. Learn what is available in your community to help support families.

- *Think of and ask about other family members.*

    1. Recognize that the needs of each family member are equally as important as the needs of the child with disabilities. Support parents with this understanding.

    2. Recognize that a family's survival and well-being depend on their ability to meet such basic needs as housing, food, transportation, and health care. Appreciate the fact that the family's efforts to meet those needs in addition to meeting the needs of the child with disabilities may be affecting the welfare of the family.

    3. Be sensitive to sibling issues and include them in your conversations.

    4. Understand that when a child is born with a chronic illness or disability, the entire family system (including its informal supports) is under significant stress.

- *Be sensitive to times and circumstances that create stress for families.*

    1. Bring sensitivity to the times that may be difficult to face: pregnancies,

birthdays, Mother's Day, the first day of school, and so forth.

2. Recognize that when parents seem quiet, sad, angry, or irritable, their feelings probably have nothing to do with you.

3. Take the time to ask how a parent is doing, and be available if a parent seems to need someone to listen.

4. Do not feel responsible for the difficult times that parents inevitably have to cope with.

Summary

This chapter addresses the unique challenges facing families of children with disabilities and the stronger, more visible thread of commonality shared by all families.

All families have dreams for their children: They want them to reach their greatest potential; to be loved and to feel good about themselves; to be fully included in all aspects of life through their family, neighborhood, and community; and to be seen as valuable, contributing members of society.

All families function to meet basic needs in the best way they can. Some families experience additional problems, such as the need for affordable, quality child care for children with exceptional care needs. Those families should have the same options and choices for child care that are available to parents of children without disabilities. To offer this choice, providers must have the degree of training and support needed to enable them to provide extra care when required.

More than a child's disability itself, a family's lack of options and choices can threaten a family's survival. Fortunately, families are remarkably resilient in the face of the most devastating or challenging circumstances. Their desire to remain a family in whatever way that has meaning for them should be trusted and respected.

The effects of disability have been examined from many perspectives in this chapter. Perhaps most significant is the conviction most families share that their children with disabilities affect their lives positively. We learn from parents about their sense of personal growth, expansion of values, and reassessment of what is important to them in life. We learn about deeply personal struggles and about decisions made in the interest not only of the child with the disability but the whole family. To be able to work with families in this way is a privilege.

This chapter lays a foundation of understanding for child care providers about how it may be for some families to have a child with a disability. This is the starting point in offering services to families. The most important role that providers can play is being available and understanding of the

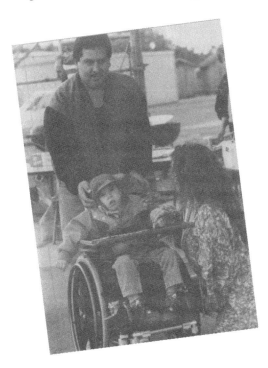

needs of families and the unique challenges they face in the parenting of a child with disabilities.

Lastly, but perhaps most important of all, is the right a family has to know what its individual rights are. They must understand that the birth of a disabled child does not take from them their rights as people. They still have the right for recreation, for time alone, for time with each other, for time to read, paint, write poetry, visit with friends, or what they will. It must not take away their right to complain, to bewail, to bemoan or to cry. In other words, they still have a right to be the human being that they were before the child was born and to become the human being toward which they aspire.

— Leo Buscaglia

KEY POINTS

1. Individuals experience a range of normal, healthful responses when a significant life event occurs that is unexpected or unplanned. These feelings help people cope and mobilize their internal strengths and external supports.

2. All families have basic needs. Families of children with disabilities may have additional concerns and stress related to meeting these basic needs.

3. Families unable to meet basic needs may not be able to mobilize the support, resources, time, or energy to meet any extra demands that a child with a disability places on them.

4. How a family responds to the birth of a child with a disability or to the diagnosis of a disability will depend on a number of variables. Families need both formal and informal support systems. If these are perceived as

8. Providers are helpful when they observe and understand a child within the context of the family. They are validating when they see a child as a child first and as a child with a disability second. They are exceptional when they are willing to walk in the shoes of another and to understand the world from a different perspective.

References

Buscaglia, Leo. 1989. *The Disabled and Their Parents: A Counseling Challenge.* New York: Holt, Rinehart & Winston.

Child Care and Development Needs in California Families of Children with Disabilities. 1988. Berkeley: Final Report for the California State Department of Education, Child Development Division. Berkeley Planning Associates.

Cobb, S. 1983. "Social Support as a Moderator of Life Stress," in Gallagher, Beckman & Cross. *Families of Handicapped Children: Sources of Stress and Its Amelioration,* pp. 10–18.

Cranor, L. 1988. *Preschool Special Education Program Handbook: A Resource to the Field.* Sacramento: Resources in Special Education.

Kubler-Ross, E. 1969. *On Death and Dying.* New York: Macmillan.

Kupfer. *Before and After Zachariah.* 1982. Chicago: Chicago Academy Publishers.

Moses, K. L. 1983. "The Impact of Initial Diagnosis: Mobilizing Family Resources," in *Parent-Professional Partnerships in Developmental Disability Services.* Edited by J. A. Mulick and S. M. Pueschel. Cambridge, Mass.: Academic Guild Publishers.

unavailable, inconsistent, or inadequate, the whole family is affected.

5. The need for accessible, high-quality, affordable child care for children with disabilities is staggering and is expected to increase. This need is directly related to the limited number of options and choices for parents and the need to recruit, train, and support professionals in the field of child care.

6. Families often must learn how to access needed services and make systems work for them and their child. External systems may seem to be intrusive in their personal lives. Providers can be sensitive in their requests for information from parents of children with disabilities and provide these parents with information about resources that are available to them.

7. Along with the usual concerns of all parents seeking child care, parents of children with disabilities may have additional concerns. Awareness of their concerns and efforts to alleviate their fears can be very helpful.

Trout, M. D. 1983. "Birth of a Sick or Handicapped Infant: Impact on the Family," *Child Welfare*. Vol. 62, No. 4 (July-August).

Turnbull, Summers, and Brotherson. 1983. *Working with Families with Disabled Members: A Family Systems Approach.* Lawrence: Kansas University Affiliated Facility at Lawrence, Bureau of Child Research.

Resources

Publications

Coleman, J. *The Early Intervention Dictionary*. Rockville, Md.: Woodbine House, 1993.

This useful book is a cross-disciplinary resource for clarifying and defining terminology used in early intervention services for young children. It is appropriate for professionals representing medical, educational, or therapeutic perspectives as well as for families involved in the field of early intervention.

Goldfarb, L. A., and others. *Meeting the Challenge of Disability or Chronic Illness: A Family Guide*. Baltimore: Paul H. Brookes, 1986.

Written primarily for families facing issues related to chronic illness and disability, this book provides insight and strategies that families can develop to meet the challenges of caring for an individual with special needs. The book employs a framework for problem solving, examples, and case studies to illustrate key concepts.

Lobato, Debra J. *Brothers, Sisters, and Special Needs: Information and Activities for Helping Young Siblings of Children with Chronic Illnesses and Developmental Disabilities*. Baltimore: Paul H. Brookes, 1990.

This book is a helpful resource in understanding the needs of siblings of children with chronic illnesses and developmental disabilities. Activities are suggested as well as specific strategies to support siblings in learning successful ways of coping with and adapting to family events and circumstances when there is a brother or sister with a disability.

Lynch, Eleanor W., and Marci J. Hanson. *Developing Cross-Cultural Competence: A Guide for Working with Young Children and Their Families*. Baltimore: Paul H. Brookes, 1992.

This book is a helpful resource for professionals who need to be aware of cultural factors as they work with children who have special needs and their families. The book helps to strengthen understanding of the role culture plays in establishing beliefs and shaping attitudes and behaviors. Specific strategies are provided that are crucial to developing cross-cultural competence in professionals who work with families from diverse linguistic, cultural, or ethnic backgrounds.

McAnaney, K. D. *I Wish: Dreams and Realities of Parenting a Special Needs Child*. Sacramento: United Cerebral Palsy Association of California, Inc., 1992.

This inspiring book offers the author's experiences of parenting in a way that will touch the feelings and broaden the perspectives of anyone working with families of children with disabilities.

May, J. *Fathers of Children with Special Needs: New Horizons*. Bethesda, Md.: Association for the Care of Children's Health, 1991.

This pamphlet looks at the response to parenting of fathers of children with special needs. It sensitively outlines the need for supportive fathers and identifies programs that will encourage their involvement. Strategies are suggested for building support groups, and additional resources are recommended that address the specific needs of fathers.

Miller, Nancy B. *Nobody's Perfect: Living and Growing with Children Who Have Special Needs*. Baltimore: Paul H. Brookes, 1994.

This book is a resource for parents that chronicles the experiences of several mothers as they strive to meet the needs of their children with special needs. A framework is created for identifying coping strategies for families as they meet the challenges of parenting a child with disabilities.

Neugebauer, B. *Alike and Different: Exploring Our Humanity with Young Children*. Redmond, Wash.: Exchange Press, 1987.

Powell, T. H., and P. A. Ogle. *Brothers and Sisters: A Special Part of Exceptional Families*. Baltimore: Paul H. Brookes, 1985.

Written for both parents and professionals, this book acknowledges the special relationships of siblings who are nondisabled. In addition to addressing issues that challenge those relationships and stressing the need for understanding and support, the authors recognize the contributions of the siblings to the families of which they are a vital part.

Simons, Robin. *After the Tears: Parents Talk About Raising a Child with a Disability*. Denver: Children's Museum of Denver, 1987.

Parents share their experiences in raising children with disabilities. Written to support parents, this eloquent book brings the reader closer to the experiences shared by many parents.

Training

MITCH (Model of Interdisciplinary Training for Children with Handicaps). A series designed for caregivers of infants and toddlers that deals with family functioning and the impact of a child with special needs. Tallahassee: Florida Department of Education, Division of Public Schools, Bureau of Education for Exceptional Students, 1990.

This series of 11 training and resource modules was developed to assist school districts in providing interdisciplinary training to parents, community child care personnel, and health care personnel who work with young children with disabilities from birth to five years of age. The modules include text, training scripts, and resources related to the specific topic areas.

Wolfe, B. L.; V. G. Petty; and K. McNellis. *Special Training for Special Needs*. Project ETC (Exceptional Training for Caregivers). Greater Minneapolis Day Care Association. The Portage Project, Portage, Wisconsin. New York: Allyn and Bacon, 1990.

This excellent resource for trainers is highly recommended. It is a competency-based training program for personnel who work with young children with special needs. It is appropriate for a variety of participants, including persons who work in early childhood education and special education. Each module identifies basic and special-needs competencies, uses a variety of training strategies, and includes handouts and resources.

Videos

Down's Syndrome: A Parental Perspective. Distributed by Learner Managed Designs, Inc., Lawrence, KS 66047; telephone (913) 842-9088.

Someday's Child: A Focus on Special Needs Children and Their Families. Produced by Educational Products, Inc., 7412 SW Beaverton Hillsdale Hwy., Suite 210, Portland, OR 97225.

Family Album. Portage Project, CESA 5, 626 East, Sliver Street, Portage, WI 53901; telephone (608) 742-8811.

Special Kids, Special Dads: Fathers of Children with Disabilities. SEFAM Family Support Program, Merrywood School, Bellevue, Wash.: Vision Productions, 1989.

Organization

National Information Center for Children and Youth with Handicaps (NICHCY), P.O. Box 1492, Washington, DC 20013.

This organization provides free information to assist parents, educators, caregivers, advocates, and others in helping children and youth with disabilities become participating members of their communities.

Chapter 4

Inclusion: Developmentally Appropriate Care for All Young Children

By Beth Hannaman, M.A.; and Kristin Zink, M.A., M.S.

Acceptance and belonging are the essence of a child's reality. For any child, belonging means having the same opportunities as anyone else to participate in life events. That participation has little to do with ability or disability but instead has to do with inclusion—knowing that there is but one world in which each person must play a part.

The magic of young children is that they are able to learn so much from each other. For the child with disabilities, the world

Ability is of little account without opportunity.

— Elbert Hubbard

unfolds when shared with other children in natural settings. And the worldview of children without disabilities is broadened when they understand that a person is much more than a disability. This chapter will explore the philosophy of developmentally appropriate care and provide strategies for the inclusion of children with disabilities in community child care settings.

Developmentally Appropriate Care

Inclusion is a developmentally appropriate practice for all children. Developmentally appropriate care and practice are based on knowledge of children and their needs. This care and practice include the incorporation of concepts that are individually appropriate, age appropriate, and developmentally appropriate. Regardless of the severity of their disabilities, children benefit from inclusive settings. In addition, the quality of appropriate developmental care is enhanced by meaningful involvement with the family

based on knowledge of a child's home life and family composition and by the involvement of adults significant to the child. Finally, developmentally appropriate practice involves the concept of the "whole child"; that is, understanding children within a context of age, strengths, needs, family, community, and culture.

Children share many needs in common: the need to satisfy hunger and thirst, the need for shelter and rest, the need for nurturing and love, and the need to develop a positive sense of self and self-esteem. All children need to experience belonging and friendship, to be respected and treated with dignity, to make choices and exercise personal rights, and to learn skills that help them grow into capable, contributing adults. These common needs are a part of each child's human experience regardless of ability, ethnicity, or culture. And yet, a key component in our care of and work with young children is a consideration of how they are individually unique.

How do child care and development staff honor diversity?

Our world is made up of diverse groups of individuals. As adults working with young children, we are in a position to

ABOUT THE AUTHORS

Beth Hannaman is an early childhood resource teacher in the Special Education Department, San Diego City Unified School District. She received B.A. and M.A. degrees from Ohio University in speech pathology. She has worked for the past 14 years with preschool-aged children. Her current responsibilities include developing and coordinating alternative programs for preschool children with special needs; coordinating mainstreaming options in preschool and special day classes; and serving as an itinerant teacher for identified children enrolled in private preschools and child care settings. Beth is a parent of a daughter who has Down syndrome.

Kristin Zink has worked with young children and adults for the past 25 years. She has taught in the field of early childhood development and has served as a community college instructor. Her interests focus on the whole child, developmentally appropriate curricula and environments, and the manner in which children learn. She is a full-time child development instructor at Cuyamaca College, El Cajon.

explore diversity and help children experience each other's differences as positive and interesting attributes.

Honoring diversity begins with understanding who we are and where our own values lie. We need to recognize in what ways our values might differ from the families of children in our care. If, as adults, we have not carefully examined our own expectations about all aspects of human diversity, including our feelings about disability and inclusion, we might convey unintentionally negative attitudes or messages to children in our care.

Child care providers are in a unique position to guide children in their acceptance of differences. Children develop strong and positive attitudes toward differences through their experiences and their interactions with others. For young children, this acceptance occurs when there are opportunities to be with other people who may look or sound different, who practice different customs or beliefs, or who have disabilities. Understanding and acceptance of differences are natural outgrowths of being with others who are different from ourselves.

Adults play important roles in the lives of young children by modeling respectful behaviors and by setting clear standards. Lessons in diversity can be taught through direct instruction, the "teachable moment," and selective intervention. For example, when talking about disabilities, adults should state facts simply and honestly. Adults can also facilitate learning about diversity when negative comments are made about race, culture, or disability by increasing children's sensitivity to the effects those comments can have on others. Chapter 2, "More Alike Than Different," offers a more in-depth discussion of these strategies.

Developmentally Appropriate Environments

Learning environments that support the value of individual differences are essential to developmentally appropriate inclusive care. Aspects of learning environments to be considered in the following sections include:

- Fostering participation in play

- Promoting social interactions for children with disabilities

- Allowing children to make choices

- Organizing physical spaces, toys, and materials

- Planning consistent and predictable routines

Why is play important in developmentally appropriate environments?

A child's world takes on meaning through the development of his or her senses. Accordingly, young children learn through play, which provides them opportunities to solve problems, make decisions, resolve social conflicts, practice skills, and feel competent in their world. Child care providers know the value of play and its relationship to the development of the whole child. They should also be aware of the effects a disability may have on a child's ability to use play as a means of learning about the world.

How might a disability affect a child's play?

A disability can affect the way a child plays, the quality of play, or the ability to use play as a primary means of learning and generalizing new skills and concepts. There are no specific rules on how to adapt a curriculum for a particular disability. Instead, we must be careful observers of children in order to learn about their strengths and needs. Observations will provide guidance in planning and implementing interventions. Generally, families are invaluable resources in helping us understand their children. Ask parents about toys a child enjoys and about favorite activities. Find out whether adapted toys or materials are used at home or elsewhere, such as in motor therapy sessions or special education programs. Invite parents to demonstrate techniques that have been successful at home to engage the child in play. Professionals working with children are also important sources of information. Don't be hesitant to try different approaches with children in your setting. Remember that, although guidelines do exist, recipes for working with individual children do not. The best advice that can be given is to trust the child to be your guide.

Environmental factors, personality, and even gender influence the development of play skills. The impact of a disability often becomes an additional variable in how a child develops through play. A child may use toys inappropriately, be unable to sustain a play sequence, lack spontaneity or exploration in play, or persist at a particular level of development. It may be difficult for some children to learn through play without adult help. Activities that enable all children to be successful at their own skill level should be encouraged. It is also important to know the next developmental step or sequence to that step in order to appropriately challenge children in their play. For example, when presented with toys, a child might engage in repetitive banging. The child care provider might expand the play by presenting a variety of surfaces for the child to bang,

model releasing the toys onto surfaces, or try presenting toys which cannot be banged or that require two hands to manipulate or explore. Adults play critical roles in determining the type and extent of support necessary to ensure growth. Some general considerations for enhancing play skills for children with disabilities are outlined in the chart on the next page.

Promoting Social Interactions for Children with Disabilities

Think Kid Power. Kids can do with inclusion what adults can't. It's important to start our friendships early on.

— Ann Turnbull

Few would argue the appropriateness of including children with disabilities in any aspect of life. However, children with disabilities may often be deprived of everyday opportunities to be with other children. Often, the more visible a disability is, the more restrictive opportunities become. For this reason supporting child care and development staff in the inclusion of children with disabilities is critical.

When developmental needs are being considered and appropriate environments are being planned, what is most important for all children is the opportunity to be with other children. Learning appropriate social behaviors is a fundamental task in early childhood. Self-esteem is built on a child's sense of competence, ability to make friends, and knowledge of being valued and liked by other people. Social competence does not occur in isolation of other developmental tasks but is an integral part of the developmental process. An important task of

Considerations for Enhancing Play Skills
for Children with Disabilities

Type of Disability	Play Strategies
Communication or learning	Provide good language models. Use such comments as "Show me" to help a child be understood. Listen attentively, give good eye contact, and use words for objects and places. Avoid yes or no responses by asking open-ended questions. Use a variety of ways to communicate, and allow time for the child to process information.
Physical	Provide cause-effect toys and materials children can easily access. Position children so that they can interact with others. Plan for different levels of participation. At times, proximity to others is the goal. Observe children for fatigue, allow time to complete tasks, and provide opportunities to rest. Outdoor riding toys can be modified, or bucket swings can be used.
Visual	Heighten awareness of all sensory input. Make sure that the child is able to hear at all times. Give auditory and/or tactile cues to alert a child to changes in activities or to solicit attention. Expand play behaviors if the child appears to be limiting exploration to mouthing or smelling. A child may need guidance in initiating social interactions with peers.
Hearing	Use communication strategies that parents have identified as their preferences. Always be at a child's eye level and in clear view of a child. Help the child learn the social cues of other children as well as how to approach and be involved in the play of others. If signing is used, most children enjoy learning signs to communicate with friends who have hearing impairments.
Emotional or behavioral	An important strategy is to teach a child alternative behaviors for communicating their needs or frustrations. Set clear limits and instruct all children in how to use their words to communicate what they do not like. Some children may need direct adult intervention to learn and practice acceptable play or social skills. Limit choices. Provide a mixture of quiet and vigorous activities. Be alerted if a child has a short attention span or has difficulty in organizing play.
Developmental	Use materials that allow for multisensory exploration and activities that are open-ended and that encourage imitation of higher-level skills. Children may need more experience with real objects in their play, such as clothes for dress-up, dolls, or "furniture" for house play. Involvement and proximity to other children will improve purposeful play and a child's range of play skills. Play sequences or tasks may need to be taught in small steps.

childhood is to become socialized within the family, culture, and community.

Social skills are learned behaviors that begin soon after birth. Adults respond to an infant's cries, smiles, and vocalizations. By rewarding or ignoring certain behaviors, adults help to shape a child's social development. As an infant grows, social development follows a predictable pattern. Through play, infants and toddlers become interested in the world around them. They watch other children but do not yet "play" with them. At about three years of age, children become more socially aware of other children. Beyond that age they begin learning from other children as well as adults. By age five most children have developed a foundation of social skills that will last a lifetime.

Regardless of the setting, opportunities for social interaction occur throughout a child's day through both adult-directed and child-directed activities. Bos (1990) suggests that we ask questions about the socialization aspects of our learning environments. Does this activity encourage a child to work with another? Can this individual activity be expanded to include more children? Does this activity encourage one child to ask another for help?

How does the environment promote social integration?

All children benefit from being with other children. However, being together does not automatically imply that children will interact and become friends with one another. Many children with disabilities will need additional help in developing social skills. The role of the adult is to help bring children together in ways which support their growth and development, particularly as to socialization.

The concept of environment and its relationship to learning includes not only how physical space and materials are organized but also how the space facilitates interactions and accommodates individual needs. The design of a developmentally appropriate environment must focus on planning for the whole child. Although a disability may need to be an important consideration in the implementation of a program or the care of a child by an adult, it is only one component among many to be examined in attempting to understand the child.

The design and setup of all child care and development environments include inside and outside activities. How the environment is organized has a significant influence on the quality of children's play, learning, and socializing. A child-directed environment offers opportunities for self-selection and initiation, encourages young children to explore and experiment with materials and ideas, and brings children together in cooperative and interactive play. Child-initiated environments foster problem solving and decision making and empower children to exercise control within a safe setting.

The environment reflects a provider's understanding of the individual needs of children. For example, there may need to be both a traditional block area for building on the floor and a block table situated nearby so that a child in a wheelchair can access the materials. Play spaces for small groups of children to engage in cooperative activities can also be designed to include a child with disabilities. A book area that includes tactile materials for children with low vision will allow small integrated groups of children to gather.

While the philosophy of open-ended activities is promoted, it is also acknowledged that learning occurs when experiences do not turn out as expected. An atmosphere that allows for healthy failure teaches children that it is all right to "mess up" and not to complete activities perfectly, or to complete them differently by, for example, adapting materials to meet their needs. Children learn through practice and repetition. Adults sometimes believe that they have to provide new and different activities every day. But children gain confidence and security when there is a balance of familiarity and novelty, such as replaying a scenario with a new ending. Play and hands-on experience foster learning and competence. As children work with objects and ideas, they learn to manipulate and master their environment. As a result, they feel good about themselves and others and discover answers to questions through their interactions with materials and with one another.

Important goals in planning activities are to support children in positive learning experiences and involve them in the joy of self-discovery: "I can do this," "The paint is red," "Play dough can be shaped like a ball," or "Blocks can be stacked and knocked down." Children learn by doing. It is as simple as that. They develop positive self-concepts and self-images when they are provided developmentally appropriate activities that encourage meaningful interactions within their environments.

Specific strategies for promoting social interactions through daily activities and scheduling are discussed in Appendix 4-A. Appendix 4-B provides guidelines for promoting socialization opportunities for children who have disabilities.

Why does the environment need to include child choice?

Children learn best through experience, exploration, and experimentation. This type of learning is meaningful and enjoyable. Care providers are responsible for creating environments in which children discover new ideas and facts. Burton White (1975) offers the analogy that adults are the architects of the child's environment—set designers for the production in which children are the stars.

Providing children with a choice of activities involves planning and preparation. *Child choice does not work if the adult is not prepared.* The keys to success lie in setting up the activity or center, providing environmental cues, and organizing areas and materials. Open-ended activities in which the materials involved can be used in a variety of ways without a predetermined outcome are especially appropriate for self-selected learning opportunities. These activities can be simplified or made more complex as individual children require. The child controls the outcome and the adult does not present a model or example of the completed project.

Some children may require adult help in learning to use materials. Adults may also need to help expand a child's skill level by challenging her or him during a chosen activity. For example, if a child continues to mark with crayons repetitively on paper, the adult might model broad strokes or circular strokes. Or the child might require hand-over-hand assistance from an adult.

The concept of choice for children with disabilities is especially important in encouraging a positive sense of self. All children are empowered when provided control or opportunities to choose what to wear, what to eat, what toys to play with, or even what friends to be with. For some children, however, choices are limited by the nature of their handicap. Perhaps they are unable to move independently toward a group of friends, are unable to use words as a means of communication, or are withdrawn and have difficulty including others in their world. As adults we give very clear messages about a child's capabilities when we provide choices at every opportunity. A child can indicate choice in many ways: by looking, reaching, touching, pointing, using words or gestures. The adult's task is to be creative in building on every child's ability to make choices in daily routines. It is very easy to "act on" children or "speak for" children when days or routines become busy. However, in whatever ways possible, adults need to model the importance of child choice.

How might a disability affect child choice?

Not all children are ready to come into a room and immerse themselves in an activity, even if the activities are enticing and interesting. Some children need to have their choices limited to a couple of good alternatives. If a child appears overwhelmed or too stimulated by the activities, try limiting choices. "Would you like to paint or play with the sand?" Or "Chantrelle, sometimes it's hard to choose. Let's start by looking at this book about animals."

A child's self-initiation and sense of curiosity about the environment are fostered by rich, challenging materials and experi-

ences. Exploring, creating, and acting help children feel good about learning and their ability to make things happen. Having choices in activities and materials leads to confidence and positive self-esteem. Every child has an individual style of approaching activities and learning. Some children may need more structure than others. Watch for their individual rhythms as they move through the day's activities. Be sensitive to each child's avenues of self-discovery and "safe bases" (places where the child can escape, rest, or regroup from the buzz of activity in the rest of the room). Note when a child needs individual encouragement, assistance, or motivation. Look for ways in which children can control their learning experiences or achieve success through minor adaptations. For example, a child with fine-motor difficulties might need to have drawing paper taped down in order to draw; and a child with low vision may need to have drawing paper placed in a tray with edges. Remember that the adult is the architect of the child's environment.

How should the environment be organized?

In considering how environments should be organized to support play and the inclusion of children with disabilities, begin with what are appropriate considerations for all children. For many children with disabilities, the environment will not have to be modified.

Use the tools of organization and space to increase the potential of a learning environment. The environment should tell the child what to do by how it is organized. Ask yourself: Are like materials together? For example, each type of manipulative toy could be stored in a separate container, clearly labeled with a picture of the item glued to the outside of the container. This strategy encourages independence in many children with disabilities by providing helpful visual clues about the environment. Careful consideration of traffic patterns can facilitate social interactions and ease transitions from area to area. Is there enough space for children to freely explore the environment and use the materials safely without excess interference from others? Children's internal sense of organization seems to be helped by defining important areas, such as quiet spaces and eating areas. For children who have difficulty with internal controls, as demonstrated by impulsive behaviors or hyperactivity, the organization of the environment will contribute significantly to their management of their behaviors and their availability to learn.

In selecting toys and educational materials, care workers need to consider whether they support the involvement of children with disabilities. For example, an ever-increasing array of books and children's magazines are available that communicate the positive aspects of diversity and help address children's questions or concerns. Also commercially available are toys and materials that have been adapted or are easily adapted for children with disabilities. Family members or specialists working with a particular child can usually provide excellent suggestions or lend toys that have been adapted, such as battery-operated toys with switches.

The adult role is critical in teaching and modeling positive social interactions and in designing and implementing activities that support inclusive, developmentally appropriate environments. Chapter 2, "More Alike Than Different," offers further discussion on this topic, particularly in regard to selecting appropriate books for young children.

Any modification of the environment will depend on the individual needs of the child or children in your care. The chart on the next page lists points to consider.

How can the environment help to build trust and independence?

Through stability, routines, and predictability, a young child develops a sense of trust in the environment. Limits and guidelines for behavior build trust when they are consistent and simple: "Play dough stays at the table," " Keep the paint on the paper," or "Books are for reading. Come throw bean bags to me." In these ways, children come to know the environment and to trust the adults within it.

A child's sense of competence and independence is encouraged by opportunities to make appropriate choices and through the development of trusting relationships. Independence develops as children increase their language skills, problem-solving abilities, physical development, and social-interactive skills. In the planning of supportive environments, direction can be provided by:

- Spending time with parents or other significant adults to design interventions that might be helpful to the child. Often, others have experienced similar concerns and have found workable solutions.

Considerations in Modifying Environments
for Children with Disabilities

Type of Disability	Planning Strategies
Learning	Arrange space in ways that help a child to focus on learning activities. Reduce unnecessary visual distracters (materials). Consider a quiet space to work.
Physical	Space may be needed to accommodate movement of special equipment, such as a walker or a wheelchair. Special chairs or positioning equipment may be needed throughout the day, requiring extra space. Children may need to be placed away from areas where they might be bothered by loud or sudden noises, such as a telephone.
Visual	Children must be familiarized with the room arrangement. Clutter should be minimized. Look for ways in which the child can be as independent as possible by using auditory and tactile cues as guides. Provide work space that has reduced noise and movement for children who are easily distracted.
Hearing	Capitalize on visual and tactile cues to help guide a child in daily routines and activities. Seat a child so that there is a clear view of the speaker. Good lighting is also important. Learn how to use any hearing the child does have in ways which will foster independence and interaction with others. If a child can hear the sound of a particular bell, use it to signal transition.
Emotional or behavioral	Children may need very predictable environments and structured routines. Rooms may need reduced stimulation, and choices may need to be limited. Some children are helped by having very concrete cues for transitions, such as a ringing bell or pictures of the next activity. Some children are helped by having a special area where they can go when they feel the need to be away from others. For others, having an adult nearby may help them maintain a focus and sense of control.
Developmental	Children may need more multisensory experiences and space that invites open-ended exploration and play. Familiarize the child with the space and provide tactile and visual cues as guides. Be aware of safety considerations for a child who is not cognitively aware and who may place objects in his or her mouth or touch objects that might cause injury.

- Ensuring that daily routines and expectations of child behaviors are consistent and are matched appropriately to the developmental levels of each child.

- Helping children to realize what consequences will result from unacceptable behaviors: "Biting hurts your friends. When you bite, you need to sit here with me."

- Learning to identify events that may adversely affect a child's behavior, such as noise levels or overly stimulating environments. Intervene before there is a problem.

- Trying to redirect children when they are apparently having difficulty in managing their level of participation in an activity or with friends.

Typically, caregivers learn to read children's cues before difficulties arise and are able to intervene in helpful ways.

Building a sense of trust in young children becomes increasingly important and challenging for children whose constitutions place them at risk for normal growth and development. Equally at risk are those children whose family lives do not provide stability, routines, or predictability. Often, these are children whose needs do not qualify them for additional educational services but, nevertheless, may place them at risk for later developmental problems. These children are often unavailable for learning. A more in-depth discussion on children at risk is included in Chapter 7, "Caregiving Strategies: Building Resilience in Children at Risk."

Observing Children: The Key to Quality Practice

"Observation of children and looking at children are not synonymous—observation is noticing and paying attention to the character-

istics, behaviors, and circumstances which occur during the period of observation" (Richarz 1980). The richest sources of information about children are the children themselves. Information on family and culture, special needs, areas of interest, and motivation can be gathered through observations of the child.

Why is observation important?

No better tool exists for individualized planning than observation. To meet the needs of an individual child most effectively, try to incorporate regular and systematic observation into each day. Irwin and Bushnell (1980) suggest that observation be used to gather information about children to:

- Generate ideas about the children. (What interests do the children have?)

- Answer specific questions. (Why does Susanna seem to spend so much time wandering around the room?)

- Provide a more realistic picture of behavior or events. (What can Lionel do in spontaneous play that he appears unable to do on request?)

- Better understand children's behavior. (What are the learning styles of specific children?)

- Evaluate behavior and performance. (How does Martha respond to a new situation? or Is Tom able to eat with a spoon?)

Undoubtedly, observation facilitates planning and learning. By observing children, we are better equipped to meet their needs. We are more sensitive to **who** they are and **what** they need from us and their environment.

Good ways of gathering information through the observation process include the following:

- *Informal notes:* Write notes about a particular child or setting. Try keeping an index card for each child close at hand and jotting down key words about what is observed. Later, you can go back and fill in the details. One use of this technique is to keep track of what activities are especially interesting to an individual child.

- *Specific events:* Watch for a particular behavior or interaction. Record exactly what preceded the event, what happened, and what occurred subsequently. This observation technique can be useful in dealing with problem behaviors, such as biting or hitting.

- *Checklists:* List the skills or areas you want to observe and check them off as they are observed in individual children. These observations may provide valuable information about children for parent conferences.

Good observation is unbiased and nonjudgmental. Record your observations in an objective manner without incorporating your interpretations, beliefs, or expectations into what you observe. To use observation as a guide to understanding and planning for children, you must be objective.

The best curriculum-planning and guidance techniques are rooted in good observational practice (Hendrick 1989, 1991). Observe the children, notice where their strengths and concerns lie, and write down examples and strategies. Is Jason *always* spilling the paint? Through systematic observation you may discover that the brushes are too long for him. How can Erika, who uses a walker, be included in the music and movement experience? Observe her capabilities for movement, and plan a specific sequence for the group based on those abilities. Observing that Lupe seems to avoid eating certain foods may lead you to ask her parents about "family favorites" or food that Lupe likes to eat at home. Use observation to learn about children!

Summary

Each friend represents a world in us, a world possibly not born until they arrive; and it is only by this meeting that a new world is born.

— Anaïs Nin

Inclusion of children with disabilities in child care and development settings is developmentally appropriate for all children. Everyone benefits through inclusion. What must be considered is how we will direct ourselves to meet this goal. Essential to the successful placement of any child with disabilities is a positive attitude and a willingness to support children. Success depends on several important factors. Practical and hands-on support through staff development, collaboration with other agencies and professionals, access to resources, and information are the foundations from which our efforts begin. Successful inclusion will also be affected by the capability of child care and development staff to enhance the skills they already have to respond appropriately to the needs of all children. Success will depend on having care providers who value and respect each child's individuality; who model appropriate responses and interactions with children having diverse needs; and who possess the knowledge required to be effective providers—knowledge gained through careful observations of children in collaboration with families and specialists. These relationships will help set the foundation for ensuring a warm and welcoming place for all children to grow and develop—a place to belong, to be included, to be with friends.

KEY POINTS

1. Inclusion is a developmentally appropriate practice for all children.

2. Child care providers are in a unique position to guide children in accepting differences in people.

3. A disability can affect how children play and to what extent they use play as a means of learning.

4. A critical role of child care and development staff is to foster social relationships among children through the careful planning of daily activities and structuring of the environment.

5. For children with disabilities, choice and open-ended activities are especially important in developing a positive sense of self.

6. Creating environments that demonstrate stability, routines, and predictability helps children to develop a sense of trust and mastery.

7. Regular and systematic observation is an important tool in determining the individual strengths and needs of children.

8. Ongoing communication among family members, child care providers, and other professionals supports developmentally appropriate inclusive care.

9. Practical and hands-on support, collaborative efforts, and access to resources and information are necessary to developing successful child care placements.

References

Bos, B. *Together We're Better*. Roseville, Calif., 1990.

Hendrick, J. *Total Learning*. Columbus, Ohio: Merrill Publishing Co., 1989.

Hendrick, J. *The Whole Child*. Columbus, Ohio: Merrill Publishing Co., 1991.

Hohmann, M.; B. Banet; and D. P. Weikart. *Young Children in Action: A Manual for Preschool Educators*. Ypsilanti, Mich.: The High/Scope Press, 1979.

Irwin, D. M., and M. M. Bushnell. *Observational Strategies for Child Study*. New York: Holt, Rinehart & Winston, 1980.

Richarz, A. *Understanding Children Through Observation*. New York: West Publishing Co., 1980.

White, B. L. *The First Three Years of Life*. New York: Avon Books, 1975.

Resources

Alike and Different: Exploring our Humanity with Young Children. Edited by B. Neugebauer. Redmond, Wash.: Exchange Press, Inc., 1987.

Allen, K. E. *Mainstreaming in Early Childhood Education*. Albany, N.Y.: Delmare, 1980.

Arenson, B., and B. Hannaman. *Hand in Hand*. San Diego: San Diego City Unified School District, 1983.

Carta, J., and others. "Developmentally Appropriate Practice: Appraising Its Usefulness for Young Children with Disabilities," *Topics in Early Childhood Special Education*. Vol. 11 (1991), 1–19.

Cohen, D., and L. Stern. *Observing and Recording the Behavior of Young Children*. New York: Teachers College Press, 1958.

Cook, R.; A Tessier; and V. Armbruster. *Adapting Early Childhood Curricula for Children with Special Needs*. Columbus, Ohio: Merrill Publishing Co., 1987.

Derman-Sparks, L. *Anti-Bias Curriculum: Tools for Empowering Young Children.* Washington,, D.C.: National Association for the Education of Young Children, 1989.

Developmentally Appropriate Practice in Early Childhood Programs Serving Children Birth Through Age Eight. Washington, D.C.: National Association for the Education of Young Children, 1987.

Doerre, D. "Selecting Materials for Mainstreamed Preschools," *Topics in Early Childhood Special Education,* Vol. 2 (1982), 33–42.

Dunlop, K. "Mainstreaming: Valuing Diversity in Children," *Young Children,* Vol. 5 (1977), 26–32.

Fallen, N. H., and J. McGovern. *Young Children with Special Needs.* Columbus, Ohio: Merrill Publishing Co., 1978.

Fewell, R. R., and R. Kaminski. "Play Skills Development and Instruction for Young Children with Handicaps," in *Early Intervention for Infants and Children with Handicaps.* Baltimore: Paul Brooks, 1988, pp. 145–58.

Friel-Patti, S, and J. Lougeay-Jottinger. "Preschool Language Intervention: Some Key Concerns," *Topics in Language Disorders,* Vol. 3 (1985), 46–56.

Gillis, H. "Observations of the Play Behavior of Infants and Young Children," in *Team Assessment in Early Intervention.* Sacramento: Resources in Special Education, 1990, pp. 117–38.

Hazen, N.; B. Black; and F. Fleming-Johnson. "Social Acceptance," *Young Children,* Vol. 9 (1984), 26–36.

Including Children with Special Needs in Early Childhood Programs. Edited by M. Wolery and J. Wilbers. Washington, D.C.: NAEYC, 1994

Mainstreaming Children with Special Health Needs in Child Care Settings. San Diego State University, 6505 Alvarado Road, Suite 108, San Diego, CA 92120, (619) 594-4373, n.d.

Odom, S. O., and M. A. McEvoy. "Integration of Young Children with Handicaps and Normally Developing Children," in *Early Intervention for Infants and Children with Handicaps.* Baltimore: Paul Brooks, 1988, pp. 241–67.

Pitcher, E.; S. Feinburg; and D. Alexander. *Helping Young Children Learn* (Fourth edition). Columbus, Ohio: Merrill Publishing Co., 1989.

Reynolds, V., and L. Brekken. *Preschool Special Education Program Handbook.* Sacramento: California Department of Education, 1988.

Reynolds, E. *Guiding Young Children: A Child-centered Approach.* Mountain View, Calif.: Mayfield Publishing Co., 1990.

Safford, P. *Integrated Teaching in Early Childhood: Starting in the Mainstream.* New York: Longman, Inc., 1989.

Smith, C. *Promoting the Social Development of Young Children: Strategies and Activities.* Mountain View, Calif.: Mayfield Publishing Co., 1982.

Souweine, J.; S. Crummins; and C. Mazel. *Mainstreaming Ideas for Teaching Young Children.* Washington, D.C.: National Association for the Education of Young Children, 1981.

Appendix 4-A

Strategies for Promoting Social Interactions Through Daily Activities

A variety of opportunities exist for facilitating social interactions among children. Through directed observations of children during the day, child care and development staff can be guided in planning and implementing activities that promote social skills and development. The following suggestions are organized by typical daily routines: circle time, small-group activities, option time, snack and lunch time, outside time, and transitions.

- *Circle time.* Circle time provides ideal opportunities for all children to participate and to be socially involved. Finger plays, stories, puppets, and sharing activities can be structured to facilitate social interaction among children. Prearranged seating in the circle is one way to discourage isolation. Some children should be in clear view of the teacher and, when appropriate, seated next to strong role models. Songs such as "If You're Happy and You Know It" can be adapted to "If You're Happy and You Know It, Hug a Friend." The song "Down in the Valley Two by Two" (Bos 1990) provides opportunities for children to imitate motions in groups of two. Many other songs can encourage children to reach out in a positive way. Using puppets can help to involve a child with more severe disabilities. Assigning children roles from stories or nursery rhymes involves children in group activities. For example, a very young or nonverbal child can be part of "Humpty Dumpty." The entire group could be taught sign language for a familiar song.

- *Small-group activities.* Most child care and development programs incorporate small-group activities into their daily routines. Children who have difficulty participating in larger groups may be more successful in groups of two or three. Plan open-ended activities that support heterogeneous groupings (grouping children of varying skill levels together). Whenever possible, arrange activities in which a child with a disability is able to help another child learn a particular skill.

- *Option time.* During option time activities are generally set out for children to select. Consider individual needs and interests so that all children can participate at some level, either together or near one another. In most instances the process of the activity will take precedence over any product resulting from the activity. The types of materials provided will affect the nature of the social interactions. Providing duplicate sets of materials will help to eliminate waiting and may encourage a child with special needs to imitate or model others.

- *Snack and lunch time.* Snack and lunch are ideal times for socializing, developing language skills, learning self-help skills, and fostering independence. Adults can model language in many different ways. They can communicate a child's intention: "You're looking at the milk. That tells me you want milk." They can expand a child's request: "Rachael said 'milk.' You're telling me that you want milk." Adults sitting at the table can facilitate conversation, specifically including a quiet or nonverbal child. Provide only as much help as needed for each child. If a child wants to help another child, the adult may want to occasionally redirect by saying: "Mary is learning to pour the milk by herself, just as you are learning to tie your shoes. You can pour the milk yourself, Mary." Remember that some children may need additional time to be as independent as possible. Adapted seating and utensils are available for children with specific motor needs. The use of special utensils may enable a child to be an independent feeder. Even when children are unable to feed themselves, being at the table with other children is important for social integration.

- *Outside time.* Outside time, an important part of a child's day, should provide opportunities to practice fine and gross motor skills, social skills, sensory awareness, and language skills. Sensory play, such as that involving water or sand, outside painting, or play with large cardboard boxes are excellent and encourage interactions among children. Children can be entertained for long periods of time with materials as simple as buckets of water and paint brushes. Dishpans filled with water and placed on a table can bring children together to wash dolls and toys. Tire swings on which two or three children share a ride can provide the setting for a very social activity. Installing a bucket swing may allow a child with motor difficulties to participate with friends. Providing wagons with room for two encourage children to play together and take turns pulling each other. Riding toys that do not require pedaling are also helpful. The sandbox is a natural gathering place for all children; in this setting, sharing toys and helping one another happens naturally. However, encouragement from an adult may be needed: "Alysse is filling her

bucket with sand. Jenny, you try it. Fill your bucket, Jenny." Applying rules consistently in this situation will help children who have difficulty with unstructured play. Be clear and consistent: "Mario, sand stays in the sandbox."

- *Transitions.* Transitions between activities can be helped through consistency and predictability in the routines. However, the nature of a child's disability may make transitions difficult. If a child is unable to hear, see, understand, move quickly or independently, or tolerate rapid changes, ways should be determined to help that child. The following are suggestions for transitions from free play to cleanup:

—An oral reminder a few minutes before cleanup may help prepare children for an upcoming change.

—A child helper might ring a bell, a light might go on and off, or an adult might physically help a child clean up.

—A cleanup song pairing children might be devised. ("Jimmy, Sam will help you pick up the Legos.")

—Children may be given choices to make the cleanup more enjoyable. ("Do you want to pick up the blocks or the trucks?") Offering a choice will also provide guidance and reinforce the security of routine.

—When transferring from a quiet activity, adults might give each child directions and specifically match a child with disabilities and a peer to encourage social interactions in a positive way: "Tanisha, find someone who is wearing pink shoes and walk to the snack table."

Appendix 4-B

Guidelines for Promoting Social Skills in Young Children with Disabilities

Throughout the day, regardless of the activity, every child can feel successful by being provided a balance of direction, support, and opportunity to be independent. Partial participation or even proximity to an activity may be what is encouraged for some children who have more significant needs. The following may be helpful strategies for promoting socialization in young children with disabilities:

- *Consistently reinforce small steps toward social interaction.* If a child is watching others play, the teacher can comment on the activity: "Bobby and Dion are rolling their play dough. Would you like some too?" Your attention and comments may encourage the child to play at the play-dough table. Remember that even sitting at the same table and watching others play may be a positive step in a child's social development.

- *Find another way.* If a child is not able to participate in an activity in the same way as other children do, look for an alternative. Children benefit from participation in different ways, including partial participation. For example, a child who is not walking may help the other children march by beating a drum. Whenever possible, give the child a choice of ways to participate: "Would you like to ring the bells or wave the scarf?"

- *Help the child enter the play situation.* In the dramatic play center, you might say: "Jimmy has a stomach ache. Is the doctor in?" Or give a child a sentence to imitate: "Jimmy, tell them, 'I feel sick.'" One of the "doctors" will probably respond. Try to interfere as little as possible to avoid disrupting play or causing the child to be dependent on you.

- *Let the children know when they are doing well.* If a child can enter the play on his own, specific verbal statements about the desired behavior,

such as: "Juan, you and Matt are working together to make a very tall sand castle," give positive, unobtrusive feedback. Words, smiles, and hugs are always excellent reinforcers of positive social interactions.

- *Model good social behavior.* Speak out to show children how to engage others in social interactions: "Say Corey's name to get his attention," or "Tap him on the shoulder and say his name again," or "Tell Yolanda how you built the road."

- *Set clear expectations for respecting and including all children.* Rejection or exclusion should not be allowed. Help children through difficult situations by encouraging them to figure out how a child with a disability can participate. For example, Mark (who uses a walker) wants to play kickball with the boys. But they say, "He can't run. We don't want him to play." With adult help the boys decide that Mark can be the goalie.

• *Teach all children, regardless of their abilities, a few simple rules about playing together*. Learning these rules may not always be easy for some children. The rules must apply to all children in the group—those with disabilities and those without disabilities. Caregivers can guide children in solving problems and following through on agreed-upon consequences in helpful ways. Some children will need specific guidance. For example, if a child knocks over an elaborate block structure, the adult may wish to lead the child away and say, "Janet asked you to find another place to play." Janet should be praised for asking the child nicely to leave.

Despite careful planning and selection of materials, caregivers may need to focus on a child's interactive skills with adults or with toys before moving on to social interactions with peers. Child care providers may need to allow more time than expected for young children with disabilities to develop relationships. Do not be concerned if not all children choose to be friends with a child who has a disability. Children typically choose not to be friends for many reasons. Friendships cannot be forced on children. What is important is that we support inclusive settings. If we do not provide these experiences, we deny all children the opportunity to learn about others who are different from themselves.

Chapter 5

Family Caregiving Partnerships

By Kate Warren

Introduction

All we know about who we are and who we might become begins with the capacity to form and sustain human relationships. This process of developing relationships unfolds throughout our lifetime in many different ways.

From the beginning the most significant relationship is that created between parents and children. Beyond

One of the ways professional caregivers can be most helpful to parents of newborn or newly identified children is to encourage and support parents as parents. Such reinforcement does as much as anything else to build a parent's self-confidence as a parent, as a decision maker, and as a partner in the care and nurturing of the child.

— J. Gallagher

this most intimate of relationships, young children will also be influenced by relationships involving other significant caregivers, including extended family members, friends, and child care providers.

Children must be considered within the context of their families because the quality of adult relationships affecting children plays a significant role in children's sense of security and well-being. Our consideration of the importance that relationships between family members and professional caregivers play in the lives of young children with disabilities begins here.

Options for families seeking quality child care programs for children with special care and/or developmental needs have been identified as extremely limited. Many families feel that a lack of options compels them to take whatever they can find. Sometimes, families must piece together services from multiple caregivers. Too often, a family may find no suitable care at all (Berkeley Planning Associates 1988).

The barriers to finding and maintaining care are complex and may involve financial considerations, lack of physical accessibility, or reluctance on the part of providers to offer care to children with disabilities. This reluctance may translate more meaningfully to the providers' lack of experience and training in caring for children with disabilities. Providers may not know how to interact with and relate to families, another barrier to successful placements of children with disabilities.

Building and maintaining collaborative partnerships between families and professionals are often considered the most important factors in successful inclusion of children with disabilities in community child care settings. This chapter is intended to create a framework for building such relationships. It discusses critical aspects of developing partnerships with all families, including families of children with disabilities. Strategies for good practice are also discussed. Throughout each of the chapters, a consistent theme is presented: Children are more alike than different, and families of children with disabilities are more like other families than different.

Family First

Just as caregivers consider children within the context of their families, families must be seen within the context of broader social systems which include their neighbor-

ABOUT THE AUTHOR

Kate Warren's background includes parenting three sons, one of whom has a disability. She has worked as a parents' advocate for more than a decade to increase choices and opportunities for children with disabilities and their families and to develop partnerships with the professionals who serve them. At the time this chapter was written, Kate was counselor and coordinator of special needs services with BANANAS, a child care resource and referral agency in Alameda County. Her main interests are increasing the awareness of the needs and strengths of diverse populations, including individuals with disabilities; developing effective family-centered services; and strengthening communities through parent/professional partnerships. She is the director of the Family Resource Network.

hoods and communities. California's families are among the most diverse in the nation. In addition, the structures of today's families vary greatly, offering new perspectives and experiences for professionals who work with young children and their families. Children enrolling in child care and development programs reflect the diversity of strengths and challenges in our changing communities. Child care and development staff, learning to expand and adapt to meet changing needs, provide a supportive community resource that strengthens the family and society. Child care "increases community building because it brings children with handicapping conditions and their families together with other children and their families, highlighting commonalties and shared values" (Gallagher 1990, p. 87).

The family: The definition of family has broadened over the past years. The word *family* no longer brings to mind the singular image of two parents and their children in one household. A single mother and her baby, foster parents, blended families, adoptive parents, married couples, grandparents with childrearing responsibilities, and co-parents are all families. Today, we might more appropriately define a family as a group of individuals whose purpose is to provide a primary relationship of care, responsibility, support, and love to its members. Each family is unique—with its own values, culture, and ways of operating. In working with children, we should strive to understand how a family's values and culture influence its relationship with its children and with others.

In addition to having individual structures and values, families are unique in other ways. Life experiences and circumstances affect a family's expectations and outlook. All families bring a range of strengths,

abilities, and needs to child care partnerships. All families, regardless of circumstance or need, are families first. From this point of reference, child care and development staff must take their first steps forward in building and understanding the nature of relationships with families. By exploring the context of similarity, we can better understand families having children with disabilities and the unique challenges they may face.

Families of children with disabilities: Having a child with a disability does not define a family. Families with children who have exceptional care needs "exhibit the same range of resourcefulness, parenting strengths, and flexibility as other parents" (Lynch, Mendoza, English, 1990). They also want what is best for their children. They want to know that they are seen as important and capable in the lives of their children. Often, their need for reassurance that they are good parents will be greater than the need of parents of other children.

There are two primary reasons why parents of children with disabilities may need more reassurance: First, these parents did not arrive at parenting their children with disabilities with any special knowledge or training. Most likely, they had to adjust to a unique, often traumatic situation—one for which they had little or no preparation. Second, the parents may be in a position of just learning about their child's disability and having to deal with different professionals and systems in order to help their child. This situation can often be overwhelming and discouraging. Families typically respond with a range of emotions to handle these new stresses and cope with their feelings. If family members have had limited acquaintance with other individuals with disabilities, they may experience feelings of increased anxiety and isolation.

Professional support and reinforcement of a family's capacity to care for its children are priorities. Families need honest and accurate information. Understanding family coping strategies as healthful and normal encourages positive parenting. Professional attitudes and actions must encourage and affirm a family's own capacity to meet challenges. A more in-depth discussion on the impact of disability is included in chapter 3, "Living with Disability: The Family Perspective."

Building Blocks for Successful Relationships

Relationships between child care professionals and families, including those with young children with disabilities, develop over time and are based on a foundation of trust, mutual respect, good communication, confidentiality, and an acknowledged agreement to work together in the best interest of the children. Supportive relationships are rooted in attitudes of nonjudgment and flexibility. Through the process of building relationships, families and caregivers encourage the development of working partnerships. Consideration of these aspects of positive relationship building should lead to the understanding that no two relationships will ever be the same. Families will bring their own unique needs and strengths, and providers will reflect their own individuality in providing what they believe to be important in the care of young children. *It is not children alone who benefit from a positive child care experience. For every child whose life is touched in a positive way, support is provided to a family.*

There are several key characteristics which support the concept of "capacity building." These characteristics become the building blocks for successful partnerships.

Trust

Trust is the foundation of all successful relationships. It is a result of consistency, predictability, and follow-through. Mutual trust between caregivers and families is based on the premise that both want to do their very best in caring for children.

Trust is a reflection of what we say and do. Child care providers trust that families will follow through on agreed-upon responsibilities (for example, picking up and dropping off children at agreed-upon times); meet their financial obligations; and inform the providers of significant circumstances that may affect the children (such as illnesses, new medications, separations, or absences of family members). Families trust that reliable caregivers will be consistently available, that they will share information regarding significant events of the day, and that the children in their care will be safe, valued, and liked.

Establishing trust in relationships begins long before families come to child care. Policies and practices that ensure this aspect of quality caregiving should be evident in the child care setting. Trust is demonstrated when care providers are shown to value not only their own experiences and perceptions but also those of families.

Mutual respect

Mutual respect, as observed through the interactions of children, families, and other staff members, begins with self-respect. The value child care and development staff members place in themselves is reflected in their work. "When you respect yourself and your position, parents will respect you, and building a relationship through good communication will become a priority for both of you" (Kishel 1986, p.11).

Partnerships are characterized by appreciation and respect for new or different points of view. Caring for children is neither simple nor predictable. The very nature of child care requires working together and sharing information and ideas that support families and caregivers in their respective roles. When an equal partnership is the framework within which caring for children is approached, responsibilities become shared, concerns are resolved, discoveries are made, and successes are appreciated.

Child care providers and families bring their own experiences, values, and preferences to the partnerships. Professionals must have opportunities to explore personal feelings and attitudes about working with children and families so that their interactions with families are communicated sensitively and respectfully. Similarly, participation in community child care settings will broaden families' perceptions through new experiences and through exposure to a variety of backgrounds that may differ from their own. In this context mutual respect and acceptance takes hold.

Open communication

Ongoing communication is critical to supportive relationships. It is important to recognize that communication skills are learned and practiced and that they may not come naturally. Most people have experienced some level of difficulty in saying what they mean or in understanding what others are saying. What is transmitted through conversation is not only information but also the underlying feelings behind the spoken message. What we hear others say, how we share information, and how we respond to one another all influence communication. Generally, we know we are successful when

we arrive at a common understanding of each other's points of view.

In this arena of relationship building, child care providers may bear the greater responsibility. Understanding the ways in which communication can be facilitated is important. *Active listening is one of the most valuable skills to bring to relationships with families.* Active listening is the ability to be attentive to a family's concerns or priorities and to reflect accurately what the family has shared.

Communication is also enhanced when information is shared in ways that are consistent, sensitive, and honest. Often, responsibility for setting the tone of conversations and creating safe environments for families to share information will rest with child care providers. Their awareness of effective communication strategies as well as their willingness to meet families more than halfway will help to create strong working partnerships.

Confidentiality

A family's right to privacy must be honored, especially as to medical, social, or educational services and records. This right is protected by law that prohibits the sharing of personal information without the express written permission of a parent or legal guardian. Thus, a social worker, doctor, or special educator is prohibited from providing information about a family or child without permission. Respecting confidentiality is vital to every aspect of the relationship between family members and professional caregivers.

Caregivers and families must also use good judgment and be mindful of the sensitivity of information they relate outside the child care setting. Parents do not want to hear about their divorce, financial difficulties, drinking problem, or a child's bedwetting from anyone with whom they have not personally chosen to share this information. Carelessness about personal information can be devastating to all concerned.

An ongoing process

Ongoing relationships are an investment in time and energy. They demonstrate flexibility and a capacity to grow. A mutual commitment to children brings the partnership between families and child care providers into focus. Relationships reflect a balance of give and take, a willingness to listen and to understand one another's perspectives, and a desire to find solutions that feel mutually beneficial.

Special Considerations

Developing a level of awareness of factors that may create barriers or present challenges to a partnership between a family and professional caregivers is especially important when serving a child with a disability. The following discussion addresses some of the circumstances that caregivers and families may encounter.

Feelings and experiences

Parents and providers caring for a young child with disabilities may experience anxieties that lie just below the surface. Fears about their own abilities can be translated into feelings of insecurity about the success of the child in the child care setting. A family's fear of rejection may be based on past experiences in a society unaccepting of differences. Feelings of anger and "unfairness" often result from a lack of choices. Parents may feel that the value of their child is diminished each time they are told, "No. I'm sorry, but I just don't think it will work out."

"When people have been deeply and frequently wounded, they grow sensitive. Words and glances can jar raw nerves even when no unkindness is intended" (Featherstone 1980, p. 39). The vulnerability of a family may lead to feelings of doubt and a lack of confidence. In an effort to restore their own self-confidence, parents may minimize their children's needs. This strategy is a sound coping mechanism in response to society's assumption that the abilities and health of children are directly related to the effectiveness of the parent. It says, "I am still a good parent." In addition, a family whose primary concerns are focused on meeting basic needs for food, clothing, shelter, and safety may not consider a child's special-care needs a priority. Caregivers need to be aware of why parents may give mixed messages. Careful listening and sensitive questioning will help to overcome some of the misunderstandings that may occur.

Sharing of expectations

All parents requiring child care services have questions about such matters as hours of operation, holiday care, and sick care. Families also need clarification about their financial obligations to providers when their child is not in attendance because of appointments or illness. Parents of children with disabilities may have additional concerns about coordinating their need for child care with early intervention services, medical or therapy appointments, necessary assessments, or meetings with agencies providing services to their children or the family. The need for providers to be flexible in helping parents meet family needs and priorities is frequently a concern. Parents may also worry about what fee will be charged and may be too anxious even to discuss the matter. There are a number of ways by which families can be helped to address these concerns. For example, some providers give families written information about policies regarding fee schedules, holidays, and absences. By anticipating these concerns, providers will be in a better position to respond to parents or be more comfortable initiating the conversation.

Parents' expectations of what a program can accomplish must be realistic and appropriate. Group care requires adaptation and compromise on the part of everyone, including the child with exceptional needs. It is fair and necessary for providers to explain to parents that the well-being of all the children in care must be attended to and that this situation affects the level of assistance available. The process of clarifying expectations will help parents make decisions about the appropriateness of the program or help them realign their expectations. Written contracts between families and caregivers as well as parent handbooks which include program policies can serve as vehicles for communicating ground rules and mutual expectations.

Families and child care providers may have unrealistic or different expectations of one another or of the child. In almost every arena of caregiving, misunderstandings or poor communication can jeopardize children's placements and lead to judgmental stances on the part of families or providers. Ongoing communication then becomes a critical factor in addressing expectations such as how a child is viewed, how caregiving and developmental needs are met, how roles and responsibilities are understood, and how constraints affecting both families and caregivers are shared. Discussion of appropriate program expectations for children from the perspectives of both the provider and the parent is also important. Examples of program expectations which should be considered include the following:

- A child with disabilities should have opportunities to participate fully in all activities unless otherwise indicated.

- Children should have access to all areas of the program used by other children.

- Social and behavioral skills should be developmentally and age appropriate.
- Cooperative behaviors should be encouraged.
- Interventions should be based on careful observations and assessment of each child's needs.

Family involvement

Families come to child care settings wanting the very best for their children. During the child's initial entry into a child care setting, families should be included as much as possible. There is little debate regarding the positive effect of active parental involvement in community child care settings. However, the participation of families whose children have disabilities will vary greatly. These families may be expected to participate and communicate more frequently but may be unable to do so because of the variety of demands on their time and energy.

Families frequently need to be involved in other disability-specific services. Multiple-agency involvement in the lives of the child and family members, although supportive, can also be experienced or felt as intrusive. For these reasons, thought and care must be given to the nature and level of involvement requested or expected. Fostering a sense of belonging is important, but understanding the demands placed on families may require flexibility. Families should be encouraged to participate to the extent to which they are able or interested.

Child care providers may also observe that family involvement fluctuates and changes over the course of time. Families with very young infants may be more involved with additional activities than are families with older children. There may also be periods of time when the focus of the family is on meeting the needs of their children in different ways. For example, a child may need surgery and a long convalescence, or a family may have overriding financial concerns related to meeting the needs of the child. Whatever the circumstance or need of families, it is important to agree early that parents and caregivers will each strive toward a relationship of open communication and flexibility.

Myths or stereotypes about disabilities

A label or diagnosis does not tell much about who a child is or what a child's care needs may be. Labels often do no more than limit our perceptions of children. The needs of children with similar diagnoses can vary greatly, and the impact of a disability can affect different aspects of a child's growth and development. One child who has cerebral palsy may have very involved physical and developmental needs; another may have mild physical needs requiring little or no intervention. It is unreasonable to think that, on hearing a diagnosis such as cerebral palsy or Down syndrome, one will know very much at all about a particular child.

Families are in positions to detect the level of acceptance and consideration that caregivers are willing to offer in caring for their children. A certain amount of hesitancy can be honest and appropriate, especially when there is a lack of information. However, fears about caregivers' rejecting or accepting children with special needs will be communicated. Words used and tone of voice are subtle communicators of fears and will encourage either openness or reluctance on the part of families to establish relationships.

Considerations on separation

Caregivers may sense initial tension or discomfort in their relationships with families. Leaving a young child in the care of someone else may raise legitimate issues of separation for families. Many parents of young children are reluctant to seek child care and return to work after the birth of a baby. Feelings of guilt for leaving a child may arise. Often, parents of children with exceptional care needs who seek child care do so with additional reservations and fears. Issues about separation can be especially painful to parents for the following reasons:

- Little or no choice in selecting the child care program.

- Increased guilt and ambivalence about returning to work.

- Feelings of being irreplaceable. Many parents have needed to learn specialized caregiving strategies for their children.

- Concerns about whether the caregiver can handle the child: Can anyone do it as well as I can? These feelings may also initiate a revisiting of how difficult or overwhelming parenting a child may be.

- Feelings of overprotectiveness based on real needs to protect the child.

- Increased anxiety resulting from fear that their child's condition may deteriorate, necessitating repeated hospitalizations, or from fear that they will lose the child to death.

Respect for professional boundaries

For a variety of reasons, families may become overwhelmed by their responsibilities, especially when they do not have reliable support systems. As a result child care providers may be faced with situations they do not feel prepared to deal with. What is most important for care providers and ultimately most helpful for families is the ability to recognize the need for further assistance. Knowing when a family may need additional resources or referrals to other professionals or community agencies is essential to maintaining healthful relationships.

Other strategies should be considered by which caregivers can respond appropriately to families' needs. For example, in center-based programs opportunities are available to talk with other staff members regarding family concerns or to have consultants available to meet with staff. Family day care providers might also seek out their local resource and referral agency for information, resources, and support. Working with families and children who have multiple pressures in their lives requires adequate levels of support at the direct service level.

Sharing concerns

Child care providers often worry that sharing a concern with family members might be upsetting to them. Family members may also be reluctant to disclose their concerns because of fears that their child will be excluded from the child care setting. Circumstances that arise when caregivers are working with children whose health is failing or whose development is compromised by unforeseen events are difficult for caregivers as well as for families. It may help caregivers to talk with coworkers, peers, or other support persons. Caregivers should find ways to share concerns with families on a regular basis. Postponing a discussion of concerns or difficulties may result in more long-term problems. Issues that are neglected will most likely resurface at another time. Decide early on, with all parents, how situations will be handled. In chapter 6 of this volume, "When Concerns Arise: Identifying and Referring Children with Exceptional Needs," strategies are suggested to help child care and development staff address their concerns with families.

Strategies for Good Practice

Building successful partnerships for the benefit of young children with disabilities is based on foundations of respect, trust, communication, confidentiality, and willingness on the part of caregivers and families to work collaboratively with one another. The following practices are based on these foundations. Actions and attitudes should reflect these practices as families turn to caregivers for guidance and support.

Focus on the family

Families of children with disabilities are families first. They are also groups of people who may be faced with a variety of challenges or stresses in caring for their children. Child care and development staff need skills in recognizing the sources of parental stress. If what a parent of a child with a disability is experiencing seems to relate more to just being a parent than to anything else, then this is probably the case. When the disability appears to be the source, empathy goes a long way with most families. Recognize the other responsibilities and functions of individual family members. Ask about how things are going at work or in school. If appropriate, inquire about other children in the family. Lighthearted remarks by caregivers about never getting the laundry done or deciding what to have for dinner can reassure family members that you know that their life extends beyond their responsibilities for this particular child. If you know of a parent's hobby or favorite activity, talk about it. You may find that you share an interest. Ask if the family had a chance to do something enjoyable or different on the weekend, or how the recent move to a new apartment is working out. Viewing the family as a whole is one of the important ways providers can help family members to feel acknowledged and valued for who they are without being made to feel different.

Caregivers cannot "cure" children, and they cannot make disheartening circumstances go away. But they can make a significant difference in the lives of children and families by modeling an attitude of acceptance for every child in their care. In all successful relationships empathy and mutual support are essential, as are reassurance, recognition of a family's strengths, and support of children.

Positive initial contact

It is typical for parents to have concerns about their child's adjustment to the child care setting. All parents want their children to be loved and accepted and to "fit in." This is particularly true of parents of children with disabilities. They may have concerns about how the provider or staff will view their child: Will their son or daughter be seen as a child first? Or will he or she be viewed only in the context of a disability. Parents may have additional fears about how other children will treat their child, and they may worry about how the other families will react. Parents may fear that no one will notice or help their child deal with these special challenges.

An open, caring, and sensitive response to a family's first telephone call or visit is one of the first steps in building a positive relationship. During the initial contact, a genuine interest in the child and the family is important. As they do with all families, caregivers should discuss the needs and services requested, including the hours of care needed, meals to be provided, and languages spoken. The program's philosophy and the options or requirements for parents' participation should also be dis-

cussed. A written contract and written program policies can be useful in clarifying mutual expectations. Once these areas are covered, questions about the child's specific strengths and needs can be raised. A list of questions to consider asking families when initially enrolling a child is provided in Appendix 5-A. Appendix 5-B outlines a step-by-step collaborative decision-making process for enrollment.

Caregivers can use this initial information-gathering and conversation process to get a sense of the child, the family, and the family's circumstances. Parents are more likely to discuss their child's special-care needs with less anxiety or defensiveness when the initial contacts have been respectful. Caregivers benefit by being as informed as possible regarding the child's skills and needs and by determining how the program or environment might be adapted to meet these needs. The key to allowing a parent to feel comfortable in disclosing information is to be as accepting as possible.

Caregivers may also want to share the program's policies on confidentiality in order to reassure families that their privacy will be protected. Families of children with exceptional caregiving needs may have specific concerns about confidentiality in regard to what is said about their sons or daughters and to whom it is said. Parents are naturally curious about the other children in the program and their families. They may be especially curious about the details of the development, diagnosis, and care required for childen with disabilities.

Ongoing communication

Use a variety of approaches to communication. Most communication between parents and caregivers takes place during transitions—when children enter care in the morning and when they are picked up in the evening. These can be very hectic times; lengthy discussions or problem-solving sessions should be scheduled for more appropriate times.

The need for ongoing daily communication with parents whose children have disabilities is critical. Parents rely on their children's caregivers for important practical information, such as how much or how little a child ate during lunch or snack times, and when the child napped and for how long. Parents also need to hear about the general tone of the child's day. Was the child distressed by an event or especially excited about an activity? Share information such as who the child played with, which toy or game sparked the child's interest, how successful the child was at trying something new, or how well the parent's suggestion for soothing the child worked.

A notebook that goes back and forth between the home and the child care facility is an excellent medium for sharing information. Some entries might be lengthy and include important and detailed information. At other times, a simple "great day!" will do. A notebook also allows a parent to add comments or suggestions or to ask questions. A caregiver should not discuss serious or negative issues in a notebook without first having addressed those issues with the parent in person. The use of a notebook can also be expanded to include notes or information from other professionals who work with the child. For example, an occupational therapist might update the provider on new positioning or feeding techniques. A speech therapist might include notes on language concepts being taught.

When speaking with families, care providers should try to use open-ended questions that require more than yes or no answers, which usually provide little in the way of helpful information. If questions are asked that call for thoughtful and informative responses, such responses are more likely to be forthcoming. Instead of asking "Does your child talk?," ask "How does your child let you know what she needs?" Responses might include: "She shows me by pointing," "He tells me," "We are both beginning to learn sign language," or "He cries or acts fussy, and after that it's a process of elimination." Open-ended questions provide more qualitative, useful information.

For children whose health and daily routines require close monitoring, a more formalized approach is necessary. Changes in medication, new procedures or treatments, observed improvements in the child's condition, or increased difficulties must be reported clearly and immediately. Neither the caregiver nor the parent is likely to overlook or neglect these important concerns.

Family involvement

Family activity days or special events should be planned with attention to the physical access needs and the interests of families whose children have disabilities. Outings and celebrations should be held in places where all children, including those who are nonambulatory, can participate. There are many ways to carry the spirit of inclusion to all activities in which parents and children are asked to participate. Too often, support activities for families of children with disabilities have been developed around disability issues and concerns. As a result, many parents have not had opportunities to be with other families in enjoyable ways, further isolating them from their communities. If we embrace the concept of inclusion for children with disabilities, we must also include members of their families at every opportunity.

Community child care facilities are settings in which this inclusion can occur.

When parents come together, they often discuss common problems and remedies. A mother whose child has disabilities may find that her own concern is one shared by other parents as well. A mother who worries about her child's defiant NO response is supported by other parents who are struggling with the same behavior in their own toddlers' pursuit of independence. Opportunities to share with others reduces isolation and encourages camaraderie among families. And, although it may take some time, parents of children with disabilities will begin to feel more comfortable with parents whose children are developing typically. Friendships may develop as parents share the common challenges of juggling work, children, and other family responsibilities. The inevitable guilt that working parents feel can be reduced when they recognize that they are not alone. Discovering common experiences encourages a sense of belonging. Parents who are provided with opportunities to meet and spend time with other parents are more likely to become involved in child care programs.

Ask for help when you don't know

It is common for parents to be particularly anxious about the future abilities of their children. Their desire for reassurance or validation about this concern is appropriate. But caregivers must resist the temptation to extend their skills and roles beyond the boundaries of child care and their documented knowledge of or experiences with a particular child. The most helpful course is to share observations of progress or to validate a concern expressed by the parent. Caregivers need to be aware of community resources in order to make appropriate referrals. Chapter 6 in this volume, "When Concerns Arise: Identifying and Referring Children with Exceptional Needs," provides information that is useful in developing additional strategies and support.

Summary

The intent of this chapter is to encourage awareness and recognition of the role that child care providers play in the lives of young children and their families. This role has been considered from the perspective of building relationships between child care providers and families of children with disabilities. The strengths and capacities generated by these relationships are often the most important factors in the successful placements of children with disabilities in appropriate community child care settings.

Families of children with disabilities have the same desires, capabilities, and dreams as other families. All families share common concerns regarding parenting and child care. What may differ in the process of working with families whose children have disabilities may be the need for increased flexibility in approaching solutions.

Clearly, what will help are training, support, and information that is specific to the needs of families who have young children with disabilities. The appreciation of the family perspective, along with the development of caregiving skills, will make partnerships with families meaningful and rewarding endeavors.

What will be most appreciated by families are experiences that reflect acceptance and respect. Above all else should be the goal of serving all families in an environment of mutual trust and collaboration.

You give but little when you give of your possessions.

It is when you give of yourself that you truly give.

— Kahlil Gibran

KEY POINTS

1. The ability of families and professionals to build and maintain collaborative partnerships may be the single most important factor in the successful inclusion of children with disabilities in community child care settings.

2. All parents have concerns about parenting and issues that relate to child care.

3. The process of building relationships between families of young children with disabilities and child care professionals is the same as the process used with families whose children are developing typically.

4. Relationships develop over time with the establishment of a foundation of trust, mutual respect, effective communication, confidentiality, and an agree-

ment to work together in the best interests of children.

5. What is good practice in working with other families is also good practice when working with families whose children require exceptional caregiving.

6. Parents of children with exceptional care needs "exhibit the same range of resourcefulness, parenting strengths, and flexibility as other parents."

7. Developing an awareness of factors that may create barriers or present challenges to a partnership between a family and child care professionals is especially important in the care of children with disabilities.

8. An understanding of the child care provider's role and an appreciation of the family's perspective is important when the provider begins a partnership with families who have children with disabilities.

9. What will be most appreciated by families will be the acceptance and respect they are shown.

References

Berkeley Planning Associates. 1988. "Child Care and Development Needs in California Families of Children with Disabilities" (Final report). Sacramento: California Department of Education, Child Development Division.

Featherstone, H. 1980. *A Difference in the Family.* New York: Basic Books, Inc.

Gallagher, J., and others. 1990. *Policy Implementation and P. L. 99-457: Planning for Young Children with Special Needs.* Baltimore: Paul H. Brookes Publishing Co.

Kishel, S. 1986. *Making the Connection: Parent/Provider Communication.* n.p. Child Care Resource and Referral, Inc.

Lynch, E.; J. M. Mendoza; and K. English. 1990. *Implementing Individualized Family Service Plans in California: Final Report.* Sacramento: California Department of Developmental Services. (Copies available from the department, 1600 9th Street, Sacramento, CA 95814.)

Resources

Anderson, P., and E. S. Fenichel. *Serving Culturally Diverse Families of Infants and Toddlers with Disabilities.* Washington, D.C.: National Center for Clinical Infant Programs, 1989.

This publication is designed to help policy makers and practitioners develop programs and serve families with infants and toddlers with disabilities within the families' own cultural frameworks and individual lifestyles. The concept of culture and specific cultural issues (e.g., family definitions, roles) are discussed.

Bailey, D., "Collaborative Goal-Setting with Families: Resolving Differences in Values and Priorities for Services," in *Topics in Early Childhood Special Education,* Vol. 7, No. 2 (Summer, 1987), 59–71.

This article discusses value conflicts between parents and professionals as well as strategies for effective collaborative goal setting.

Bruder, M. B.; P. Denier; and S. Sachs. "Models of Integration Through Early Intervention/Child Care Collaborations," *Zero to Three,* Vol. X, No. 3 (February, 1990). National Center for Clinical Infant Programs.

Carson, A. T. *A Professional Challenge: Working with Multi-Problem Families.*

San Diego: San Diego State University Foundation, 1986.

This manual is based on the work of Project IINTACT, a model demonstration project funded to provide home-based services to high-risk families with young children who are developmentally delayed or are at risk of developmental delay. The manual is intended as an overview and sampler of three major problem areas (problems within the family, problems between the family and the home visitor, and problems of the home visitor) and as a guide to possible points for intervention.

Dunst, C.; C. Trivette; and A. Deal. *Enabling and Empowering Families: Principles and Guidelines for Practice.* Cambridge, Mass.: Brookline Books, 1988.

This book describes social and family systems theory, but it also provides a practical framework, a set of guidelines, and sample forms and procedures for family-focused assessment and intervention.

Equals in This Partnership: Parents of Disabled and At-Risk Infants and Toddlers Speak to Professionals. Washington, D.C.: National Center for Clinical Infant Programs, 1984. 2000 14th Street, North, Suite 380, Arlington, VA 22201-2500, telephone (703) 528-4300.

This booklet contains presentations made by parents at a national conference in 1984. The parents eloquently express their experiences, hopes, and desires.

Fewell, R. R., and P. F. Vadasy. *Families of Handicapped Children: Needs and Supports Across the Life Span.* Austin, Tex.: Pro-Ed., 1986.

The developmental nature of families' experiences in caring for children with disabilities is the focus of this book. Excerpts from interviews and statements by family members offer insights into the experiences of family members that service providers often lack.

Hanline, M. F. *Rationale for Integrating Young Children.* San Francisco: Project STIP, San Francisco Unified School District, 1989.

Journal of Early Intervention, Vol. 14, No. 3 (Summer, 1990). Reston, Va.: Council for Exceptional Children, Division of Early Childhood.

This journal's special issue on families includes data-based studies and innovative intervention strategies that address many of the questions that face service providers.

Moses, K. *Lost Dreams and Growth: Children with Disability: Parent Issues, Parents' Concerns* (Video, 72 minutes). Evanston, Ill.: Resources Networks, Inc., 1988.

This 72-minute videotape follows the processes of grieving and coping that parents go through when their dreams are shattered by the birth of a child with disabilities. Vignettes of parents sharing their personal experiences are included.

National Early Childhood Technical Assistance System (NEC*TAS). *Guidelines and Recommended Practices for the Individualized Family Service Plan.* Washington, D.C.: Association for the Care of Children's Health, 1989.

An Individualized Family Service Plan (IFSP) task force, composed of leaders in the field of early intervention, recommended best practices for the development of the IFSP. The recommendations,

as outlined in this document, include developing a philosophical and conceptual framework, building positive relationships, identifying child and family strengths and needs, developing outcomes, and implementing practices. Case studies and sample forms are included.

"Separating from Infants and Toddlers." A BANANAS Growing Together handout. BANANAS Inc., Child Care Information and Referral and Parent Support, 6501 Telegraph Avenue, Oakland, CA 94609, (415) 658-0381, 1989.

Turnbull, H. R., and A. P. Turnbull. *Parents Speak Out: Then and Now* (Second edition). Columbus, Ohio: Merrill, 1985.

Parents Speak Out is a collection of stories that describe how those who sought help for persons with disabilities and their families, and those who tried to provide it, met with a mixture of success and failure. Most of the contributors are parents or relatives of someone with a disability and work directly or indirectly in organizations and professions that serve disabled citizens. A number of the essays include the original essay written in 1978 plus an updated version written in 1983.

Westby, C. E., "Ethnographic Interviewing: Asking the Right Questions to the Right People in the Right Ways," *Journal of Childhood Communication Disorders.* Vol. 13, No. 1 (1990), 101–111.

This article examines the influence of culture on the interviewing process and describes an approach to "ethnographic interviewing" of families of handicapped children. Using this approach, professionals ask the right questions of the right people in the right ways so they can assist these families in meeting the needs of their children.

Appendix 5-A

Questions to Ask Family Members

When child care providers enroll a child in their programs, it is important that they take time to discuss with family members both the program's policies and procedures and the individual needs of the child. The initial questions that providers will ask about a child with a disability are not that different from the questions that providers should ask all parents.

Additionally, when a child has a disability and/or an exceptional health care need, it may be important to gather further information from parents (and sometimes professionals) prior to enrollment. This information-gathering process will help ensure a smooth transition to the new setting and facilitate quality planning that is designed to meet each child's needs.

Following are questions to consider when enrolling a child. It is not recommended that this list be used as a form for parents to fill out. It is advised that family members be interviewed in person whenever possible and that families be advised about their right to confidentiality prior to any interview.

What type of care is the family looking for?

Request that parents share with you their priorities and concerns in seeking child care. Ask them to discuss the characteristics of child care that are the most important to them. Open communication about the family's priorities allows for both parents and caregivers to discuss and mutually determine if what the family is looking for matches what the program offers.

Does the child have any exceptional caregiving needs?

Asking all parents if their child has special needs gives them an opportunity to share the unique insights they have about their child. Begin by suggesting that parents share what makes their child special or unique. If a child has a diagnosed disability or is coming into child care with health and/or developmental concerns, parents may provide this information at this point.

What special considerations and accommodations does the family feel the child may require in the child care setting? Are there any special equipment needs?

Does the family anticipate or meet the child's basic needs in any special way at home that would be useful for the provider to know about? Are there specific accommodational needs that should be discussed and explored in order to ensure optimum opportunities for the child's participation in all activities?

How would parents describe their child's personality and temperament?

Is their child social or shy, active or quiet? Does he or she warm up slowly in new situations or immediately seem comfortable? Does she prefer one-on-one interactions, small groups, or large-group settings? Would they describe their child's temperament as easygoing, difficult, or fluctuating?

What are the child's favorites—toys, games, and so forth?

Does he have a favorite toy, a special place to play, or something he particularly enjoys doing? Who does she spend the most time with? Who is his best friend? Who does she seem to enjoy being with the most?

What skills has the child mastered?

Has he recently learned something new? Are there signs of emerging skills? Which activities can be self-initiated and which are independent? Does the child enjoy practicing anything special? Do the parents or other family members have any concerns about their child's overall development?

What does the child like to do during the day?

What makes the child the happiest? What is her favorite time of the day? What is he curious about?

What is the child proudest of? What are favorite activities? In which ways will adults need to help facilitate play? How should toys or activities be introduced?

(List things children do in a daily routine and ask if their child likes or enjoys each one.)

How does their child interact with others—with peers, older or younger children, other adults, and strangers?

Has their child previously been cared for in group settings? Does he have sisters or brothers? What are their ages? Has the child been with older or younger children? Has that worked well? Is she equally comfortable with male and female children and adults? Does their child typically initiate interactions, or does he wait until approached by others?

What does the child do when the parents are unavailable—when, for example, they are in the bathroom?

How does the child respond and behave if an adult cannot be seen or heard? Are there concerns about the child's safety if an adult is not in immediate physical proximity? How much supervision does the child need?

How do parents guide their child's behavior?

What frustrates the child, and how does she react when frustrated?

How does the child communicate?

What are the primary languages spoken in the home? What are the cues of a nonverbal child? What is the extent to which the child understands what is said? How does the child indicate choices—by touching, looking, signing, or speaking? Is the family working toward specific communication goals? How can the child care provider encourage growth toward these goals?

What is the child's history regarding medication, allergies, and other physical or health-related conditions?

What medication(s) does the child take (prescription and nonprescription)?

• When are these medications administered?

• Does the child need to have any medication during program hours? On what schedule?

• Are there any side effects (including behavioral)? From which medicines?

Does the child have health problems, chronic illnesses, or allergies?

• If so, what happens to the child when he has a crisis related to this condition?

• What procedures would the staff follow to:

—prevent these crises?

—deal with them when they occur?

Does the staff need to be trained in any particular emergency procedures in order to ensure the child's health and safety?

What communication or feedback would parents find important?

How does their child eat?

Are there any dietary considerations? What are the child's likes and dislikes? What are her favorite foods? Does he need assistance with feeding or drinking? What have been the child's typical snack and mealtimes?

What are the toileting skills of the child?

Are there special considerations during diaper changing or toileting? How does the family know when to toilet? Does the child give any verbal or physical indication? Are the parents currently working toward independent toileting skills?

Does the child have any special physical or positional needs?

In what ways will the provider know that the child is uncomfortable or tired? Is the child physically active, or does she tend to like less activity and movement? Does he prefer to rest or sleep in a certain position? Does she eat in a high chair, child's chair, or adult seat? Is he comfortable playing on the floor? Does she like to be held in a special way? Are there any other special handling considerations?

Are there things that, if brought from home, would make the transition to the new child care setting easier?

Does the child have a favorite blanket for nap time or a special toy? Would bringing photos from home of family members, friends, neighbors, or pets be helpful? Are separations difficult? Is there anything the provider should know about separations in general?

Will the child be involved in other programs or transitions during the day?

Will the child be attending child care full-time or part-time? Will he be involved in any other programs? Are there things the provider should know about the child's typical day or week? What is the child's most stressful time of day?

Is the child and/or family receiving services from other agencies or professionals that should be coordinated with child care?

What are these services? What steps should the provider take to collaborate with representatives of these agencies? How may the family be able to assist with this networking?

Are there other significant caregivers or professionals from whom information should be gathered?

Who are other important family members the provider should know about or meet? What are the names and telephone numbers of professionals who should be consulted? What information should be discussed with these people? Should the provider request and review reports or files from professionals or agencies?

In serving a child with special-care needs, providers should gather information from all sources that a parent feels would be helpful. It is critical to be mindful, however, of the priorities and concerns of individual families. Parents, for a multitude of reasons, may not

want all information about their child or themselves shared with other family members, professionals, and/or agencies. It is essential to honor parents' wishes in this regard. Additionally, because the initiation and coordination of multiple services can be overwhelming for families of young children with disabilities, it is imperative that all service providers be understanding and respectful of how demanding and difficult this process often is. It is for this reason that federal legislation mandates the coordination of services for young children with disabilities and their families. In many communities, agencies are developing single-entry intake forms so that family members do not have to fill out multiple forms or tell their stories over and over again. Collaboration on behalf of children must begin with developing successful partnerships with parents. Assisting families in ways they feel will be most helpful to them is the first step.

Remember that, before concluding the family interview, parents should be asked specifically:

1. **To list the agencies and persons they authorize you to provide with information about their child**
2. **To sign a release-of-information form for each professional person or agency that you will need to contact for information**

Resources

Doggett, L., and J. George. *All Kids Count.* Arlington, Tex.: The ARC National Headquarters. 1993.

"The Chronic Illness Health Record Form," from *Healthy Young Children: A Manual for Programs.* Washington, D.C.: National Association for the Education of Young Children, 1991.

Appendix 5-B

A Collaborative Decision-Making Process for Inclusion

Enrolling young children with disabilities in community child care settings

1. An Outline of the Process

A. Review policies, procedures, and program philosophy.
- Internally
- With families

B. Conduct family interview.
- Discuss accommodational and inclusion needs.

C. With permission, contact:
- Other family members and caregivers
- Professionals
- Agencies

D. Review information gathered.
- Outline exceptional accommodational needs.
- Review legal mandates and licensing regulations.
- Clarify questions with families and professionals.

E. Consider all available resources.
- Examine possible solutions.
- Explore reasonable alternatives.

F. Develop an inclusion plan.
- Action plan: who, what, when
- Involve all key people.

G. Make enrollment determination.
- When unable to accept:
  —Review with parents the reasons for the determination.
  —Refer parents to other resources and sources of support.
- When enrolling:
  —Implement an inclusion plan with families, specialists, and other caregivers.

2. Implementing the Process

A. Review policies, procedures, and program philosophy with family members.

It is always helpful for families seeking care for their child to have a clear understanding about the type of program that is being offered. Given options, families of children with disabilities will typically have the same criteria for selecting child care as other families do. By reviewing the philosophy of your program and presenting an overview of its policies and procedures, you and the parents will be able to mutually consider whether the program matches what the family is looking for. Family and program handbooks are especially useful for this purpose.

B. Gather information from family members about their child. Discuss and identify accommodational needs.

The initial questions that a provider will ask families about a child who has a disability are not that different from questions asked of all parents. Many programs have designed their own questionnaires for the purpose of interviewing parents prior to their child's enrollment. Project EXCEPTIONAL has also developed a list of questions to ask families, which interviewers can review.

Through this information-gathering process with parents, specific accommodational needs of children should also be explored and identified. In many cases children with disabilities will not require any special accommodations in the child care setting. All children with disabilities, however, benefit from collaborative planning.

This process helps to ensure successful placements and ongoing quality caregiving.

Some children's enrollment will, however, be contingent on your meeting their accommodational needs. In these instances further questions clarifying the unique needs of the child should be asked of parents. This will enable providers to fully understand the whole child in the context of his or her disability, age, personality, culture, and family. Parents and providers should consider how a child's individual needs might best be met in the child care setting and discuss specific accommodations. Specialists who are working with the child may also be of assistance in this assessment.

C. **Follow up and consult with other significant caregivers and professionals whom the family has given you permission to contact.**

Contacting other significant family members and/or professionals who are currently providing service to the child is often very helpful. Remember that a release of information must be signed for each agency or professional that is contacted. Additionally, it is preferable to have written parental consent to contact others.

D. **Review records and other pertinent information about the child received from these sources.**

All records that have been requested should be thoroughly reviewed. Medical records, therapy reports, and Individual Education Plans (IEPs) or Individual Program Plans (IPPs) are possible sources of helpful information for caregivers. Providers should follow up with parents or requesting agencies if necessary to obtain clarifying answers to questions.

E. **Consider all available resources that may enable your program to successfully care for this child and meet her or his inclusion needs.**

Each child's unique needs must be considered on a child-by-child basis. Logical accommodational solutions should be examined and reasonable alternatives explored.

F. **Develop an inclusion action plan. Outline the steps that will facilitate a successful transition to the child care setting.**

Develop a plan for how, when, and by whom the accommodations will be provided, and establish a process for ongoing monitoring. Collaborate with the persons who will be involved.

G. **Make enrollment determination.**

If your program is unable to provide the necessary accommodations, review with the family (in person, whenever possible) the reasons why and the specific steps taken to make this decision.

Refer the family to other family child care homes or child care and development programs in your community that would more likely be able to meet their child's needs. For example, a larger agency may be able to absorb accommodational costs that a small family child care business cannot. Offer emotional support and assistance in any other meaningful and appropriate way.

When accepting a child's enrollment, review and discuss the details of the inclusion plan with family members and other significant professionals who will be involved in the care of the child.

Follow-through and ongoing evaluation of how well the child's needs are actually being met is critical to successful inclusion. When collaborative planning is fully valued and implemented through thoughtfully laid-out plans, all children, all families and all professionals benefit from the rewards fostered by the true spirit of inclusive child care.

Chapter 6

When Concerns Arise: Identifying and Referring Children with Exceptional Needs

By Eleanor W. Lynch, Ph.D.

Introduction

For most children development is a fairly straight path traveled at about the same speed. Developmental milestones, the major accomplishments in the infant and preschool years, are usually described within a range of years or months according to the average age at which children reach those destinations on the path of development. For example, we expect the normal range for children to sit without support to be six to nine months of age; to walk alone, twelve to fifteen months; to use about 50

It's hard when you suspect that there's something wrong with a child. You want the child to get help, but you're afraid to tell the parents. Sometimes you wonder if maybe it's just you. But when you get help, it really feels good.

—A child care provider

words, by the time they are two years old; and to draw recognizable pictures, during their third year. By the time children are four years old, we expect that they will be able to use the toilet independently, and by the time they are five, we expect that they will be choosing friends and playing imaginative games. These milestones, or norms as they are sometimes called, are used to help us confirm that children are following the expected developmental path and to identify those children who seem to be moving too slowly or taking a detour.

Achieving these developmental milestones within the normal range of time is influenced by such factors as opportunity, culture, and disability. Opportunity plays a large role in how quickly children accomplish developmental tasks. If a child lacks an opportunity to try new skills, such as drink from a cup, bounce a ball, or ride a tricycle, he or she will be delayed in learning those skills. Children whose families are unable to provide certain learning opportunities or whose parents may not encourage them to try new things may appear to fall behind others their age. If you notice that a child is unable to do something that other children are able to do, you may need to ask yourself whether the child has ever had an opportunity to learn that particular skill.

Culture plays a large role in determining when children reach developmental milestones. Some cultures may value self-sufficiency and encourage children to be independent very early. Families from other cultures may not expect children to be self-sufficient or independent until they are six or seven years old. Thus, we may see children who have been weaned, toilet-trained, and conditioned to sleep alone in a room at a later age but who have nonetheless reached these developmental milestones normally in the context of their own cultures. When you compare a child's performance to what you know or what you have read about developmental norms, it is important to ask yourself how that child is expected to perform at a particular age in his or her own culture.

We must account for the individual growth and development of all children. Some will be good at some things but have trouble with others. Children with disabilities may take longer traveling the developmental path toward school readiness. For example, one child with cerebral palsy may be good at solving problems and may talk very well but will have trouble doing tasks that require the use of eyes and hands in a coordinated way. Another child with cerebral palsy may have no trouble with eye-hand coordination but may have trouble understanding concepts, solving problems, and speaking. Children with multiple disabilities may have trouble with all of the developmental tasks that are expected of young children.

ABOUT THE AUTHOR

Eleanor W. Lynch is a professor of special education at San Diego State University, where she coordinates the program in early childhood special education. Her professional interests include child assessment that is family-centered and family-friendly, strategies for developing cross-cultural competence, interagency collaboration, and transdisciplinary teams. She is convinced that in all aspects of life it is important to celebrate diversity without forgetting that all people are more alike than different.

In many instances, a child will be identified as having exceptional needs prior to being placed in a day care center or family day care setting. The role of the provider in the care of these children becomes one of learning about the disability and its impact on their development. Often, however, a child's disability may not be identified prior to entering child care. This chapter is intended to provide support and direction to providers who have concerns about a child's development and growth. Child care providers have the opportunity to see many children travel the developmental path and they typically have experience with the wide range of normal development. For this reason, they may be among the first to notice that a particular child is having trouble that may require special help. Determining whether a child is in need of help may require both informal and formal assessments or evaluations. In this chapter, assessment is defined, behaviors that may suggest that an assessment is needed are discussed, and hints on how to present developmental concerns to parents are provided. In addition, community resources are identified and expectations during and following a formal assessment are discussed. Key points are summarized at the end of this chapter, and a list of references and resources is included.

An Overview of Assessment

Throughout this chapter the words *assessment* and *evaluation* are used interchangeably. An assessment or evaluation is any systematic effort to gather information about a child's performance, ability, or development. Informal assessments provide a quick overview of the child's performance. Formal assessments are much more compre-

hensive and provide a sophisticated, in-depth analysis of the child's behavior, performance, ability, or development. Formal assessments generally build on information that has been gathered informally, over time, from a variety of learning contexts.

Informal assessments

Informal assessments may be conducted by anyone who is knowledgeable about typical child development. Child care providers often conduct informal assessments as they observe children's behaviors, gather information from parents, and make comparisons to the behaviors of other children that they have known. Typically, informal assessments will involve teachers and/or providers who use skills built on their understanding of typical child development. From the perspective of experts in the field of early childhood education, informal assessments play a vital role in the understanding of the young child and in the planning and monitoring of developmentally appropriate environments.

In a program advisory (FSB 91/92) entitled "Appropriate Assessment Practices for Young Children," issued by the California Department of Education, strategies and guidance are provided on both the basic criteria for appropriate assessments and methods that are useful in appropriate practice. The advisory suggests specific language that defines the legal obligation of all publicly funded child development programs to conduct developmental profiles in order "to appropriately identify the emotional, social, physical, and cognitive growth of each child served in order to promote the child's success in [school]" (1992, p. 9). This advisory gives wording to the concept and describes the practice of "authentic assessments." It is within this context that most child care providers will make informal assessments and will be in position to identify those children for whom concerns are being raised. Informal assessment combines observing and recording children's behaviors over time and in a variety of settings. It involves compiling information that may include written observations and anecdotal notes, communications with parents, examples of students' work, and, when appropriate, the use of developmental profiles. Informal assessments may be enhanced using audiotapes or videotapes of children's behaviors.

The quality of informal assessments is directly dependent on the abilities and skills of the observer in understanding the range and variability of young children's development. Informal evaluations help the provider plan activities that the child will enjoy, match activities to the child's skills and abilities, and may serve to signal that a particular child is having problems that require a referral for formal assessment. In the event that a formal assessment is planned, the information obtained will provide valuable insight regarding the child over time and include both the child's strengths and areas of concern.

Formal assessments

Formal assessments are conducted by professionals trained in assessment methodology and in typical and atypical child development. In addition, each assessor has training in a specific professional discipline such as special education, psychology, speech and language, nutrition, physical or occupational therapy, nursing, or medicine. Depending on the problems that the child is having, one professional, or more professionals working as a team, might be needed to assess the child.

There are three reasons to conduct a formal assessment of a child: (1) to learn more about the child's strengths and needs; (2) to determine whether a child is eligible for special services; and (3) to make a formal diagnosis. For child care providers the first two reasons are the most important. Learning about the child's strengths and needs enables the family and the child care provider to build activities around the child's strengths and provide special help in those areas in which the child is having difficulty.

For example, at three years old Marcus was not talking, and he often had tantrums when playing with the other children. Supported by the provider's observations and parental concerns, he was referred to a psychologist and a speech and language therapist for a formal evaluation. The psychologist was able to determine that Marcus had normal intelligence, so his language delay was not due to limited cognitive ability. In her interviews with Marcus's mother, grandmother, and family day care provider, she learned that except for the frequency of tantrums, his behavior was quite typical for a three-year-old. After a number of observations and special tests, the speech and language therapist was able to determine that Marcus had a condition called aphasia that was causing a serious delay in language development. His tantrums were related to his inability to express himself, not to a specific behavior disorder. In this case, his family members and his family day care provider were taught some strategies for helping him express himself through a communication board, an adaptive device that a child can manipulate to enhance verbal communication. (For the young child the board generally has pictures of common needs, wants, or activities.) In addition, Marcus was enrolled in a language therapy program. This intervention capitalized on his strengths (normal cognitive ability) and helped to strengthen his skills in the area of need (language).

The second reason to conduct formal assessments is to determine whether the child is eligible for special services. In Marcus's case, the evaluation findings indicated that he was eligible for speech and language services from the public school system. These services were provided for Marcus free of charge because of Public Law 94-142 and its amendments. In addition, his mother had a health insurance policy from her employer that covered speech and language services. Learning that Marcus was eligible for these services gave his family someone and someplace to turn to for help.

The third reason to conduct an assessment is to determine a diagnosis. In Marcus's case his diagnosis was normal intellectual development with aphasia. Although families are often very eager for a diagnosis, labeling a child's problems usually provides little help in deciding what to do. For example, knowing that Marcus has aphasia is not nearly so helpful as knowing what to do to help him learn to communicate. In addition, many young children with developmental problems may have disorders that are not amenable to a specific diagnosis.

What is assessed?

Any developmental area, such as cognitive, social and emotional, receptive and expressive language, fine and gross motor, and self-help development, can be assessed. So, too, can a child's health, medical and nutritional status, vision, and hearing. The areas selected for assessment depend on the concerns raised. For example, if a child care provider notices that a child is very clumsy and cannot do many of the things that his or her peers can do, such as run, jump, and play

catch, an assessor would probably choose to evaluate the child's gross motor functioning and skills. If parents expressed concern about their daughter's interactions with others, describing her as shy, clinging, and silent in all group situations, the assessor would probably want to assess her social and emotional development and skills. Assessments should always be directly linked to the concerns that were expressed in the referral. Although an assessor may wish to expand on the referral concerns, it is his or her obligation to address primarily those concerns that led to the referral.

Developmental Indicators for Assessment

Whether assessment is required may depend on several factors.

When is an assessment necessary?

Child care providers see many children traveling the developmental path; and sooner or later all child care providers work with a child who does not seem to be traveling the path in the same way or at the same rate as the others. He may lag behind his peers; she may behave in unusual ways; or the provider may just have a feeling that something is wrong. Unfortunately, there is no rule book that can tell one what to do, when to wait and see, and when to recommend to parents that a child be assessed. The only guideline is to base decisions on specifics—behaviors that can be described, such as examples of differences in performance or social interactions. Gathering the specifics needed to make a referral often requires observations. Specifics should include (1) a verbal or written description of the child's skills, performance, or behavior that you are concerned about; and (2) comments on what was observed compared to what is expected of a child of the same age from the same culture.

Typically, children who need to be referred are developing very slowly or very atypically. Slow development simply means that the child is behind other children of the same age, such as a twelve-month-old who has made no attempt to stand or a four-year-

old who is not using sentences. Atypical development suggests that the child's progress differs in some qualitative way from what is expected; for example, an infant who seldom cries and seems not to like being cuddled or a five-year-old who has a tantrum every time he doesn't get his own way.

A smaller but equally important group of children who may need assessment are those who seem to have a specific difficulty, such as those who are not hearing or seeing well, experience shakiness (called tremors) when they reach for something, or may seem to "tune out" for short periods of time. Although all of us tune out now and then, frequent episodes may indicate that the child is having petit mal seizures. These seizures could indicate that the child has a form of epilepsy and that a medical evaluation is definitely required.

When is an assessment unnecessary?

Perhaps the most important thing to remember is that a single behavior that seems inappropriate or immature is usually not enough to suggest the need for referral. It is only when a child's performance or functioning is consistently different from or behind that of other children that an assessment may be needed.

Talking with Families About Your Concerns

The first step in suggesting that a child be assessed is to talk with the parents about your concerns. Before an assessment can be made, the child's parents or legal guardian must be informed and agree to the evaluation. The value in early identification of developmental problems is that it can lead to early intervention, thereby ameliorating or preventing further developmental difficulties. The child care provider may help parents find an agency or person to do the assessment, may help the parents make the connection, and may even be asked to participate in the assessment. But nothing can be done without the parents' or a guardian's permission. Assisting in the referral of a child does not, in any way, legally obligate you to provide or pay for services.

Informing parents that you have concerns about their child is not easy, but it may be the most important thing that you do for that child and family. For some parents, it may even be a relief to know that someone else has noticed a problem that has concerned them. The important relationship between child care providers and families is both an advantage and a disadvantage in sharing your concerns. Because providers are generally known, trusted, and important people in the family's life, parents may be able to heed concerns more easily from you than from a stranger. On the other hand, it may be more difficult for providers to approach parents because of the close ties that may exist among families, children, and providers.

If you have ever had to give someone bad or threatening news, you know how difficult it is and how anxious it can make you feel. Telling parents that you are concerned that their child is not developing like other children is one of the most difficult pieces of information to communicate. However, a lot has been said and written about how to talk with parents about developmental concerns, and parents themselves have shared their feelings on the ways in which they would like to be approached. The following paragraphs suggest some strategies that can help providers express their concerns.

Preparing for the conversation

Before talking with parents about your concerns, you need to make some preparations. The first is to record some objective notes about your observations of the problems that you believe the child is having and to role-play how you intend to present your concerns. The notes don't have to be elaborate or formal, but they allow you to review how and why you reached your conclusion and demonstrate that you have thought about what you are sharing. This is one of the informal assessment strategies discussed earlier.

Checklists provide a quick way to record information regarding young children about whom you have concerns, and they can help identify areas that may need further observation or assessment. Record your observations, including questions about developmental domains, behavior, and interaction.

When you are making notes or talking with families about their child, it is important to be objective and avoid any expression of negativism toward the child or family. For example, avoid writing or saying:

During free play last Wednesday, Marcus was mean. He bit Sarah and Roberto and knocked down a block tower that Kaleesha was building.

Although that was certainly not acceptable behavior, expressing the judgment that the child was mean does not help solve the problem. Words such as *mean, hateful, nasty,* and *bad* will make parents feel defensive and less receptive to what you are saying. In reporting Marcus's behavior, it would be better for you to say:

During free play last Wednesday, he bit Sarah and Roberto and knocked down a block tower that Kaleesha was building.

Parents do not want to hear that their child is not developing as quickly as others or is behaving in ways that are unacceptable. It is extremely important to be nonjudgmental; negative comments only serve to make people feel bad.

The second way to prepare is to request a convenient time to talk with the parents. Catching them on the run while they are dropping off or picking up their child is not a good way to share information of such significance. Such consultation requires uninterrupted time, thoughtfulness, and a quiet, private spot. Although child care providers seldom have the luxury of a quiet place or time, it is important to make the setting as calm and relaxed as possible. It is also best to talk about concerns with families without the child being present. For many child care providers, it may be easier to talk with the family on the telephone. However, sharing concerns about a child's development or behavior is too important for anything other than a face-to-face meeting.

A third way to prepare is to consider any cultural or language issues that may enhance or obstruct communication with the parents. If the parents speak a language other than the one you speak, a translator or interpreter will be necessary. Simply knowing the language is not enough. Interpreters or translators should be able to communicate the content and the context in ways that are culturally appropriate. Information about developmental or functional concerns cannot be communicated through gestures. You may also want to consider information about the parents' culture that relates to decision making. For example, if elders or other individuals within the cultural community are the decision makers, parents will not be able to respond to the idea of an assessment until the decision makers have been consulted. However, in a desire to be polite, some families may appear to accept everything you say but, in fact, do nothing. The more that you know about the family and the cultural values and beliefs that they hold, the more effectively information can be presented (*Developing Cross-Cultural Competence: A Guide for Working with Young Children and Their Families,* 1992).

The fourth way to prepare is to learn a little about some of the assessment resources in the community that families could use. You don't have to be an expert, but it can be helpful to offer parents a few specific suggestions. The child care resource and referral networks in most communities maintain information on agencies that conduct assessments, and a later section of this chapter suggests other community resources. In addition, your community's public school district may have assessment and placement capabilities for young children with special needs.

Finally, spend time gathering your own thoughts and calming your nerves. Everyone is nervous in these situations, but it is the manner in which nervous energy is used that is important. Using it to tell the parents, openly and honestly, of your specific concerns and the observations that led to these concerns is an approach that may motivate them to hear what you are saying. However, allowing nervous energy to cause you to insist that something is wrong, that something must be done, or that you don't like the response that you are getting will not help. As you prepare for the conversation, it may be important to remember that the purpose of the meeting is to share your concerns and to listen to what the parents say. Several additional discussions may be required before parents agree to have their child assessed. If the first conversation ends without their enthusiastic support for assessment, the effort is not a failure—it simply means that they were not ready to make the decision at that time. The door should always be left open for future conversations.

Expressing your concerns

There are several important strategies to keep in mind when meeting with parents. The first is to make the setting as private and comfortable as possible (Turnbull and Turnbull 1990). As mentioned earlier, although it is often difficult to find peace and privacy in child care settings, both are important to an effective conversation with parents. Try to find a space that will allow you to talk uninterrupted by children and other staff. None of us would want issues about our children discussed where others might overhear, nor would we want a serious conversation interrupted. The thoughtfulness and respect that a private, relaxed setting conveys is an immediate sign of your caring.

The second strategy is to provide specific, nonjudgmental examples of your concerns. Examples that include how the child's functioning differs from that of other children of his or her age and culture will clarify the concerns. These examples may be especially helpful to parents who do not have other children and may not have much information about typical child development. One parent of a child with developmental disabilities talks about this strategy as bringing the best information that you can bring to parents (Cranor 1986). The more good information that parents have, the better equipped they will be to make a decision and to share their concerns with the assessment team.

A third strategy suggested by Cranor (1986) is to "be human." Imagine how you might feel if the roles were reversed, and try to present the information with care and sensitivity. The experience may be new for parents, so recognize that they may be

surprised to learn of your concerns. People handle surprise in many different ways, ranging from denial to anger to a gradual adjustment to the situation. Be prepared for a range of emotions. If parents deny that a problem exists or if they become angry, do not feel that you must defend your position. Instead, listen to them, acknowledge their feelings and point of view, and do not push. It may take many examples and discussions for parents to move from surprise to action.

A fourth strategy is to allow time for questions. Many parents will want to ask a lot of questions about your concerns. They may want information repeated or they may present alternative explanations. For example, it is not uncommon for parents to appear to brush aside your concerns by saying something like, "Mark's dad was slow to talk too, and he turned out just fine," or "Josie has always been a handful—she just has a mind of her own." Some parents will not have immediate questions but will tell and retell their own stories. Although it takes time, listening to parents is an important part of the interaction. It can provide insights into the child's functioning and will give parents a chance to begin processing the information.

A fifth strategy is to have suggestions and referrals prepared for parents who say they are ready to consider an assessment. The section on resources later in this chapter includes the names and locations of agencies that are available in most communities and that offer comprehensive assessments. If possible, parents should be given the names of agencies and contact persons, their telephone numbers, and copies of the agencies' brochures, if available. In order to create an opening for further discussion, you may want to say that you'll call them in three days or a week to see what they have decided or suggest that you meet again in two weeks to continue the discussion. This strategy allows the parents time to consider what has been suggested, talk together or with others, and to feel assured that you are not trying to pressure them. It also gives you an opportunity to follow up without feeling that you are nagging or pestering them. You can encourage parents to call you if they have additional questions.

Taking the next steps

The next steps will vary for every family. For some there will be more conversations and discussions about your concerns, and ultimately they will decide to have their child assessed. Others may ask you to help them contact an agency, to provide information to assessors, or to allow an assessor to observe the child in the child care setting. Still others may decide that they do not want to have their child assessed. All of these options are reasonable and must be honored. Even when the family makes a decision that is different from the one you prefer, your concerns and your conversation with them are important. Whatever the family decides, you have planted the seeds that will help them observe their child more carefully and

think about what you have said. Sensitively showing your concern for a child and family is never a bad thing to do.

Community Agencies Providing Assessments

Assessment resources vary from community to community, but there are some public agencies available to families throughout California. Each agency has different rules and requirements, but those described below are generally available and likely to be able to provide help.

School Districts

By law (PL 94-142 and its amendments), school districts must assess children from birth through twenty-one years of age who are suspected of having a disability. To make a referral, the parents or legal guardian should contact administrators at the child's school, explain that they think their child may have special needs, and request an assessment. School districts have psychologists, special educators, speech and language therapists, nurses, and other professionals who provide assessments. Assessments are free to families.

California Children's Services

For children with physical disabilities under twenty-one years of age, California Children's Services (CCS) provides specialized medical care and rehabilitation services, including diagnostic evaluation, treatment services, physical and occupational therapy, clinical orthopedic and pediatric services, and medical case management.

Regional Centers for the Developmentally Disabled

Every area in California is served by a regional center for the developmentally disabled. These centers provide assessments for individuals, from birth through adulthood, who are suspected of being developmentally disabled and for children under the age of three who are at risk for developmental disabilities. To make a referral, the parents or legal guardian must contact the regional center in their area and request an assessment. Regional centers have a full complement of professionals, including psychologists; physical, occupational, and speech and language therapists; nutritionists; social workers; nurses; and physicians who provide assessments. Assessment services are free to parents.

Local Interagency Coordinating Areas

There are 32 local interagency coordinating areas (LICAs) in California that were established by the Department of Developmental Services. Staff of these LICAs are responsible for assisting the lead agencies in implementing the comprehensive, coordinated local plan for providing services to families with children through three years of age who have special needs. They are often quite knowledgeable about local resources for children through age five and can suggest resources for assessment in the local area. Anyone can contact a LICA for information.

Some parents may want to talk with their pediatrician or family physician before contacting an agency. Physicians with whom families are comfortable can be very helpful in discussing and explaining developmental norms and expectations; however, many of the problems that become evident in child care settings are not medical in nature. A valid assessment requires a relevant specialist or a team of specialists, and the physician may or may not be the most appropriate assessor. In the event that the concern is medical, such as suspected hearing difficulties or seizures, the family's primary physician will play the leading role in referring the child for additional diagnostic examinations with, for example, a pediatric neurologist or an audiologist. These decisions for additional diagnostic information will be enhanced by the careful observations others have made of the child at home or in a child care setting.

Some families may have insurance plans that cover assessments. Health maintenance organizations (HMOs) often provide comprehensive developmental, physical, and behavioral assessments at no cost or at low cost to families. Depending on the community and the family's insurance, the HMO may be a resource that families may elect to use.

To learn more about the assessment resources in their communities, caregivers may want to contact local child care resource and referral agencies. Such agencies often have information related to developmental and behavioral concerns that includes referrals.

The Assessment Process

Assessments of young children differ depending on what is being assessed and what type of professional is conducting the assessment. However, comprehensive assessments of young children usually include three elements: (1) observations of the child in many situations and settings; (2) interviews with the parents and primary caregivers; and (3) tests that often look more like puzzles and games.

As the child care provider, you may be asked to share your observations or concerns, to allow the assessor to observe the child when he or she is with you, or to assist during the assessment. Your involvement can be extremely important to the family and the child, and the information you provide can be very helpful to the assessor. If you are asked to be involved, you will probably be asked a lot of questions, and you may want to refer to the notes that you made about the child before you talked with the family. Some of the questions may seem repetitive; others may seem unrelated to the concerns that you presented to the parents. But such questions may be used to rule out certain problems or to make sure that all of the important information has been gathered.

What does an assessment look like?

An assessment can take place at an office, a clinic, or an agency; in the child care center; or in the home. Assessments of infants and toddlers are often done in the home, where the child is most comfortable and surroundings are familiar. Assessments of preschoolers and additional assessments of younger children are often done in an office or special playroom. Assessments of young children are usually conducted by a team of professionals.

When the assessment team is working with the child, the assessment looks like a combination of play and more structured questions and games. Often the assessor will begin the assessment in a room with the child's parent or someone else that the child knows well. This gives the child time to get used to a strange person and allows the assessor to observe how the child and adult interact. During this time the child is typically allowed to play freely with her own toys or those that the assessor has brought.

As the assessment becomes more specific, the assessor(s) may ask the parents or participating adults to do certain things with the child. For example, the assessor may have the parent give the child several consecutive directions to see whether or not he can follow them. The assessor may ask the parent to read a story to the child and ask specific questions, or the assessor may ask the parent to play peek-a-boo with, roll a ball to, or play catch with the child. Occasionally the assessor may ask to work with the child alone to see how the child works with a stranger, how the child handles the separation, and how long the child can work without a familiar person present.

Assessments of infants and toddlers involve examination of the ways in which children move, get attention, solve problems such as obtaining toys that are out of reach, and respond to familiar and unfamiliar people. Preschool assessments include these same factors at more advanced levels and include examinations of how children respond to and use language, do simple tasks for themselves, and control their own behavior. Assessments in specific areas, such as motor development, may involve moving the child's body to evaluate muscle tone or determine how limber the child is.

Although children may balk at some of the games and questions used in assessments, the exercises are usually designed to be fun for a young child. Experienced assessors work very hard to create an environment that is comfortable and safe for the child and family members.

After the assessment, what then?

Immediately following the assessment, parents should expect to receive some general information about the child's performance and information about next steps. Within several weeks, they should expect to meet with the assessor(s) and to receive a written report of the findings of the assessment. At that meeting parents should be included as equals on the team, and their questions should be answered. The three most important clusters of questions for parents to ask assessors are:

1. What did you learn about my child's functioning? How does her performance compare to expectations?

2. Do the results of the assessment suggest a need for any special intervention or action? If so, what are the options? Of the options, which do you recommend? How do we make the necessary contacts? Will you assist us in making these contacts? What exactly will happen next? What

specific suggestions do you have that will help our child function more effectively at home, in a child care setting, and elsewhere? Are there books or pamphlets that we can read, other parents we can talk to, or tapes or videos that will help us understand the problems and the interventions? If we have additional questions, who can we call? When will we receive a copy of the report?

3. If no action or intervention is recommended, how should we continue to monitor our child's progress? Are there things that we and/or other care providers can do to address the original concerns without special assistance? Should another assessment be scheduled in a year? Who should we call if we have additional questions?

Sometimes it is difficult for parents to be assertive in an unfamiliar situation, but most professionals want parents to be equal members of the assessment and intervention team. As a child care provider, you can encourage parents to speak up and get their questions, and yours, answered.

Everyone wants the best for young children, so discovering that a child is not developing or behaving typically is upsetting. It's difficult to share concerns with families, and sometimes it's difficult to manage a child who is having problems. But as a child care provider, you are in an especially important position to identify children who may need extra help. Encouraging families to consent to an assessment when their child's behavioral development is not keeping pace or is very different from that of other children of the same age and culture is an important role for the child care provider. Nobody said this role would be easy, but it does afford the opportunity to make a difference.

Summary

The purpose of this chapter is to provide information on assessments of young children. It presents strategies that providers can use when they have concerns about the growth and development of children in their care.

The role of the provider is one of obtaining information about the child over time and in a variety of settings through informal assessments. The process of sharing difficult information with parents was given particular emphasis because of the important role the provider plays in the life of the child and the family.

This thorough discussion of formal assessments was provided not only to increase the provider's knowledge and understanding of the assessment process but also to enhance her ability to support the family as it investigates or proceeds with a more in-depth assessment of the child.

Finally, a list of community resources typically available was discussed as well as a framework for asking questions following the assessment. Providers can further help families by familiarizing themselves with local resources or sources of information. Through early identification and referral, providers can help initiate early intervention services designed to minimize the impact of developmental concerns or disabilities on a child's growth and potential for learning.

KEY POINTS

1. Most children develop at about the same rate and in the same way as other children of the same age and culture. For some children, however, the quality or rate of development may differ from that of their peers.

2. Differences in development may be due to differences in the opportunities to learn, differences in cultural expectations, or differences within the child.

3. Child care providers typically have experience observing the range and variability of normal development in children of many different ages and backgrounds. This experience places providers in key positions to identify those children who may need additional help.

4. An assessment or evaluation is a systematic effort to gather information about a child's performance, ability, or development. It involves both informal and formal practices.

5. Informal assessments generally occur in the child's day care or preschool setting and are made by professionals who work with the child on a regular basis. These assessments occur over time and in a variety of settings.

6. Formal assessments are conducted by professionals with expertise in both typical and atypical development. Their expertise may include specialized training in psychology, special education, speech and language therapy, occupational or physical therapy, social work, nursing, or other health-related fields.

7. Formal assessments are conducted to learn more about a child's strengths and needs, to determine eligibility for special services, and/or to make a diagnosis. They usually include observations in a variety of situations and settings, interviews with parents and primary caregivers, and formal tests.

8. Children can be referred for assessment, and information about them can

be shared with others, only with the written consent of parents or legal guardians.

9. Child care providers should consider any cultural or linguistic differences that may influence how a child is perceived as well as the ethnic, cultural, or linguistic differences that may enhance or interfere with communications between providers and the child's family.

10. When child care providers approach parents with concerns about their child, it is important that they share all observations in a nonthreatening and nonjudgmental manner. They should invite the parents to meet in a quiet and private setting. Several meetings may be necessary in order to share information and address concerns.

11. Parents are vital members of a formal assessment team. Their participation will be enhanced if the process is explained to them and if they know how they can be involved and what they can expect following the assessment.

12. Providers play a vital role by helping to identify, early, those children who may benefit from a more in-depth assessment.

References

Cranor, L. "Early Childhood Assessment Parent Fact Sheet." 1986. (Available from California Infant Preschool Personnel Development Programs, 650 Howe Avenue, #300, Sacramento, CA 95825.)

Developing Cross-Cultural Competence: A Guide for Working with Young Children and Their Families. 1992. Edited by E. W. Lynch and M. J. Hanson. Baltimore: Paul H. Brookes.

Program Advisory FSB 91/92—California Department of Education. July, 1992. "Appropriate Assessment Practices for Young Children: Implementing the Recommendations of *Here They Come: Ready or Not! Report of the California School Readiness Task Force.* 1988; and *It's Elementary! Elementary Grades Task Force Report.* 1992."

Turnbull, A. P., and H. R. Turnbull III. 1990. *Families, Professionals, and Exceptionality: A Special Partnership* (Second edition). Columbus, Ohio: Merrill.

Resources

For more detailed information about the identification and assessment of children with exceptional needs and related issues, the following books and articles are recommended.

Cohen, D. H.; V. Stern; and N. Balaban. *Observing and Recording the Behavior of Young Children* (Third edition). New York: Teacher's College, Columbia University, 1983.

This comprehensive guide for observing and recording the behavior of young children contains technical and practical information to assist care providers. Of special interest is Chapter 12, "Recording the Behavior of Children with Special Problems."

Greenspan, S. I., and S. Meisels with the Zero to Three Workgroup on Developmental Assessment. "Toward a New Vision for the Developmental Assessment of Infants and Young Children," *Zero to Three,* Vol. 14, No. 6 (June-July, 1994), 1–8.

This short article presents the most recent recommended guidelines for the assessment of infants and young children. Developed by an interdisciplinary work group convened by the National Center for Clinical Infant Programs, the work represents a major shift in the way in which professionals think about and conduct assessments.

Hanson, M. J., and E. W. Lynch. *Early Intervention: Implementing Child and Family Services for Infants and Toddlers Who Are At-Risk or Disabled* (Second edition). Austin, Tex., PRO-ED, in press.

Written for early intervention professionals, this book discusses programs and services for children from birth through age three who are at-risk or disabled and their families. Chapters on coordinating screening and identification efforts, assessing children and identifying family strengths and needs, cultural diversity, and working with families provide information related to identification, assessment, and interactions with families.

Leavitt, R. L., and B. K. Eheart, "Assessment in Early Childhood Programs," *Young Children,* Vol. 46, No. 5 (July, 1991), 4–9.

This short article provides excellent suggestions for collecting informal assessment information in the child care setting. The article is clear and specific and provides helpful guidelines for care providers on gathering and recording information.

Meisels, S. J., and S. Provence. *Screening and Assessment: Guidelines for Identifying Young Disabled and Developmentally Vulnerable Children and Their Families.* Washington, D.C.: National Center for Clinical Infant Programs, 1989.

This booklet provides technical information about legislation and best practices for assessing young children. Chapter 2, "A Perspective on Young Children's Development"; Chapter 3, "Processes and Procedures for Screening and Assessing Young Children"; and Chapter 4, "Vignettes"; are of interest to child care providers.

Ripley, S. "National Information Center for Children and Youth with Handicaps (NICHCY)." *Exceptional Parent,* Vol. 20, No. 4 (June, 1990), 52, 54.

This short article describes the services of NICHCY, a central information agency that provides free information about disabilities. Child care providers may want to request information about certain disabilities or management techniques or they may want to refer parents to the NICHCY toll-free telephone number: (800) 999-5599.

Turnbull, A. P., and H. R. Turnbull III. *Families, Professionals, and Exceptionality: A Special Partnership* (Second edition). Columbus, Ohio: Merrill, 1990.

Wilcox, D., "Heather's Story: The Long Road for a Family in Search of a Diagnosis," *Exceptional Parent,* Vol. 21, No. 2 (March, 1991), 92–94.

This article describes, from a family's point of view, the assessment process, the roadblocks, and the final outcome of years of seeking answers about their daughter's differences.

Chapter 7

Caregiving Strategies for Building Resilience in Children at Risk

By Marie Kanne Poulsen, Ph.D.

Introduction

"José is such a jittery infant. He cries a lot and is hard to cuddle."

"Kelly whined all day and wet her pants."

"Tommy just wandered around touching everything and everybody. He didn't focus on any play activity."

"Marco bit Joey for the third time today."

"Tamika just stands and watches the other children play."

The behaviors of José, Tamika, Marco, Kelly, and Tommy are typical of some children in our care. Although their behaviors differ greatly, these children are all telling us that something is going on in their lives that is too difficult for them to handle. Parents and caregivers are usually most sympathetic to children like Tamika, whose distress is easy to see. Adults will patiently try to comfort them and make their lives a little easier. But we may just give up on José and let him cry, and we may be impatient with children like Kelly and Tommy. We often respond to Marco with anger or frustration, seeing him as an aggressive child who acts that way on purpose, rather than as a child who is also stressed beyond his capacity to handle himself in a positive way.

It is through their behavior that children tell us how they are feeling about their world. All children have their good days, when everything goes smoothly, and their bad days, when stress becomes overwhelming and everything falls apart. Difficult behavior often indicates that a child is feeling stressed because of fatigue, poor nutrition, discomfort, pain, or illness. A child may also be showing stress because of a family situation, such as an absent parent, a new baby, a family argument, or a family member's illness. Most children are able to deal with the stress in their lives and are their old selves in a day or two. This is particularly true if there are adults who help them deal with people and events in an adaptive or positive way rather than focus on their negative behaviors.

However, some children's difficult behaviors are numerous, extreme, or persistent, indications that they are overwhelmed by the stresses in their young lives and have not yet learned positive ways to express their feelings or deal with challenges. These children are at risk of developing learning, behavioral, and/or emotional problems in later life. As caregivers, we can support children at risk by helping them to deal more effectively with their daily situations.

The discussion of at-risk children in this Project EXCEPTIONAL document is based on several beliefs regarding the prevalence and scope of the needs of these children. Children at risk of developmental problems constitute a large and growing population of children who are overwhelmed by the stresses in their environments or by biological risk factors such as prematurity, low birth weight, or prenatal substance exposure. This increase in the numbers of children at risk has an enormous impact on child care and development programs that may not be prepared to accommodate their needs. Child care providers may identify these children as difficult to handle, children requiring additional support from staff. Because these

ABOUT THE AUTHOR

Marie Kanne Poulsen is a licensed psychologist at the University of Southern California, Center for Child Development, University Affiliated Program, Children's Hospital, Los Angeles. She has developed a community-based early intervention program for drug-addicted mothers and infants and is a mental health consultant for Head Start and the Los Angeles Unified School District. Her interests include infant and early childhood mental health, mother-child interactions, children at risk, perinatal substance exposure, and family foster care.

at-risk children function at about the same levels on the continuum of development as their peers, their difficulties do not fit into traditional definitions of disabilities, and often they do not meet eligibility criteria for special education services. Nevertheless, their behaviors or emotions interfere with their learning. These are children who often "fall through the cracks" of support systems when they are young and could be helped significantly. Thus, children at risk may need extra support from their caregivers. In some ways, at-risk children may require even more attention from child care and development staff than children with clearly identified disabilities.

The levels of awareness and skills needed to care for children at risk parallel those needed in caring for all children, including youngsters with more identifiable disabilities. In this chapter we discuss common risk factors in young children and suggest strategies that are helpful in working with all children, and particularly those children whose behaviors and emotions are of concern. With no intervention, help, or support, this population of children will most likely continue to be at risk for later school problems.

How children become "at risk"

The sources of stress in a young child's life may be internal or external. Internal stressors, such as developmental immaturity, may be the result of birth-related (neonatal) or early childhood problems. Children may have immature, poorly organized, or extremely sensitive nervous systems resulting from:

- Infection in infancy
- Low birth weight or prematurity
- Lack of prenatal care for the mother
- Prenatal exposure to toxic substances (alcohol, drugs, or lead)
- Poor maternal nutrition during pregnancy
- Maternal infection during pregnancy
- Birth complications

Difficulties may also result from early childhood experiences, such as:

- Severe illness or injuries
- Malnutrition
- Extreme neglect

It is important to note that many young children who have experienced these problems show no evidence of immaturity or delay of nervous-system development. Those who do manifest effects of these problems may become easily upset or stressed by noise, commotion, fatigue, changes in daily routine, or new people and situations.

Some children for whom there is no evidence of neonatal or early childhood problems are by nature intense, sensitive, and overreactive. These children also tend to become easily stressed and, therefore, need more attentive caregiving.

In addition to internal causes of stress, external situations may cause stress in children and affect their behavior. These external stresses include:

- Separation from parent, significant caregiver, or siblings
- Substance abuse by parent
- Domestic violence
- Homelessness
- Mental, physical, or sexual abuse
- Extreme poverty
- Parental depression
- Multiple foster placements or multiple caregivers
- Foster care placement in situations in which children are constantly leaving

There is no direct relationship between a child's intense temperament, neuro-developmental immaturity, and/or family problems and a child's later behavior, but we know that the more stresses children experi-

ence, the more help they will need to cope with the everyday challenges of growing up.

Characteristics and needs of the child at risk

We consider children healthy when they have the internal and external resources to deal with stressful situations and when they have developed the initiative to explore, discover, learn, and solve problems. When children deal with the world effectively, they become competent and confident; they develop the self-esteem that allows them to cope with the demands of others and to handle conflict in effective ways. They may not always get their way, but they do not fall apart. They don't have to win all the time in order to feel competent; they can compromise. In assessing a child's ability to handle stress, one must consider the child's age. A two-year-old warrants different behavioral expectations than a five-year-old. Similarly, the skill with which a child uses resources is important. Is the child able to handle requests or conflicts independently or with minimal adult help or redirection? Or does the child require complete adult supervision and intervention in new or challenging situations?

Children are at risk to the extent that they have not developed the self-esteem and skills needed to handle everyday stresses, to the extent that they have poorly organized or immature nervous systems, and to the extent that their family and child-care experiences manifest stressors. Children "tell" us that their stresses are overwhelming when they *consistently* are "unavailable" for learning or interaction in the following ways:

- They are overactive.
- They have difficulty focusing on or completing a task.

- They become easily frustrated or anxious.
- They have difficulty making decisions.
- They have difficulty following directions.
- They hit, bite, grab, or push to solve problems with peers.
- They have uncontrollable tantrums.
- They cling to adults.
- They avoid new challenges.
- They demonstrate inadequate play skills.
- They show signs of regression (i.e., crying frequently, wetting, or soiling).
- They do not eat.
- They have sleep disturbances (i.e., nightmares, night terrors, wakefulness).

It is important that caregivers interpret these behaviors as signs of stress and an inability to cope rather than as indicators of "willfulness" or defiance. We must remember that children would prefer to deal with their world in effective ways. But children who are living with extreme stress may not have learned easily from prior experiences. They may need to be taught and re-taught the simple social expectations other children learn naturally, such as taking turns, sharing, and verbally resolving conflicts.

Children at risk may become easily stressed by demanding and threatening physical and emotional situations. They may need a protective environment that shields them from too much excitement or stimulation until they develop effective ways of coping.

Finally, children who are experiencing a chaotic home life, separation and loss of family members, unstable living conditions, family substance abuse, or family illness are at increased risk for developmental and emotional difficulties. These children's families need help to address these problems, help which the caregiver may be able

to provide through referral to social service or health agencies. And these children need positive experiences to help them cope with the negative stresses they cannot avoid.

Working with children at risk

There are no easy ways to help children resolve internal or external conflicts in adaptive ways. Children are individuals, with unique experiences—what works with one child may not be the best approach to meet the needs of another.

The suggestions given in this chapter for working with children at risk are based on the following beliefs:

- Every child has strengths and feelings that need to be acknowledged.
- All children need help in dealing with stressful events such as separation, divorce, illness, and death.
  —Discuss the event in an age-appropriate manner with the child. To deny or pretend the event did not happen will only increase the child's anxiety.
  —Put words to the feelings that the child is experiencing.

—Offer the child reassurance, understanding, and support.

• Many children need to be taught and retaught appropriate ways to express anger, disappointment, frustration, fear, or sadness. They need support in resolving their conflicts.

• An effective way to help children cope with stress is to build on their sense of self-mastery.

To illustrate strategies that caregivers have reported to be effective, we return to the at-risk children described at the beginning of this chapter.

José

"José is an irritable baby. He seems to cry at the drop of a hat. He's jittery and hard to cuddle . . . and when I try to 'talk' to him, he just kicks and squirms."

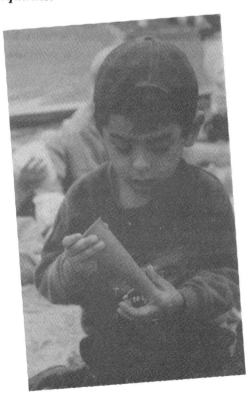

José's birth history is very important in understanding his behavior. José's mother had no prenatal care and did not maintain proper nutrition during pregnancy. José was born six weeks premature and had respiratory difficulties. As a result, his nervous system is poorly organized. He becomes easily overstimulated by lights, noise, and movement and may cry for long periods. At times, he arches his back instead of cuddling when he is carried, and he becomes excited instead of paying attention when caregivers try to interact or play with him.

Babies with poorly organized nervous systems are easily overwhelmed and may:

• Close their eyes to commotion.

• Turn their heads when someone gets too close.

• Flail their arms and legs instead of calming down to play with a person or toy.

• Cry during usual routines.

• Breathe rapidly.

It is important for caregivers to realize that these are not "leave-me-alone" messages, but indicators of a need for help. For example, José needs a protective environment that will keep him from being overwhelmed. He needs a care provider who will facilitate his capacity to organize his behavior the way most infants do without extra help. Recognizing that parents generally know their children best, José's child care provider learned from them some effective ways to care for him. Gradually, as she began to know José, his provider discovered additional effective strategies, such as:

• Protecting him from too much noise, bright lights, and sudden movement.

• Approaching him slowly and speaking in a soft voice.

- Holding him wrapped in a blanket with his arms and legs bent to help him become calm enough to engage with her.

- Responding to José whenever he looks at her, makes sounds, reaches, or smiles so that he learns that he can be effective.

- Pausing and letting him "rest" when he turns away from an interaction and gradually reengaging him when he is ready.

- Responding to José as soon as he begins to whimper, because he has difficulty calming himself once he starts to cry. (This response will not "spoil" the infant; it is an immediate response to his signals of distress and discomfort.)

- Helping José bend forward slightly at the hip before attempting to cuddle him and placing a small pillow under his head during diapering to inhibit his arching.

It is critical in caring for a high-need infant to understand the most effective ways to help. This knowledge will require ongoing communication among care providers and family members. It is important that all caregivers continue to learn from each other.

If José's parents do not know how to effectively respond to their baby, a cycle of difficult parent-child interaction may develop. An experienced care provider can act as a mentor to inexperienced or overwhelmed parents. Talking together and having common goals in the care of José will better enable all his caregivers to provide more effectively for his needs.

Kelly

"Kelly can play calmly with the other children. But there are many days when she whines, grabs children's toys, and wets her pants—all more typical behaviors of a younger child."

After keeping a log on Kelly's "difficult days," her child care provider noted that on these days, some change in routine had occurred, the result of an absent caregiver, an ill parent, or a new child at the center. Most children are able to regulate their behavior and can tolerate normal changes in the routines of their households or child care centers. However, Kelly tends to be overly sensitive to the physical and emotional world around her. Changes in routine agitate her beyond her capacity to cope, resulting in regressive behaviors. Her caregiver now does several things to help Kelly learn to cope with changes in routine:

- The caregiver notes changes in the child care program and discusses Kelly's "sensitivity to changes" with her mother, who now also alerts the caregiver about any changes in routines at home.

- Knowing that a reason for atypical behavior may not always be evident, the caregiver observes Kelly every morning to see whether there are any behavioral indicators that Kelly may need some extra help that day.

- The caregiver prepares Kelly for any anticipated change in routine by talking to her about the change, asking Kelly what she might be feeling, and offering her support and reassurance.

- The caregiver keeps Kelly close during parts of the day and solicits her help, which strengthens Kelly's sense of self on days when she is feeling insecure.

- The caregiver coaches Kelly to use words when she wants to play with another child's toy rather than grabbing. The caregiver also encourages the other child to say either "OK" or "when I'm done."

- The caregiver ignores the whining behavior but lets Kelly know that her "big-girl voice" is more appropriate.

- On a regular basis, the caregiver monitors the number and interest level of toys so that Kelly's needs and those of the other children can be met easily.

Consistency and family involvement play important roles in the ongoing support Kelly may need. Child care providers need to pay close attention to how well the family is able to deal with Kelly's needs. Because of her age, Kelly's regressive behaviors may be frustrating to adults. Parents and care providers will need to monitor how well their intervention strategies are working. If ignoring Kelly's whining worked initially but is later found to be ineffective, then a new approach may be needed. When parents and child care providers feel they have exhausted their repertoire of strategies, a referral to a child guidance specialist may be useful. It may also be that Kelly's family is involved with other agencies, such as public health or social services. If this is the case, providers should ask the parents for permission to share observations of Kelly's strengths and needs. Families, child care providers, and the child specialist should work together to develop a consistent intervention plan.

Tommy

"Tommy always seems very busy. At times he doesn't focus on play but wanders around touching everything. Often, he does not pay attention to the directions given to children. When he gets into a conflict, things quickly escalate out of control. He usually ends up hitting someone or having a tantrum when things don't go his way!"

Tommy's child care provider noted that Tommy has difficulty modulating his activity and emotions. Once Tommy's behavior is out of control, it is difficult for him to calm down. Her best strategy for dealing with out-of-bounds behavior is to prevent his distress from escalating and resulting in overactive behaviors or tantrums. His caregiver now does several things to prevent Tommy's behavior from reaching the out-of-bounds point:

- The caregiver has learned to detect subtle clues that Tommy is in distress or near conflict, and she "talks him through" events.

- The caregiver diverts Tommy's energy by giving him a choice of active but constructive tasks, such as helping to move boxes or wash toys. She remains close to him during the process until he settles down. She expresses verbal praise.

- The caregiver has instituted a relaxation game after outside play: Lights are dimmed, soft music is played, and a quiet song is sung. She has Tommy stay next to her and assist her in setting up "relaxing time."

- The caregiver has arranged a quiet corner that Tommy has learned to choose when he needs quiet time. The quiet corner is equipped with a bean bag chair, a comforter, pillows, books, and a tape recorder with soft music.

Initially, the child care provider joined Tommy in the quiet corner, which is used by the group as a rest place, not for time-out. Gradually, Tommy used it by choice or as an option presented to him before things got out of hand.

- The caregiver lets Tommy know that his hitting children cannot be tolerated ("I cannot let you hit.") and coaches him to use words to solve conflict ("Tell Marco what you want.").

• The caregiver establishes eye contact with Tommy or stands near him before she gives directions to the group. Sometimes, she places her hand on his shoulder to help him attend to the task.

What is significant in the child care provider's strategies is that they allow her to observe Tommy's behaviors from a supportive point of view. Tommy's sense of self is preserved, and he is not labeled a "bad" child. It is important to observe the critical junctures at which intervention occurs— before Tommy's behaviors get in the way of his learning or interacting with others. Tommy is learning important lessons about himself. He is learning that he is capable of handling difficult moments.

By discussing with Tommy's parents his strengths and his difficulties in child care, the provider can open the door for Tommy's parents to express concerns they may have. Of primary importance is to ensure that all significant adults in Tommy's life share a similar view of him and are able to interact with empathy and comfort. This is no easy task. It requires good communication, mutual respect, and support for all involved.

Marco

"Marco came this morning in a very cranky mood. He grabbed Angela's ball and ran. When Joey pushed him, Marco bit him. This is the third time Marco has bitten Joey!"

Marco's caregiver noticed that his frustration tolerance is very low. When he comes to child care in a "cranky mood," almost all his interactions with peers are negative. Biting—at any age—cannot be allowed; the intervention of the caregiver is always necessary. After a parent conference, Marco's mother and the provider realized

that Marco was having difficulty adjusting to his parents' divorce and acted out more following visits with his father. They concluded that he was having difficulty adjusting to the change. The child care provider now does several things to help Marco deal with his low frustration tolerance:

• The caregiver spends extra time with him when he arrives. Often, this alone reduces his stress and allows time for Marco to make a smooth transition to the environment.

• The caregiver firmly but not angrily tells Marco that he hurt Joey and that he cannot bite other children. ("Use your words, not your teeth. Biting hurts. See, Joey is crying.")

• The caregiver keeps Marco and Joey separated from each other, because Marco has bitten only Joey.

• The caregiver coaches Marco to use words to let Angela know he wants to play with the ball and to tell Joey not to push him.

- Marco's mother lets the caregiver know when a visit with his father has occurred. Now Marco and the caregiver discuss "Daddy's visit." Marco draws a picture of Daddy, which he keeps in his cubby. The caregiver and Marco look at it together when they talk about the visit.

Often, circumstances arise in children's lives over which care providers have little or no control. Marco's behaviors, for example, appear to be related to his relationship with his father. When the child-care provider and Marco's mother discussed the problem, they tried to solve it together. They identified strategies that validated Marco's experience and his anger while redirecting him to more appropriate ways to express his feelings. Sharing books or stories about other children who sometimes feel anger or who have experienced painful separations may help Marco to not feel so alone and may show him additional ways he can communicate how he is feeling. Helping Marco to understand his own feelings may help him in future years to deal successfully with other difficult or sad experiences.

Marco's mother may also need support in understanding his behaviors. Sometimes linking parents with other parents in similar circumstances is helpful. Sometimes simply providing a listening ear when the occasion arises will help a parent feel supported.

Tamika

"Tamika seems so sad. She clings to her mother and cries for long periods of time after her mother leaves. Tamika doesn't join the other children in play but merely stands and watches. She ate only a few bites at lunch today."

Tamika is overwhelmed by a recent 12-month separation from her mother during which Tamika lived with relatives. Tamika will need extra help to establish trust with new adults in her life. She will also need reassurance that her mother will pick her up at the end of the day. The caregiver now does several things to help establish Tamika's trust and to help her deal with separation.

- The caregiver has some photographs of Tamika and her mother playing together (she asked the mother for them) and she spends time each day looking at them with Tamika.

- The caregiver discusses Tamika's stressful experience with her. ("Did you miss your mama when you lived with your auntie?")

- The caregiver acknowledges Tamika's feelings. ("You're feeling sad because you want your mama.")

- The caregiver reassures Tamika that her mama will pick her up at the end of the day.

- The caregiver allows Tamika (as well as all the other children) one toy of her own that she doesn't have to share for the day.

- The caregiver engages Tamika in play when Tamika is too immobilized to initiate play on her own.

- The caregiver does not force Tamika to eat but has Tamika help with the lunch preparation.

It is important to understand a child's sadness, anger, and/or confusion over separation or abandonment. A young child may not be able to fully understand the circumstances or may not have the words to describe needs or fears. In Tamika's case, the care provider's strategies will help the child cope with her past experiences. Of greater importance is that the provider understand the vulnerability of this young child and her mother in relation to their attachment to each other. It serves no purpose to judge the separation and its impact on Tamika. Rather, every effort must be made to support the mother in reestablishing a bond and a relationship of trust.

Tamika's mother may need help in understanding Tamika's overt behaviors, which may include her sadness or her rejection of the mother's advances. The provider can support the mother by helping her to observe changes as they occur and by sharing the events of Tamika's day and the strategies that seemed to be most helpful in caring for her. The task is to help both Tamika and her mother to feel successful in their interactions and secure in their renewed relationship.

There is no question that the caregivers of José, Marco, Kelly, Tamika, and Tommy used extra time, patience, and energy to meet these children's special emotional needs. They each took extra time to confer with parents, to spend time alone with the child, and to acknowledge feelings. Such a relationship allows the child to build positive coping skills to deal with the challenges of growing up.

Additional suggestions

The attentive caregiver of the child at risk should:

- Develop a mutually respectful relationship with the child's family.

- Learn about the child's birth, social, medical, and developmental history.

- Have the parents provide information about past and present family events that can influence the child's sense of self and his or her reaction to stress.

- Keep a log of the child's behavior in order to identify "triggers" and patterns of stress in the child's life, and share these

observations of the child's progress with the family.

- Identify the environmental and interactional stressors and the supports you can provide as a caregiver.

- Identify community resources that can further assist children and their families.

Finally, the attentive caregiver should take care of herself or himself and find ways to replenish the energy it takes to meet the needs of children at risk and their families.

Components of healthful caregiving

Quality caregiving depends on an understanding of the process of children's growth and development; the importance of an enriched, child-centered environment; and the significance of the relationship between children and emotionally available adults. The following charts compare quality caregiving to at-risk caregiving with reference to characteristics of caregivers, caregiving environments, and interactions between caregivers and children.

Caregivers' Characteristics

Quality caregiving	At-risk caregiving
Quality caregiving often includes many of the following factors:	*Caregiving that puts children at risk includes the following factors:*
The presence of a consistent primary caregiver over time	The presence of different primary caregivers over time
A nurturing, emotionally responsive caregiver	An overwhelmed, stressed, and emotionally unavailable caregiver
An understanding of child development and how a child learns	Naiveté about a child's developmental needs and ways to facilitate development
A view of a child's behavior as an expression of how the child copes with the world	Negative attribution ascribed to child when behavior is noncompliant
The acceptance of the "urgency" of a young child's needs	Expressions of annoyance when the toddler's needs interrupt the caregiver's needs
An understanding of the importance of a child's learning to assert himself or herself	Discouragement of the child's development of autonomy, self-dependence, and self-assertion
The possession of a broad repertoire of soothing strategies	The practice of giving the child a bottle or food when the child is upset
Encouragement for the child to make choices	Lack of opportunities for the child to make decisions
An emotionally balanced caregiver who enables the child to predict adult behavior	Unpredictable reactions by the caregiver to the child's behavior

Caregiving Environments

Quality caregiving	At-risk caregiving
Environments that contribute to quality caregiving:	*Environments that put the child at risk:*
Protect the child from too much stimulation.	Have no restrictions on amount of noise or movement or on the number of people, objects, and events.
Are continuously monitored for the safety of the climbing, exploring, curious child	Have no protections against potential hazards as the child develops new skills.
Offer toys and/or household objects for child play.	Lack objects to occupy the child when he or she is left alone for long periods of time.
Provide objects the child can call her or his own.	Allow clothes, toys, beds, and so forth to be communal at all times.
Have consistent routines for daily living activities.	Do not have family or day care rituals that center on sleeping, eating, departures, and special events such as holidays and birthdays.
Offer the child a quiet space for relaxing play.	Do not offer quiet or relaxing play areas.

Interactions Between Caregiver and Child

Quality caregiving	At-risk caregiving
Actions by caregivers that contribute to quality caregiving include:	*Actions by caregivers that put the child at risk include:*
Modeling for child how to play with objects, look at pictures, use language	Providing no opportunity for adult or peer modeling of language and play
Encouraging, acknowledging, and accepting child's expressions of emotions	Discouraging expressions of disappointment, distress, anger, or sadness
Anticipating child's nonadaptive behavior and diverting child to other activities	Delaying intervention until child's behavior is out of control
Initiating primary interaction between caregiver and child	Initiating only minimal eye contact, cuddling, smiling, touching, talking, stroking, and singing
Responding promptly to child's adaptive attention-seeking signals	Focusing on negative behavior and limiting attention to child's tantrums and behaviors such as crying, head banging, hitting, biting, and throwing
Guiding child in adaptive ways of dealing with objects, people, events, and emotions	Limiting directions that tell child what not to do
Encouraging and praising all attempts at self-dependence as the root of self-mastery and esteem	Failing to tolerate frustration, dawdling, and messiness in daily living, play, and learning activities
Viewing clinging behavior as child's request for reassurance, and responding to it accordingly	Discouraging clinging behavior as babyish
Ignoring misbehavior when appropriate	Commenting on all misbehavior

Summary

Children who have poorly organized nervous systems or who have experienced separation and loss, domestic or community violence, or emotional neglect or abuse are particularly vulnerable to being overwhelmed by events in daily living. Chronically overwhelmed children often do not deal with everyday challenges in age-appropriate and adaptive ways. Their negative behaviors can become very upsetting for their families, their peers, their care providers, and themselves.

These children will need to be taught and re-taught appropriate ways to express and resolve the conflict, anger, fear, disappointment, and sadness they feel. If their nonadaptive behaviors are not addressed in effective ways, they will remain at risk for later problems in school and in relationships. Child care and development staff members play significant roles in helping young children learn how to deal with life's stressors in constructive ways.

KEY POINTS

1. Children are at risk to the extent that they have not developed the self-esteem and skills needed to handle everyday stresses, to the extent that they have poorly organized or immature nervous systems, and to the extent to which their family and child care situations are filled with current stressors. Children tell us their stresses are overwhelming when they consistently behave in nonadaptive ways.

2. It is important that caregivers interpret negative behavior as an inability to cope rather than as an indicator of "willfulness" or defiance. We must remember that children would *prefer to deal with their world in effective ways.*

3. Every child has strengths and feelings that need to be acknowledged.

4. All children need help in dealing with stressful life events such as separations, divorce, illness, and death. Providers help when they discuss such events in an age-appropriate manner with the child, put words to the feelings that the child is experiencing, and offer reassurance and support to the child.

5. Many children need to be taught and re-taught appropriate ways to express anger, disappointment, frustration, fear, and sadness. They need support in resolving their conflicts.

6. An effective way to help children cope with stress is to build on their sense of self-mastery.

7. Additional tips for attentive caregiving:

- Develop a mutually respectful relationship with the child's parents.
- Learn about the child's birth, social, medical, and developmental history.
- Ask parents to inform you of past and present family events that might influence the child's sense of self and stress levels.
- Keep a log of the child's behavior in order to identify "triggers" and patterns of stress in the child's life. Share observations of the child's progress and other developmental concerns with the parents.
- Identify the environmental and interactional stresses the child is experiencing and the supports you can provide as a caregiver.
- Identify resources within your community that can further help children and their families.

- Take care of yourself. Find ways to replenish the energy it takes to meet the needs of children at risk and their families.

8. Quality caregiving depends on an understanding of how children grow and develop, of the importance of an enriched, child-centered environment, and of the significant relationship between an emotionally available adult and the child.

Resources

Chalufar, Ingrid, and others. *As I Am.* Ellsworth, Maine: Action Opportunities, Inc., 1988.

This book focuses on the relationship between care providers and preschool children. It provides guidance for care providers in modeling mental health skills, observing development, building relationships, and facilitating growth. The author suggests activities and recommends children's books that encourage emotional and social development in young children.

Dinkmeyer, Don, Sr., and Don Dinkmeyer Jr. *Parenting Young Children: Parent's Handbook.* Circle Pines, Minn.: American Guidance Service, 1989.

A wealth of helpful strategies for caregivers of children under age six is provided in this book. Understanding children's behaviors and teaching young children self-respect and personal responsibility are central themes. The material is particularly applicable for family day care providers.

Just Kids: A Practical Guide for Working with Children Prenatally Substance-Exposed. Sacramento: California Department of Education, 1994. *Just Kids Video* (29 minutes, closed captioned) California Department of Education, 1993. (Available in Spanish and English language versions.)

This guide and accompanying video were developed out of a need to dispel stereotypes and myths regarding young children who have been prenatally substance-exposed. Offered are effective and practical strategies that support these children in preschool and child care settings.

Poulsen, M. K., and others. *Child Development Issues and Implications for Shelter Care.* Sacramento: Children's Research Institute of California, 1988.

The section on early childhood focuses on the needs and characteristics of healthful development. The author also discusses abuse and neglect as sources of stress in young children and suggests strategies that ensure quality care for insecure children.

Saifer, Steffen. *Practical Solutions to Practically Every Problem: The Early Childhood Teacher's Manual.* Mt. Rainier, Md.: Gryphon House, 1990.

The author suggests strategies for classroom teachers and for center-based and home care providers who deal with challenging and difficult behaviors in young children.

Chapter 8

Caring for Young Children with Physical Disabilities

By Nora Snowden, O.T.R.; and Karla Snorf, R.P.T.

Introduction

We live in a world significantly impacted by advances in technology. Few members of our society have been more positively affected by these advances than persons with physical disabilities. Those who, at one time, may have been significantly limited by their disabilities are gaining access to the world in new and remarkable ways. We are also witnessing significant attitudinal changes in our society toward persons with disabilities. At the same time,

> "Sometimes I wish people would talk to me first, before they ask what's wrong with me or what happened to me. It makes me feel like my wheelchair is more important than I am."
>
> — Jade Calegory, 1987 Easter Seal Scholarship Winner

advocacy efforts and legislation mandating accessibility have helped to pave the way for equal opportunities within our communities.

It is also true, however, that many children with physical disabilities historically have been excluded from many community settings, including child care and development programs. Both the visibility of the disability and concerns for how to care for these children have contributed to the lack of child care options for families. According to a survey conducted for the Child Development Program Advisory Committee in 1988, only 15 percent of programs offered child care for children who were nonambulatory. Additionally, state licensing regulations in California have played a significant role in the exclusion of children from community-based programs, particularly for children who have severe motor or cognitive impairments.

The opportunity to learn through both play and positive social interactions is important to the optimal growth of all young children. This need is accentuated in children with physical disabilities because their options and opportunities are often limited by movement, cognitive, or communication difficulties.

Regardless of ability, all children benefit from opportunities afforded by inclusive care. The Americans with Disabilities Act, as well as other significant pieces of federal legislation, has clearly laid the philosophical and legislative groundwork for assuring children equal access to child care and development programs.

Successful placement of children with disabilities does require a thoughtful planning and implementation process. This process involves a number of critical considerations. These may include, but are not limited to (1) review of legal regulations and legislative mandates, as well as program practices, procedures, and policies; (2) assessment of each child on an individual basis through consulting with families and other professionals; (3) determination of the inclusion/accommodation needs by identification of both physical and programmatic considerations; and (4) the development of ongoing collaborative partnerships with families and specialists who are serving the

ABOUT THE AUTHORS

Nora Snowden is a registered occupational therapist (O.T.R.) who works in the Napa Infant Preschool Program in Napa, California. She enjoys the rewards that come from establishing respectful relationships with families in ways that empower them as the experts for their children. Her interests are in team assessment and collaboration with a special interest in assessing behavior and movement from the perspective of both the child's external sensory environment and the child's internal sensorimotor strategies and abilities.

Karla Snorf, R.P.T., is a physical therapy consultant with the Napa Infant Preschool Program. She previously worked with California Children's Services and as a field consultant for Personal Development for Infant Preschool Programs. Presently, she provides consultation services and training to parents, staff, and interagency members on a variety of subjects. She also provides consultation and resource information to staff who work with children in typical preschool and child care settings.

child. Careful thought must also be given to the range of resources, support, and ongoing training necessary to enable child care and development staff to provide quality care in developmentally appropriate settings for children who may bring a range of needs.

Understanding the effects that disabilities may have on children's growth and development is important for successful caregiving. This chapter will consider the development of motor skills and provide information specific to caring for children with physical disabilities. In addition, this chapter offers suggestions to promote successful inclusion of all children in community child care settings and addresses the importance of careful assessment of child care environments and the need to work closely with families.

Who Are the Children with Physical Disabilities?

Poh, an active four-year-old, runs into things and falls frequently while playing with her friends. The teacher in her Montessori preschool program and her parents have observed these behaviors but believe they do not interfere with her daily activities.

Lamara is a two-year-old diagnosed with mild cerebral palsy. She has somewhat awkward gross motor movements and fine motor difficulties that affect the use of her right hand. She is currently in a family child care home and receives weekly therapy from a California Children's Services therapist. When playing with her friends, she may need additional time to move about and to complete fine motor activities.

Four-year-old **Miguel** has spina bifida. Miguel is enrolled in a full, four-day-a-week Head Start program. Special education and

therapy services are provided directly in this setting. He currently wears leg braces that do not interfere with opportunities to be with his friends or to participate in activities such as playing at the sand table.

Tara is a gifted five-year-old who is enrolled in a local kindergarten program. She has cerebral palsy and uses a wheelchair. She activates her wheelchair through a head switch because she has very limited use of her arms. She is bused in the afternoon to her family child care home. Her favorite thing to do when she arrives at child care is to have lunch with her friends.

Zachery is a three-year-old enrolled in a child care center. He sustained significant injuries as a result of an accident and has undergone multiple surgeries and castings. Zachery is now in a full-body cast and must remain prone on his stomach. He enjoys being pulled around the playground in a wagon by his friends.

Lindsey is a 16-month-old who was born with severe multiple disabilities that include a seizure disorder. Her care is being provided three days each week by her aunt through an alternative payment program. She is very responsive when her young cousin plays with her.

All of these children are unique. They bring a range of considerations to their caregiving for a variety of reasons. What is most significant is that they are interacting successfully in different community child care settings through the availability of resources and adequate levels of support.

Children with mild to severe cerebral palsy, spina bifida, skeletal deformities, arthritis, loss of limbs, or multiple disabilities all have conditions that may limit their physical abilities in either large or small motor skills. These conditions may be highly visible, either because the children have awkward or uncontrollable muscle movements or because they use devices such as wheelchairs, braces, or artificial limbs. Some children who are unable to move independently may be unaffected in other areas of development. Others may have difficulty expressing themselves through words or movements; still others may have multiple disabilities that include conditions such as mental retardation. There are many factors that contribute to each child's growth and development; children with physical disabilities should not be categorized under one label. Recognizing this diversity among children will encourage their placement on a child-by-child basis.

Considerations for Successful Inclusion: Questions to Ask Families

Children do not come to child care independent of their families. Children are usually accompanied by the true experts in their care—parents or other significant caregivers. The importance of establishing positive relationships with families has been stressed throughout each of the preceding chapters. These relationships are vital for any child, but particularly if there are special handling, positioning, and/or equipment needs. Coordinated planning by families and providers, including the careful assessment of individual needs, will help to facilitate successful placements of young children with physical disabilities in typical child care settings.

Questions asked of families who have a child with a disability are not that different from questions asked of any family enrolling their child in care. However, if a child has a physical disability, gathering specific information from families about how daily caregiving routines are provided, how a child is to be handled or positioned, the degree to which a child can participate or help in activities, and strategies that facilitate communication is part of a successful planning experience. Following is a list of questions that caregivers may ask a family member who has a young child with a physical disability. Remember to always advise parents of their right to confidentiality prior to any interview.

What special considerations and/or accommodations do you feel your child may need in the child care setting? Does the child have unique needs that should be considered in order to ensure optimum opportunities for participation in typical activities? Does the family assist the child in any special way at home that would be useful for the provider to know about?

Understanding how parents anticipate and meet basic needs is an important factor in ensuring that children feel safe and secure in their child care setting. This is particularly true for children with physical disabilities. Because parents may adjust to meeting some of their child's exceptional needs almost intuitively, it maybe useful to help parents think through how they care for their child in the routines of the day.

What is your child's medication history; what other health-related conditions should I be aware of? Be sure to ask what medications have been prescribed, when they are administered, what side effects to expect, and what feedback parents would find important from the caregivers. While not all children with physical disabilities may be on regular medications, some may. Some children with physical disabilities will need corrective surgeries or perhaps castings that may require temporary accommodations in the child care setting. Understanding the whole child in the context of how the physical disability may affect overall health is critical to quality caregiving.

How does your child interact with others—with peers, older or younger children, other adults, and strangers? How have families helped others to play and interact with their child?

Children who have poor balance, stiff or weak muscles, or a body that is in constant motion are often distracted by the task of managing their bodies and by differing or variable levels of physical comfort. These distractions often interfere with children's abilities to pay attention, focus on tasks, or interact with others. When children are more comfortable and physically secure, their focus shifts appropriately to playing and to being with friends. They are then more likely to experience successes and develop positive self-esteem.

How does your child communicate? How does the child indicate choice—by touching, looking, signing, or speaking? What are the cues of a nonverbal child? What is the extent to which a child understands what is said to him or her? Is the family working toward any specific communication goals? How can the child care provider encourage growth towards these goals? For many children with physical disabilities, communication is not problematic. For other children physical or cognitive handicaps may make communication difficult or virtually impossible. In either case, soliciting information from families is critical.

Some children may have, or be working toward, augmentative communication devices. In these circumstances, parents and/ or therapists will need to provide additional direction and assistance.

How does your child eat? Does he or she need assistance with feeding or drinking? Will adapted utensils or special cups be

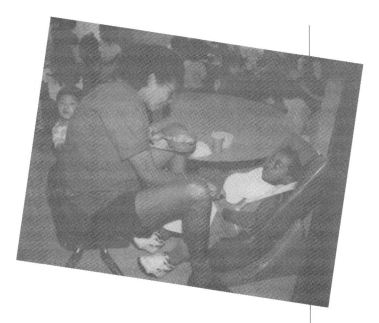

necessary? Some children with physical disabilities require special food preparation (chopped, mashed, or puréed); other children may require special diets. Does the child require a special seat or position while eating? Who will demonstrate or teach the child care provider how to feed the child? Caregivers should also know the child's favorite foods as well as the foods that should not be given.

Caregivers may also need to know the feeding schedules of children who need assistance. Some children may require an increased intake of fluids or smaller amounts of food at more frequent intervals than other children. It may take longer for a child to feed herself or himself, or to be fed, than the time allotted to feed other children.

What specific pieces of equipment will I need for your child? Does the child use a hearing aid, adaptive toys, a computer or communication board, a wheelchair, a special toilet seat, or other health-related equipment (such as a nebulizer for breathing treatments)?

The meanings of the terms *adaptive equipment* and *adaptive technology* are often overlapping. The terms are often used interchangeably. *Technology* has generally referred to devices for communication and/ or electronic devices. *Equipment* has generally referred to devices which assist with positioning, seating, and movement.

Determining a child's adaptive equipment needs is typically the responsibility of families and specialists providing services to the child. Of importance to discuss with families is who will be responsible for providing the equipment, what equipment will be transported with the child, and what will need to be purchased. In all respects, decisions that are made about these needs must be made on a child-by-child basis. What might work exceptionally well for one child may not be appropriate for another even though the two "appear" to have similar needs.

Child care and development staff should not be expected to know all there is to know regarding specialized equipment. It is important, however, for providers to become

familiar and comfortable with the equipment that arrives with a child in their child care or child development program.

Physical and/or occupational therapists, as well as parents, can be helpful consultants for ideas on adapting equipment or the environment to accommodate a child's needs. Additionally, they can be excellent resources for problem solving and instruction on the use of equipment that accompanies a child. With few exceptions, the needs of children requiring adaptive technology or equipment can be met as long as the resources for support, materials, and labor can be found.

It is important to understand adaptive technology and equipment from the perspective of parents. Many parents may initially struggle with the fact that their child may require adaptive assistance. Pieces of equipment such as helmets, braces, walkers, and wheelchairs can be very stigmatizing.

During their children's toddler and preschool years, families often must look at the needs of their children in ways that were not necessary or envisioned during infancy when the child was easier to carry and/or feed. For this reason parents may need additional support and understanding from child care and development staff while they learn to adjust their expectations for their children and for themselves.

Does your child have exceptional physical or positioning needs? In what ways will the provider know that the child is uncomfortable or tired? Who will demonstrate proper handling and positioning techniques? Are there problems that the child care provider or child development staff may encounter?

Positioning serves several important functions and may require additional considerations for some children with disabilities. Proper positioning may enable a child to more fully participate in activities, encourage strengthening of a particular group of muscles, or act to inhibit the deterioration of muscle groups. It is important to understand why children may need to be placed in particular positions and to have a clear understanding of ways in which proper positioning benefits the child. Caregivers may need to have information about children's physical activity needs; e.g., a child may need to stretch out and rest after sitting for a period of time in an adaptive chair or wheelchair. Staff may also need to be aware of positions that may be detrimental to a child's ability to focus, grow, or develop. It is appropriate to ask family members if there are positions that should be avoided.

While many children with disabilities do not need adaptive equipment, other children with both mild and more severe disabilities will rely on specialized equipment to help them adapt to their handicapping conditions.

What are the toileting skills of your child? What are the toileting needs of the child? Are the parents currently working toward independent toileting skills? Will this be a goal in the near future? Are there special handling considerations during diaper changing or toileting? How does the family know when to toilet? Does the child give any verbal or physical cues?

Caregivers may need to anticipate the need for diaper changes or toileting by careful observation of children's cues or by determining elimination schedules. Because of their disabilities, children may not know when they are wet or soiled or may not have the language needed to alert others.

Will your child be involved in other programs or transitions during the day? Will the child be attending child care full-time or part-time? Will she or he be involved in any other programs? Are there things the

provider should know about the child's typical day or week? What is the child's most stressful time of the day?

Children may experience difficulties when making transitions from one setting to another, from a special education program to after-school care, for example. Careful observation of children will help to determine the impact these transitions may be having on their young lives. For a child with a significant physical disability, the physical act of being moved in and out of facilities and vehicles may be very fatiguing. Strategies for minimizing transitional difficulties are discussed further in this text.

Is your child and/or your family receiving any services from other agencies or professionals that should be coordinated with child care? What are these services? Should they be coordinated with child care? What steps should the provider take to collaborate with these providers and agencies? How can parents assist in these networking efforts?

Children with severe physical disabilities will likely be receiving services from a number of professionals and agencies. These professionals may include medical specialists; occupational, physical, and/or speech therapists; early-intervention specialists; and related service providers from agencies such as a regional center, a public health department, or California Children's Services.

Because the initiation and coordination of multiple services can be overwhelming for family members of young children with disabilities, it is imperative that all service providers be understanding and respectful of how demanding and difficult this process often is. It is for this reason that federal legislation mandates the coordination of services for young children with disabilities and their families. In many communities throughout the United States, agencies are developing single-entry intake forms so that family members do not have to fill out multiple forms or tell their stories over and over again.

Showing a willingness to collaborate with other professionals is often helpful to parents and providers and ultimately is very beneficial for the child.

Are there other significant caregivers or professionals from whom I should gather information? Who are other important family members the provider should know about or meet with? What are the names and telephone numbers of professionals who should be consulted? What information should be discussed with these people? Are there reports and files that should be requested and reviewed from professionals or agencies?

In serving a child with special care needs, it is important to gather information from all sources that a parent feels would be helpful. It is critical to be mindful, however, of the priorities and concerns of families. Parents, for a multitude of reasons, may not want all information about their child or themselves shared with other family members, professionals, and agencies. It is essential to respect parents' wishes in this regard. Collaboration on behalf of children must begin first with the development of successful partnerships with parents. Assisting families in ways they feel will be most helpful to them is the first step.

When meeting with parents, caregivers should ask them to specify the individuals or agencies they authorize to share information about their child. If parents agree that it would be helpful for the caregiver to gather information from other professionals or agencies, they will need to sign a release form for each request for information.

Taking the time to collaborate with families and to carefully assess each child's needs is the first step toward successful inclusion. Equally important, however, is the assessment of a particular program's capability to provide quality services for children with a range of strengths and needs.

Planning the Child's Environment

Successful inclusion involves determining what is beneficial to all young children in community child care settings. This process begins with looking carefully at our own feelings and levels of comfort about working with children who have physical disabilities. It also includes planning environments that are attentive, nurturing, and responsive to individual needs. A child's ability to learn from the environment is enhanced when her or his basic caregiving needs are met—being changed when wet, being cooled or warmed when uncomfortable, being fed when hungry, or being given the opportunity to rest when tired. Anticipating and meeting the basic care needs of children begins with understanding ourselves and examining the physical environments that we provide.

Developing awareness of the interpersonal environment

The interpersonal environment includes the milieu that is created by adult presence, tone, and interactions. It is probably the least scrutinized of all environments and yet may have the most significant impact on children. To understand the importance to and the impact on young children of their relationships with adults, the caregiver needs to be aware of his or her own personal style and decide whether it is appropriate for different children. If not, what modifications are needed to make it a more productive match?

For example, a quiet, more tentative child may not easily engage with a gregarious adult. Or a very active, busy child may need an adult who has a very calm approach but provides reasonable and clear limits for the child. In other instances, more specifically in relating to children who have disabilities, adults may find that they have unexpected responses to children who have difficulty providing or reading cues that typically engage others to interact with them. A child who may not smile readily, who averts her eyes, or who arches his back may elicit a negative response in other children or adults who are made uncomfortable and do not know how to respond appropriately. Under these circumstances we can come to know a child through careful observation, through our conversations with parents, and through ongoing interactions with the child. Caregivers must pay particularly close attention to each child's unique style of interacting. Once we know that when Mary arches away from us it is a reflexive response to movement and noise, we can learn to approach her in a quieter way or let her know that we are approaching by calling her name. Once we know that Pedro becomes overly stimulated and agitated because of an immature nervous system, we will not view gaze-avoidance as antisocial but as an effective coping mechanism that he is using to maintain his own state.

Providers might ask themselves the following questions as they consider different aspects of the interpersonal environment and some of the variables that young children present:

- What are the interactive styles of adults and of children?

- Do the loudness and emotional tone of adult voices encourage, discourage, invite, or inspire young children?

- Does touch encourage a child to cuddle more or to move away?

- How does a child respond to adults? Is the response related to the child's unique temperamental style, family culture, home environment, or past experiences?

Assessing the physical environment

Assessments of the physical environments provided for children with disabilities help planners determine the best environments for all children. Initially, however, a careful assessment of the physical environment may be required in order to determine if any changes are necessary. For example, a care center may require a ramp to accommodate a child in a wheelchair, a rearrangement of furniture to provide safe places for children to crawl, or a rearrangement of materials in activity centers. After children are enrolled, ongoing observations of how they interact within the environment are important. This means observing children as they move through their daily routines.

It is important to consider environments from several different perspectives. The following questions will help caregivers assess the appropriateness of different environments for children with physical disabilities.

Is the physical setting safe and accessible for children? Look at the physical space and activity areas both inside and outside. In addition to noting the usual safety precautions, check to see if there are other hazards or barriers (for example, sharp corners or narrow passageways) for children who may be on the floor, who are unsteady, or who use wheelchairs or other adaptive equipment.

Surfaces that children are placed on must be clean and comfortable, including toileting areas. By considering the environment from the child's perspective, caregivers will develop a greater awareness of safety and cleanliness issues that are of particular concern for children who may spend time on the floor. Alternatives to placing children on floor surfaces include placing them on soft rugs, blankets, sheepskins, or beanbag chairs.

Is the environment conducive to learning? Children demonstrate a range of responses to such things as noise, light, and room arrangements. Child care providers often observe young children in situations that decrease or increase their activity levels. Children with physical disabilities may be over- or under-responsive to environmental stimulations such as noise levels or light intensity. Some children may also experience sensory or tactile materials as pleasurable or uncomfortable. By carefully observing children, adults will more accurately assess levels of comfort. For example, does a child avoid or seek out certain sensory materials such as sand or play dough? Does a child fuss whenever anything slightly warm or cold touches his or her body? Does a child run on tiptoe when barefoot on different surfaces? Another consideration is to observe whether activities or room arrangements influence a child's behavior. Does a child's play appear disorganized or calm following sensory activities or movement activities? Does the layout of the room help to guide and direct a child's attention and play?

Is the room temperature comfortable? A room that is too warm or too cold may affect children's energy levels. When children are too hot, they lack energy. When children are too cold, they focus on their body temperatures and not their activities. Children can easily become excessively hot in adaptive equipment because it is difficult for air to circulate and movement is limited. Consider the length of time a child has spent in a piece of equipment and the placement of the equipment. While the sun may feel good to children who are moving about, to children in stationary positions it can quickly feel very uncomfortable. Parents may also dress their children in jackets or several layers of clothing for the cool part of the morning; remember to take these clothes off as the day gets warmer. For children who are placed on the floor, check that there are no cold air drafts. Make sure that the heating reaches the floor. Providers can check temperatures by simply touching a child's skin or by making note of skin color. Does the child appear flushed? Is the child sweating? Does the skin feel too cold or lack color?

Are the choices presented appropriate and accessible? Are rooms accessible for all children, and does the physical layout lend itself to interactions and making choices? Activities that are too simple or too difficult encourage boredom, disinterest, or negative behavior. Sometimes children who have physical disabilities are given toys that are infantile rather than age-appropriate. Observe to see if the toys available lend themselves to interaction and manipulation. Are toys accessible for children who are in wheelchairs or on the floor? Remember to rotate toys frequently for children who are unable to access their own choices. Finally, observing how children make choices provides valuable information for planning and designing environments.

Understanding Typical and Atypical Motor Development

Developing an awareness of motor development will help caregivers understand all young children. This awareness will also guide caregivers in adapting activities that will promote a child's successful interactions with peers in the child care environment. As children grow and develop, they follow a predictable pattern. This pattern is observed as children learn to sit, reach, grasp, walk, run, skip, build with blocks, and cut with scissors. It is useful for caregivers to understand how development typically occurs, so that they can facilitate development or assist children who have disabilities that interfere with their motor development. To help with this understanding, typical and atypical development are briefly discussed below.

Typical motor development

Motor development depends on normal muscle tone. Normal muscle tone sets the stage for movement and posture. This means that the muscles of the body are able to work together as a team to respond to the demands of the body. For example, when the body needs the muscles to be stable to hold a position or when the body needs the muscles to move in a smooth and coordinated way, such as for running, they respond accordingly.

Motor development moves from head to foot. The head, neck, and upper trunk develop strength, balance, and motor coordination before the lower trunk and legs do. During their first year, as children are learning to walk, they first practice and perfect skills such as lifting their heads when lying on their stomachs. Later, children are able to sit independently and, still later, to balance on two feet without holding on to a support.

Development occurs from the middle of the body outward. Strength and coordination first develop with those muscles and body parts closest to the middle of the body and then progress outward toward the hands and feet. This progression is easily observed in hand skills. The baby first learns to bat at an object using the whole arm (primarily movement from the shoulder). As children continue to mature and refine their grasps, they are able to use their thumbs and index fingers to pick up small objects.

Motor development is sequential. Development occurs in a definite sequence and in an orderly fashion. Each new skill is based on mastery of an earlier skill. Standing balance can be achieved only after sitting balance develops, and sitting balance follows the development of balance in a hands-and-knees position.

Developmental stages show varying degrees of mastery. As children gain mastery at one level, they are already beginning new motor challenges at a more advanced level. For example, a child might be a fast crawler and simultaneously enjoy the new challenge of pulling himself or herself up to stand.

Primitive reflexes fade out as postural reflexes develop. The newborn comes into this world with many different reflexes that serve as survival mechanisms or ways to gain some coordination and movement patterns. One such reflex is often referred to as the "fencing position." When the baby turns his or her head, the arm on the face side is extended while the arm on the skull side is flexed. This reflex helps the child develop some eye-hand movements. By four to six months of age, most babies have lost these early reflexes. Motor therapists often refer to this change as reflex integration. The body is now able to develop postural and balancing responses to help it stay upright with good balance against gravity.

Movement depends on intact sensory systems. Newborns turn toward the source of a touch and the sound of a voice, and they track a parent's face. As development progresses all of the sensory systems help direct movement and may influence the quality of fine and gross motor skills.

Atypical motor development

Atypical gross motor development follows a pattern of delayed development and/or qualitative differences that make the performance of a particular skill a more difficult task than it is for other children of the same age. Differences in development may be influenced by one or a combination of the following (Johnson-Martin, Jens, Attermeier 1986):

Abnormal muscle tone. This condition can include high muscle tone, low muscle tone, or a combination of the two. Children with high muscle tone often feel stiff and rigid. Their bodies do not appear to relax. There is resistance to the bending or straightening of body parts such as the arms, legs, trunk, or neck. Children with low muscle tone feel floppy, weak, and unstable.

Abnormal reflex activity. Immature reflexes may persist in some children beyond six months of age. Sometimes these reflexes appear to be stronger or more exaggerated compared with those of other children who are showing more typical patterns of development. The continued presence of these earlier reflexes influences how the infant or young child moves his or her body, including the development of balance responses.

Delay in development of motor skills or abnormal performance of motor skills. A child may be able to perform a particular task but not with ease, smoothness, or spontaneity. Frequently, poor balance influences the child's development and overall performance.

Sources of motor difficulties

Difficulties with movement can result from disorders that have their sources in several areas and systems of the body, including the brain, nerves, bones, joints, muscles, and sensory systems. There may be pain or discomfort associated with any of these disorders. The following section looks at the sources of common motor disabilities and briefly describes their associated difficulties.

Movement difficulties originating in the brain. Difficulties that result from brain disorders include cerebral palsy, hydrocephalus, neurological disorders, injuries to the brain from accidents, or infections from illnesses such as meningitis or encephalitis. In all of these disabilities, the area of the brain controlling movement has suffered some damage that results in the child's having varying degrees of difficulty with movement. The brain is sending a message instructing the muscles to work in a nontraditional way. Difficulties might range from very slight observed differences in how a child moves to very severe differences. Included in this latter group might be children who are very floppy (flaccid), and who give the caregiver almost no help when being lifted, to those who are very tight and stiff (spastic) and thus difficult to move. Combinations and variations of both of these ranges (athetoid and/or ataxic) also occur. Children may wear special braces or shoes or rely on adaptive equipment or devices to assist them in being more independent. In cases of difficulties that originate in the brain, it is always best to consult with parents and the occupational or physical therapist about precautions, positioning, and handling.

Movement difficulties stemming from the nerves. Names for some of these disabilities include spina bifida, spinal cord injury, brachial plexus injury (Erb's palsy), poliomyelitis, and peripheral neuropathy. In each of these conditions, the nerves that tell the muscles to work have been partially or completely damaged so that the muscles these nerves control are either weak, do not work at all (flaccid), or are tight and stiff (spastic). Some of these disabilities may also have associated deformities of the bones in surrounding areas and loss of or diminished sensation in response to heat, cold, or touch. With difficulties that stem from the nerves, it is always best to consult with parents and the occupational and/or physical therapist about precautions, positioning, and handling.

Movement difficulties stemming from the bones. These disabilities can include fractures or bones broken in an accident, a missing limb, a limb that never fully developed, or a clubfoot deformity. Children with these conditions typically move the parts that are affected in ways that are unusual. They also may wear casts, braces, corrective shoes, or other special devices for additional support. The special devices may come with instructions on length of time to be worn, precautions against getting them wet, or the best ways to put them on. Once again, the

child's parents and physical and/or occupational therapist, if one is involved, are the best sources for information on these disabilities.

Movement difficulties stemming from the joints. The most common disabilities in this category cause arthritis or arthritic types of problems. The joint surface is wearing away or being eroded, depending on the type of arthritic process. A child with this condition experiences quite a bit of pain and needs ongoing medication for pain and/or for the inflammation caused by the process. The child may also wear special supportive or corrective devices and may need more rest than other children. Parents and physical and/or occupational therapists can provide the child care and development staff with a wealth of information to help support this child.

Movement difficulties stemming from the muscles. The most common disabilities in this category include the varieties of muscular dystrophy, which results in a progressive weakness of some or all muscles

of the body. In the most common form, Duchenne, the muscle tissue is gradually replaced by fatty tissue, causing the child to experience increasing difficulty with movement over time. Children may also wear braces or other assistive devices and, eventually, may need a wheelchair to get around. The parents of these children and their occupational and physical therapists will have the best information on their abilities and current levels of endurance.

Movement difficulties stemming from the sensory systems. The most common difficulties seen in children with under- or overresponsive sensory systems include awkwardness with activities such as running and climbing, frequent bumping into walls or objects, and difficulty in performing age-appropriate skills. With overresponsive sensory systems children may experience a fear of movement such as swinging or sliding. Children with under-responsive sensory systems may crave movements such as swinging, spinning, climbing, jumping, and wrestling. It is common to observe inconsistent performance in skills that typically fall within an age-appropriate range. Such children may not respond well to what their own sensory systems are telling them and may, as well, experience difficulties with muscle tone. Illness, fatigue, or stress may accentuate a child's difficulties in the sensory areas. There are a number of children with mild to severe disabilities who experience under- or overresponsive sensory systems. Typically these children do not qualify for the services of physical and occupational therapists because they do not have an eligible diagnosis. Together with a child's family, caregivers may need to explore other sources of consultation in order to gain a greater understanding of sensory and motor systems. Appendix 8-A contains information on the impact of sensory systems on behavior. In chapter 7, "Caregiving Strategies: Building Resiliency in Children at Risk," the risk factors that may impact children with sensory difficulties are discussed.

Understanding muscle tone

Muscle tone is inborn—meaning that each of us was programmed with the muscle tone we have now prior to birth. Children and adults who have abnormal muscle tone probably suffered some sort of injury to the area of the brain that controls movement.

The performance of young children in all areas of development can be affected by muscle tone. Understanding the effect of muscle tone on children's skills can bring about greater empathy for children and facilitate better instructional planning for all children.

Muscle tone is often described as the quantity or quality of tension or tightness in muscles. Parents frequently comment, "My child seems weak," or "My child is very strong." Muscles of children whose parents describe them as seeming weak feel soft. Conversely, muscles of children whose parents describe them as seeming strong feel hard. Muscle tone can also be described as the quality of movement, coordination, or posture that an individual typically demonstrates. Parents will often comment that their infant was wiry and not very cuddly, or was very cuddly and heavy when carried. Frequently this is again a description of the child's muscle tone. There are ranges in muscle tone that help further explain difficulties a child may be having. There is average muscle tone, and there are ranges of normal high and normal low muscle tone. Beyond these normal ranges are ranges of very high and very low muscle tone.

Ranges of muscle tone

Very low. Children with very low muscle tone may be described by parents as being weak or floppy. These children seem much heavier than their actual weight when they are carried. Parents describe these children as being difficult to pick up because their shoulders do not tend to hold down as they are being lifted, and the parents fear that they will slip through their hands. These children tend to stay in one place for a long time and not want to move.

Average low. A child with normal low muscle tone may feel very heavy and not move with the caregiver while being carried. Some parents have likened carrying these children to carrying a sack of potatoes, i.e., having to enclose them in full so that they will not fall. Having low muscle tone is probably similar to how many people with average or high muscle tone feel when they are sick or physically exhausted.

Average. A child with average muscle tone flows with movement when being carried. This child usually persists with gross motor experiences in ways that reflect strength and endurance.

Average high. Children with average high muscle tone may move with the caregiver when being carried and may even lean away from the caregiver a bit. Their parents often describe them as wiry and strong. Having high muscle tone is probably similar to how people with average or low muscle tone feel on a roller coaster.

Very high. Children with very high muscle tone are usually referred to by medical personnel as spastic. These children feel very stiff and tight when moved and tend to hold their bodies in certain postures for prolonged periods of time. The spasticity is most often due to damage to the motor area of the brain. The damaged part is telling the affected muscles to contract all the time the child is in that position. These children are generally under the care of physical and occupational therapists who, along with a child's parents, can make the best recommendations to caregivers for encouraging movement and for positioning and handling.

Mixed or fluctuating. Some children have mixed or fluctuating muscle tone. They may appear to have high muscle tone at one moment and lower muscle tone at another. Also, some children who fall into this group may have movement disorders that the medical community refers to as athetosis or ataxia. These children may have low muscle tone in their trunk, shoulders, or hips and higher muscle tone in their arms and legs or parts of their arms and legs. Such children and their parents are usually receiving support from physical and/or occupational therapists who can give caregivers suggestions on positioning and handling.

How we are affected by muscle tone

Emotions. Muscle tone is very much affected by emotions. For example, on receiving bad news, adults may tend to experience lower muscle tone. Conversely, good news and a positive environment can help raise lower muscle tone for both children and adults. Illness can reduce muscle tone and some medications can either raise or lower muscle tone. Children and adults in very stimulating environments can experience an increase in muscle tone, a condition that may not be convenient for caregivers who have a roomful of children with predominantly high muscle tone. Situations perceived as threatening may cause a child either to be more alert or to withdraw, thus affecting their muscle tone.

Performance. Muscle tone affects the quality of performance. That is, when muscle tone is interfering, children may not be able to persist in an activity for as long as they would like. They may not be able to perform an activity as well as they would like. Children may struggle to remain upright and be unable to concentrate on an activity. Because of these struggles with performance, some children may not feel very good about themselves. Below is a list of behaviors that, when observed, may indicate that muscle tone is interfering with performance:

- A lack of quickness, accuracy, and precision in gross and/or fine movements

- A tendency to lean on one arm or hand for support while trying to perform fine motor or cognitive tasks when sitting on the floor, sitting at a table, or standing at a table

- A tendency to have difficulty staying in place when sitting on the floor or in a chair. Falling over or out of the chair may occur frequently.

- A tendency to sit in one place and play with a toy or observe other children at play for a longer time than expected

- A need to wrap legs around the legs of the chair in order to stay in place, or to sit on the front of a chair with feet flat on the floor

- A need to sit with one arm over the back of a chair in order to help hold oneself in place

- A tendency to hold one or both arms and shoulders back as a means of stabilizing when performing fine or gross movements, resulting in difficulty using both hands to catch himself or herself or to perform two-handed activities

- An open mouth, frequently with the tongue out, with no sign of a cold or plugged-up nose (this characteristic may also be seen in a child who has allergies or adenoidal problems)

- Language that may be difficult to understand, possibly indicating a delay in the development of oral language

- Difficulty in marking firmly on paper, especially with crayons and pencils

- A tendency to sit or stand with a very wide base of support or with such a narrow base of support that balance is frequently lost

- A state of constant movement, usually because of a lack of adequate static balance

In order to form strategies to help children whose muscle tone is interfering with performance, it is usually recommended that caregivers discuss the difficulties thoroughly with the children's parents and, if available, receive consultation from physical and occupational therapists. Some specific strategies for the care of children with high and low muscle tone can be found in Appendix 8-B.

Strategies for Successful Participation

There are many factors that contribute to participation and successful play experiences. The challenge for caregivers is to provide activities that are open-ended and allow for different levels of participation and the inclusion of all children. While there are many approaches, some are specific to children with physical disabilities.

Encouraging play

Think about the play situation and how it may be adapted to meet the specific needs of young children who have physical disabilities. Such consideration will bring further awareness of the needs of these children. Listed in Appendix 8-C are factors to consider in determining whether a child is well positioned and ready to be fully involved in activities and play.

Observe social interactions. Do children have access to situations and areas that invite social interactions? What are each child's strengths in social situations, and

how might interactions that encourage play be facilitated?

Children will vary in their abilities to initiate play and interact with peers. Along with developmental considerations and physical accessibility, providers may need to determine the best way to engage a child with a disability. For children with developmental delays in several areas, social interaction may simply involve proximity to friends and placement in different play situations.

Sometimes providers may want to enlist parents or specialists in identifying strategies that support children's social development.

Observe children's positions. Are children positioned in ways that allow for success? Are positions secure and stable? Has a child remained in one position for more than 15 or 20 minutes? Can children comfortably use their hands and easily reach for toys? Are children positioned alongside their peers?

Awareness of children's positions is extremely important because proper positioning can greatly improve a child's level of performance and ability to interact. Proper positioning can also be an important consideration for children who fatigue more easily than other children. If a child is constantly having to maintain an unstable position or has been in one position too long, all or most of his or her energy will be expended in this effort.

Check table height. As a rule, tables placed slightly below the chest or just above the waist are optimal for children. Try working a puzzle on a surface that is shoulder height—not only are you visually restricted, but you will also have difficulty keeping your shoulders and arms raised for extended periods of time. When seating a child to work at a table, make sure the child's feet are flat on the floor. Children with vision difficulties may need to have the work surface tilted or lighted in a way that maximizes their vision.

Provide appropriate toys and learning materials. Knowing where and how to purchase toys and adapted learning materials can help providers. Not all children will require special or "adapted" toys; for those who do, they will greatly increase opportunities for play. For example, battery-operated switch toys not only teach young children about cause and effect but also allow children to join with their friends in play activities. There are many educational catalogs that include toys, materials, and equipment for children with special needs. There are also simple ways to adapt or modify toys commonly found in homes or care centers. For example, attaching a large wooden bead to the end of a string on a pull toy will enable a child with an immature grasp to hold the string securely enough to pull the toy.

Use information from all available resources, including families, specialists, or others who have successfully worked with a child. Ask families, therapists, or special education staff to help identify and locate toys and materials. In many communities service clubs volunteer to adapt toys for schools and parents. Appendix 8-D includes a list of sources for adapted toys. There is almost always a way! Visit an infant or preschool special education program to gather additional ideas and strategies.

Note whether toys and learning materials are accessible. As is true of all young children, independence is fostered when the environment easily accommodates self-initiation and self-directed play. Are toys within reach or placed at levels that are easily accessible for a child on the floor or in a wheelchair?

Observe children's activity levels. At different times most children experience a need for help in changing their activity levels. Those who have a range of physical and/or sensory difficulties may experience these difficulties more frequently. Caregivers may not realize that they commonly use sensory feedback to modify the behavior of young children. Playing games such as "how slow/fast can you go," using music to change the mood, and rubbing a child's back at nap time are common activities in child care and development settings that can also help a child with special needs. If children are having difficulties regulating activity levels, caregivers may observe increased irritability, unexplained crying, or falling asleep. In very young infants these are typical patterns. For some children with disabilities, these behaviors may persist into preschool.

Observe and ask about physical needs. By developing good partnerships, caregivers can encourage families to keep staff in-

formed about how children are feeling, eating, and sleeping. Knowing about medications the child is taking is also important. These are factors that can influence children's behaviors or physical well-being. Disruptions can signal illness or cause an increase or decrease in muscle tone, activity level, and overall motivation. Caregivers need to provide similar feedback to families to alert them to any changes in a child's physical state.

Observe and ask about social and emotional needs. Child care and development staff also benefit when families are encouraged to keep them informed about children's social and/or emotional states. It is appropriate to share with families any observed behavioral changes. If caregivers feel comfortable, they may ask if anything different is happening at home. Has the routine changed? Was it a rushed morning? A change in routine or disruptive event at home that cannot be expressed verbally by a child can greatly influence muscle tone and behavior. Changes in behavior may also signal that a child is reacting to an event that occurred during child care. It is only through ongoing and open communication that families and care providers alike can make realistic attempts to understand behavioral changes in young children.

Feeding considerations and strategies

Eating is a life-sustaining activity. In most settings, meals and snacks include lunch and are important times for developing self-help, language, and social skills. For children who have physical disabilities, particularly those whose muscle coordination makes eating difficult, this primary caregiving activity takes on added significance. Eating needs to be a pleasant, interactive time for all young children. While a particular child may need to work on feeding skills, adults can help to make the experience fun and enjoyable. In situations where a child requires special seating or equipment, the caregiver should always position the child close to the other children. Staff can usually manage to provide feeding assistance to one child if the other children in the group are independent eaters or require minimal assistance. This section provides general information for caregivers that will encourage enjoyable and interactive mealtimes. The areas addressed include positioning, using a spoon, and drinking from a cup.

Positioning. For children who have difficulty eating and coordinating the feeding process, good positioning can ease the task significantly. If a child's body maintains too much extension, with the head tilted backwards and the hips and knees extended, the child will have more difficulty chewing and swallowing. Children will be more comfortable if hips are positioned deep into the chair, knees bent at a 90-degree angle, feet flat on the surface, back erect, and chin slightly tucked in. A more reclined position is recommended for the child whose head and body tend to lean too far forward.

It is important to watch a child's body for signs of comfort and overall ease in feeding. Always watch, too, for signs of distress or discomfort. When children with significant disabilities are to be served, family members and the therapist involved should be consulted as to the best positioning during feeding.

Using a spoon. Some children have difficulty grasping a thin narrow spoon handle. Others may have difficulty removing food from the spoon with their lips. Following are some helpful tips:

- Add a piece of cylindrical foam to the handle, or wrap it with masking tape.

Foam especially made for this purpose can be purchased through a medical supply company. A built-up handle can help the child focus more on feeding than on maintaining a grip on the spoon.

- Experiment with a variety of spoons to determine the size of the spoon bowl that is best for the child. Avoid thin plastic spoons. They can be dangerous if broken when a child bites.

Drinking from a cup. There are a variety of cups available for children. There are cups with lids, spouts, and handles. Generally, for a child who experiences difficulty with coordination, a cup with a handle is easiest to use. For children with either high or low muscle tone, cups with spouts are not recommended because a spout encourages taking liquid in a fashion similar to drinking from a bottle. This may confuse some children and make it more difficult to transition to a cup. Offering small amounts of liquid in a lidless cup may be the most efficient method for teaching a child to drink from a cup.

Use cups with a wide base (Tupperware makes one). A wide base makes it easier for children with poor coordination to return the cup to the table and lessens the likelihood of spilling.

Add play dough to the bottom of a cup for added sensory input. This, too, will make it easier to return the cup to the table without spilling.

Planning transitions

Transitions need to be well planned for all children, and additional planning may be necessary for children with physical disabilities. Young children often have difficulties transitioning from one activity to another, especially if they are involved and enjoying themselves. Transitions are a part of life in child care. They are often the moments when caregivers experience the greatest difficulties in the routines of the day. For children who depend on others to be physically moved to a different activity, or for children who have difficulty with change, transitions can be somewhat irritating or even traumatic. The following suggestions may ease the transition process.

Allow enough time. Allow adequate time for activities so that children are ready for a change. Children with physical disabilities usually require more time to complete activities. It often happens that these children are the last ones to be set up and cleaned up. Try to vary the schedule so that everyone has the opportunity to be first. Think ahead in planning the day. Move a child's adaptive equipment to another location ahead of time to avoid having to move both a child and the equipment during an activity change. Have toys for a particular child laid out by the activity or play area to avoid having to look for the puzzles with handles, the blocks with Velcro, or the switch toys when a group of children begins a new activity.

Provide advance warnings. Prepare children by giving a signal prior to changes in activities so that they know what is going to happen next. Physical cues, such as a gentle touch, or auditory cues, such as playing or singing a particular song, can help alert children to coming transitions from one activity to another. Signals are helpful cues for young children, especially for children who require extra time.

Acknowledge children's feelings. Look for cues about how children are feeling during transitions. Be empathetic, share with children how you think they are feeling. Be sure to keep in mind that what may be very easy for other children to do may require significantly more energy for a child with special needs. Allow extra time and acknowledge that you understand.

The following strategies can minimize difficulties in transitions from one setting to another:

- Develop good communication systems among adults within each setting so that information about a child's day is always communicated.

- Work with families to minimize the transitions for a child. Perhaps extended child care is available at the school the child attends, making it unnecessary to bus a child halfway across town.

- Offer flexibility in scheduling. A child may need extra rest periods between transitions or may need additional foods or liquids.

- Be cognizant of the positioning of each child throughout the day. If, in one setting, he or she has spent extended time in a wheelchair, ensure that there is adequate time out of the chair in the next setting. Communication is the key to a child's well being.

Summary

Providing access for children with physical disabilities to the world of child care involves opening our hearts as well as widening our doors. The inclusion of children with physical disabilities in community child care settings is a significant milestone. Recognition is due to many individuals who have advocated for legislative change and who have helped shift attitudes toward persons with disabilities.

The inclusion of children with physical disabilities in community child care settings links them to typical child care experiences—experiences that open the world of opportunity to play, grow, and develop friends. When child care is available for families, options are created to work, recreate, and carry out typical family functions.

This chapter has focused on aspects of caregiving that foster successful inclusion of young children with physical care needs. No one can do it all or has all the answers. That is why a team approach among child care and development staff, families, and other involved professionals is essential. To adequately support children in their care, caregivers need to feel comfortable in sharing ideas and concerns or in expressing needs. Both families and other service providers, such as motor therapists, can support community child care placements by making themselves available to help care providers understand children with physical disabilities on a child-by-child basis.

"Don't let what you cannot do interfere with what you can do."

— Gwendolyn Hunt

KEY POINTS

1. Historically, options and opportunities for children with physical disabilities in community child care settings have been limited.

2. Careful consideration must be given to the range of support and training necessary to provide quality care in developmentally appropriate ways.

3. It is important to understand that children with physical disabilities are not all alike.

4. Anticipating and meeting the basic care needs of children with physical disabilities may differ from doing what is required to accommodate other children.

5. In order for children with physical disabilities to have successful play and socialization experiences, it is important that child care providers have an understanding of typical motor development.

6. The ways in which environments are planned and organized will contribute to or detract from children's abilities to focus on and attend to activities.

7. Careful planning with families before children enter a child care situation is essential for successful experiences. Caregivers should become familiar with the special equipment children require and should know how to use it.

8. Appropriate positioning and a focus on social interactions should be part of play situations so that all children can be included.

9. Children's muscle tone should be considered when determining the best strategies for lifting, carrying, and positioning.

10. Safe lifting techniques should be practiced to prevent injury to children and adults.

11. Children in community child care settings will more likely be successful if specific positioning, handling, and basic caregiving routines are demonstrated and monitored by family members and/ or the child's therapist.

12. Successful caregiving involves determining the needs of each child and basing decisions on those needs.

13. Caregivers should be aware of the value of team effort, capitalize on resources that are available, and remember that it is OK to ask for help.

References

Connor, F. P.; G. G. Williamson; and J. M. Siepp. *Program Guide for Infants and Toddlers with Neuromotor and Other Developmental Disabilities*. New York: Teachers College Press, 1978.

Johnson-Martin, N.; K. G. Jens; and S. M. Attermeier. 1986. *The Carolina Curriculum for Handicapped Infants and Infants at Risk*. Baltimore: Brookes.

Morris, S. E., and M. D. Klein. *Pre-Feeding Skills*. Tucson, Ariz.: Therapy Skill Builders, 1987.

Morton, K., and S. Wolford. *Analysis of Sensory Behavior Inventory* (Revised edition). Arcadia, Calif.: Skills With Occupational Therapy, 1994.

Semmler, C. J., and J. G. Hunter. *Early Occupational Therapy Intervention: Neonates to Three Years*. Gaithersburg, Md.: Aspen, 1990.

Resources

A Circle of Inclusion: Facilitating the Inclusion of Young Children with Severe Disabilities in Mainstream Early Childhood Education Programs (27-minute video with booklet). Lawrence, Kans.: Learner-Managed Designs, Inc., 1993.

Ayres, A. J. *Sensory Integration and the Child*. Los Angeles: Western Psychological Services, 1981.

Finnie, N. R. *Handling the Young Cerebral Palsied Child at Home*. New York: E. P. Dutton, 1968.

Greenman, J. *Caring Spaces, Learning Places: Children's Environments That Work*. Redmond, Wash.: Exchange Press, Inc., 1988.

Greenstein, D. *Backyards and Butterflies: Ways to Include Children with Disabilities in Outdoor Activities*. Ithaca, N.Y.: New York State Rural Health and Safety Council, 1993.

Klein, M. D. *Feeding Position Stickers*. Tucson, Ariz.: Therapy Skill Builders, 1987.

McClannahan, C. *Feeding and Caring for Infants and Children with Special Needs*. Rockville, Md.: American Occupational Therapy Association, 1987.

Motor Development: What You Need to Know (MITCH MODULE 9—A SERIES FOR CAREGIVERS OF INFANTS AND TODDLERS). Miami: Florida Department of Education, 1990.

The Process of Communication: Facilitating Interactions with Young Children with Severe Disabilities in Mainstream Early Childhood Programs (10-minute video with booklet). Lawrence, Kans.: Learner-Managed Designs, Inc., 1993.

The Process of Instruction: Facilitating Participation of Young Children with Severe Disabilities in Mainstream Early Childhood Programs (12-minute video with booklet). Lawrence, Kans.: Learner-Managed Designs, Inc., 1993.

Thompson, B., and others. *Handbook for the Inclusion of Young Children with Severe Disabilities*. Lawrence, Kans.: Learner-Managed Designs, Inc., 1994.

Zero to Three. Vol. 13, No. 2, October/ November, 1992; and Vol. 14, No. 2, October/November, 1993. (These two issues contain pertinent articles on the sensory systems of young children.) Arlington, Va.: National Center for Clinical Infant Programs.

Appendix 8-A

Impact of Sensory Systems on Behavior

Most adults do not realize that we are at the mercy of our sensory systems during much of the day. We uncross our legs when the pressure is too much for too long; we eat when our stomachs cry out for more; we squint when we go outside into bright sun and may put on sunglasses; some of us turn up the radio or stereo volume so we can feel the music better while others of us turn it down because it's too loud; and we don't concentrate very well if our shoes or clothing are uncomfortable, or if we need to go to the bathroom. When sensory feedback is an irritant, uncomfortable, or not strong enough for us, we either do what we can to get rid of the irritant or we do what we can to control input to obtain better feedback.

Children are no different. Caregivers need to trust children's responses. For example, if there are indications that a child does not want to touch something, caregivers need to realize that the child may perceive the item to be an irritant. The caregiver can then use creativity and resourcefulness and come up with other ways for the child to experience the activity. Children who do not like to play in shaving cream may do well playing with shaving cream that has been sealed in a plastic bag with a drop or two of food coloring so that the child can squish the bag and mix in the food coloring.

The sensory systems predominate at birth, are protective and sustaining, and provide survival mechanisms for the newborn. They also become the earliest sources of movement. Newborns startle to a loud sound, turn their mouths when the side of the cheek is touched, grasp an adult finger when it is placed in their palm, and track their parents' faces or turn to their parents' voices. We all know that they also cry when hungry. The sensory systems are among the fastest neurological circuits, causing quick responses to stimuli. Most of the strong impulses that come out of the sensory system cause a fight-or-flight response, as seen when the systems are working at a typical or high level. When these

systems are working at a reduced level, one might see a child or adult pursue activities that allow them to receive more sensory input, thus attempting to bring themselves to a response level that is more typical of others.

These systems have levels of responsivity that differ in each individual:

- There are typical response levels that we see in the majority of children and adults.

- There are underactive response levels that cause a child or adult to pursue an activity in order to get enough input to feel the sensation. Such children may also demonstrate a delayed response to stimuli. For example, a response to a question may be delayed a few minutes, or behavior may escalate several minutes after exposure to stimuli.

- There are overactive response levels that cause a child or adult to avoid an activity because it is too stimulating to tolerate. If a child cannot reduce the intensity of the stimulus, her behaviors may escalate or she may remove herself from the stimulus.

Children who arouse concerns typically fall into the categories of having under- and/or overactive response systems. Many behaviors of young children may originally have come out of these response systems. When different systems are under- or overresponsive, the child may be calmed by some activities and disorganized by others. Activities that calm one child may cause another to become disorganized or even fall asleep in order to withdraw. Child care and child development staff will be able to monitor such activities and gradually discover what works best and what is to be avoided with each child.

Children with severe motor impairments that do not allow them to move with ease may have the same typical under- or overresponsive systems as other children. They need to be helped to move to relieve pressure from lying or sitting too long in one position or from being surrounded by too much activity and noise for too long a period. Such children might become irritable or fall asleep for no obvious reason because they are overstimulated by their environment and unable to remove themselves.

There are seven primary sensory systems identified at this time:

Tactile (touch) systems give information back to a person about how things feel. Is the sensation pleasant, unpleasant, or not stimulating enough to be of interest? Children whose touch systems are less responsive may seek sensory stimulation by touching everything in sight, biting themselves, or seeming to be less responsive to pain than expected. Children whose touch systems are more responsive than expected may avoid sensory activities, withdraw from being touched, dislike having their faces washed, or dislike certain textures of clothing.

Auditory (sound and hearing) systems give information about the quality and quantity of sound. Is the sound loud enough, too soft, soothing, or irritating? These responses are in the absence of a diagnosed hearing loss. Children whose auditory systems are less responsive than expected may seek toys that make loud sounds, crave loud music, and not respond to requests without face-to-face contact. Children whose auditory systems are more responsive than expected may protest over common loud noises, seek quiet areas to play in, or seem unable to pay attention in a somewhat noisy room.

Visual (sight and light) systems give information about the quality and quantity of light. Is it too soft, too bright, or irritating? These responses are in the absence of a diagnosed loss of vision. Children whose visual systems are less responsive than expected may enjoy flicking lights on and off, may frequently spin toys that are bright, or may flick fingers in front of their faces. Children whose visual systems are more responsive than expected may enjoy darkened rooms, protest going outside on a bright day, or become very excited by a lot of visual stimulation.

Gustatory and olfactory (taste and smell) systems give feedback about the taste and smell of foods and objects. Children whose gustatory and olfactory systems are less responsive than expected may explore things by smelling and licking them, may enjoy eating spicy foods, or may not be bothered by unpleasant smells. Children whose gustatory and olfactory systems are more responsive than expected may prefer very bland food, complain that common odors are irritating, or detect odors that are barely perceptible to others.

Vestibular (movement and gravity responses) systems give feedback about the amount of movement that feels good and the amount of displacement a person can tolerate against gravity. Children whose vestibular systems may be less responsive than expected may frequently jump, bounce, walk and run firmly, love spinning, or show no fear of falling. Children whose vestibular systems may be more responsive than expected may not like to have their feet off of the ground; may avoid swings, elevators, and escalators; or may prefer quiet play.

Proprioceptive (deep pressure, vibration, muscle, and joint information) systems give feedback about where one's body is in space in relationship to objects in a room and how that feels. Children whose proprioceptive systems are less responsive than expected may give hugs that are too hard, bump into people or objects unintentionally, hold their hands or bodies in unusual positions, or like the stimulation of a vibrating toy for prolonged periods of time. Children whose proprioceptive systems are more responsive than usual may avoid activating toys or equipment that vibrate, such as mixers or vacuum cleaners.

Interoceptive (feedback and balance of internal organs) systems give us feedback about our needs related to our internal organs: bladder, heart, stomach, and so forth. Children whose interoceptive systems are difficult for them to regulate may have difficulty eating, sleeping, and controlling bodily functions. Therefore, they might have difficulty reading cues accurately about bladder and bowel functions, hunger, satiation, fatigue, or alertness and control of the emotional responses that accompany these and other interoceptive responses.

Caregivers who remember that these behaviors are primitive survival responses and that the child needs input or needs to avoid input will look at these behaviors with more empathy and understanding. They will also be more likely to evaluate the child's environment to see what can be adjusted or modified in order to accommodate the child's needs. Would reducing the lighting in the room help one child quiet down? Would some lively music alert another child to a coming transition to a new activity? Would such music be too stimulating for another child? Would some active gross motor play before a cognitive task help the child with low muscle tone to participate at a higher level? These are the kinds of questions caregivers can ask when determining how to serve each child's sensory needs.

Some of the behaviors exhibited by young children are present as problems in very young infants and may interfere with their interactions with their parents and primary caregivers. Most of these behaviors are not obvious until the child reaches two or three years of age. As the child gets older, the behavior becomes more ingrained and more difficult to change unless a caregiver can bring understanding, modify the environment, and possibly provide some specific care under the guidance of specially trained occupational and physical therapists. *Specific care intervention becomes necessary when several behaviors are present to a degree that management becomes difficult.*

The different sensory systems may interrelate, causing problems in several ways:

- One system may be under-responsive and another overresponsive.

- One system can be under-responsive one minute and overresponsive the next.

It is difficult to imagine how confusing this must be for a child and how difficult it might be for such a child to maintain emotional stability throughout the day when the sensory systems are so unpredictable. It is very difficult for such children to pay attention, concentrate, and stay with activities for a long time when their basic survival responses are constantly directing their behavior rather than allowing them to learn from typical interactions with the adults and peers in their environment.

For additional information about sensory systems and their development, see Resources, on pages 163 and 164.

Appendix 8-B

Considerations for Positioning and Handling

Most of us enjoy holding young children. When carrying a child, we can generally move about the environment easily. As we move, the child we are holding typically makes the necessary adjustments in his or her posture to maintain a level of comfort for herself or himself as well as for the carrier. Holding a child whose body is stiff, rigid, floppy, or heavy can be a frightening or uncomfortable experience. Children can also sense when adults do not feel comfortable. Taking time to better know and understand a child, as well as understanding principles of good positioning and handling, will foster positive experiences.

The goal of good positioning is to allow children to interact with the environment without focusing on discomforts. Children should feel stable, and their muscle tone should be prepared for optimal functioning. When carrying and handling children, consider what makes them more relaxed or tense. It is critical to discuss with families what works best for them about positioning and handling. Children's needs should be considered on a one-to-one basis. Many children will require minimal assistance and be independent learners, while others may require a greater level of one-to-one adult assistance or support. For most of us, considering the physical needs of young children requires that we imagine ourselves in their places. Adults should refrain from acting on young children without preparing them, either with words or a gentle touch, for what they can expect. Say, "Alfredo, I am going to pick you up," or "Nicole, it's cold outside, time to put on your jacket." Regardless of what we may think children understand, it is out of respect that we always prepare them for what will happen next. Also, consider how it might feel to be in one position for extended periods of time, or how difficult it would be to be dependent on someone else to move your body.

Relax! Get to know children on a personal level. Take a moment to notice what engages you about a child. Identify what makes a child smile or what types of activities, songs, or games she or he enjoys. Establishing a positive rapport builds trust. Children will be more physically secure if there is a sense of trust and if caregivers are confident in understanding a child's needs. Good practice in handling young children begins with adult considerations in lifting.

Adult safety in lifting

All adults working with young children are involved in lifting and carrying. For children with physical disabilities, additional lifting and carrying may be required. The child may weigh more, wear braces or other special equipment, need to be placed in and out of equipment, or be more awkward to handle. Typically, children under the age of five can be easily accommodated with proper lifting techniques. Therefore, it is important that adults follow commonsense rules of lifting. Motor therapists and families share the responsibility of demonstrating lifting techniques specific to each child.

The following suggestions are specific to lifting children who are physically disabled. Whenever an adult is moving a child, the focus must always be on the safety of both.

Plan ahead. Assess each situation and plan your lifting strategy. Determine if you can safely lift by yourself or if you need help. Be aware of how your own body feels prior, during, and after lifting.

Prepare children for change. Adults can physically cue children by gently touching them. It is good practice to describe what you are going to do and what you need the child to do. Say, "Carmen, I am going to pick you up. I need you to lift up your arms." Remember to always provide good eye contact before you move or position a child.

Always get down to the child's level. Be sure to bend your legs so that you use leg power, not your back. Do not lean over with your legs straight to pick up children. This can cause back injury.

Position children correctly prior to lifting. When a child is lying on her or his back, bend the child's legs at the hip and bring the shoulders forward. Bring your body close to the child's and lift him or her into your arms. Always hold the child close to your body. This technique is safer and requires less strength.

Stand up holding a child securely. Be sure to encircle the child's arms and legs. This technique will help the child feel more secure. It will also prevent the child from thrusting or catching a loose arm or leg on a doorway, stove, or other obstacle.

Make sure the pathways are clear. Be mindful of any obstacles in the immediate surroundings that might interfere with safely moving the child. Move your body in a way that feels comfortable.

Handling children who have low muscle tone

Children who have low muscle tone feel heavy. Their bodies do not flow with yours. When you move in one direction, their bodies may move in a different direction. Some children do not have good balancing responses. Typically they will tire easily and have low endurance and strength. They tend to stay in one place playing with one toy or watching other children for longer than one would expect.

When picking up and handling a child who has low muscle tone, be sure to hold the child's body close to yours. In this way, the child is safer and so are you. Children with low muscle tone may need more time to rest and need more frequent changes of position than other children. It can be difficult to pick up a child who has very low muscle tone because it may feel as though the child will slip through your hands. With all children, but especially with those with low muscle tone, it is especially important never to pick them up by their arms, which may result in a dislocated shoulder, elbow, or wrist. Be sure to pick up all children by placing your hands around their upper chests and under their shoulders; do not lift from their arms. It is equally important to provide children with the amount of stability that allows them to feel secure but slightly challenged in their balancing responses.

Carrying. Hold the child close to your body, either facing you or facing forward. Provide the kind of support that keeps the child secure and you safe. Always use two hands; one hand supports the child's bottom while the other hand provides trunk support. Always provide maximum support initially by placing a hand or arm across the chest or shoulder blade areas. Decrease your support by bringing your hand lower down the trunk as you feel more comfortable with the child's ability to balance himself.

Sitting independently. Children can prop their hands to their sides or front or on their knees when learning to sit independently. These positions, however, do not encourage play in which the hands are used. When encouraging children to use their hands to play and explore, the adult can hold a child securely and firmly at the hips or waist level to provide stability. A child with somewhat more stability may benefit from a beanbag being tucked firmly behind the buttocks and molded around the lower body.

Sitting on an adult's lap. Place the child in a straddling position across one of your legs. Be sure your feet are flat on the floor. Provide stability by holding the child at the hips, waist, or chest level, depending on the amount of support needed.

Corner sitting. Place the child in a corner sitter with a blanket, pillow, or large beanbag propped at each side, if needed.

Suggestions for adaptation:

- Make a custom table by turning a cardboard box upside down and cutting out a half circle at the location of the child's stomach. Cover the top of the box with contact paper if desired.

- Use an infant bathtub and place the child in the narrow, rounded end.

Sitting supported in a chair. Be sure the child's hips touch the back of the chair and her or his knees are extended beyond the seat of the chair. Knees should be flexed at a 90-degree angle, with feet flat on the floor or on a footrest. The child's back should be erect. This is the best sitting position for all children and adults. It allows for maximum comfort.

Suggestions for adaptation:

- Dycem (trademark), a commercial nonskid material, placed on the seat of the chair, can prevent a child from slipping out.

- Towels rolled up or large beanbags at the sides of a chair can prevent a child from falling to the side.

- A hip strap (fastened across the hips like a car seat belt) made from two-inch webbing and Velcro will help hold the child back in the chair. Such straps need to be fastened snugly. A child's physical or occupational therapist can help with hip straps.

"W" sitting. Some children prefer to sit in a position in which their heels are behind the buttocks and out to the sides, creating the letter "W" with their legs. This position offers good stability because the child's base of support is widened. Because children feel stable in this position, they can at times concentrate better and have more coordinated use of their hands. Children should be encouraged to sit in other positions that are easier to move in and out of and that do not stretch out ligaments as much. Parents can be encouraged to consult with the child's physician if there are concerns regarding this sitting position.

Standing. When children are standing at a support, watch for signs of fatigue such as irritability, wobbly posture, or a swayed back. Standing with feet too far apart or too close together will make it more difficult for children to balance themselves.

Suggestions for adaptation:

- Use Dycem, a commercial nonskid product, on standing surfaces to decrease slipping.

- Avoid having children stand in socks.

Caring for children who have high muscle tone

Children who have high muscle tone feel stiff and rigid. Their bodies do not appear to relax. There is resistance to bending or straightening of body parts such as the arms, legs, trunk, or neck. These children often extend their bodies and arch backwards.

When picking up and handling a child who has high muscle tone, be sure to hold the child's body close to yours. It is important to provide the child with the amount of stability he or she needs to feel secure. When children feel secure, their muscle tone will relax a little so that they are easier to lift and carry. Children with high muscle tone may also need more time to rest and need more frequent changes of position than other children. It can be difficult to pick up a child with high muscle tone because they feel stiff, may not bend easily, and may arch backward. Be sure to pick up all children by placing your hands around their upper chest and under their shoulders, not by lifting their arms. Some children with high muscle tone may need to be lifted in a cradled position because of a need for full support, or may need a second person to assist with the lift. Be sure to ask for help from a parent or physical or occupational therapist to learn the safest ways to lift, carry, and position such children. With all children, but especially those with high muscle tone, it is especially important never to pick them up by their arms; this could result in a dislocated shoulder, elbow, or wrist.

Carrying. When first lifting a child, be sure the hips are bent to at least 90 degrees and the head and shoulders are forward. Handle the child so that the body is symmetrical. This means that both legs are flexed and both arms are forward. A good position in which to carry the child is around your waist. It also helps to keep the legs separated (legs should never be forced into this position, however). Over time, as the child gains more control and balance, support can be reduced from high up the trunk to lower down on the waist or hips. When transferring a child from one position to another, be sure to maintain this flexed and controlled posture. It will speed up your transition and allow both you and the child more comfort with the handling process.

Sitting supported in a chair. Proper positioning of children in chairs is important. Hips need to be at the back of the chair, flexed to 90 degrees (a right angle), and the knees need to be flexed to 90 degrees. Feet need to be flat on the floor or on a footrest. The shoulders and arms should be forward. If the child cannot be supported in this position, further adaptation will need to be provided in consultation with the child's parents and physical or occupational therapist. The child may need to be in a partially reclined position with head supports. The child may qualify for special adaptive equipment through private insurance, California Children's Services, or the local regional center.

Some tips to consider:

- Children's backs should be erect or slightly reclined, depending on the amount of head control they are able to apply. The head should be slightly forward. If a child is unable to keep the head from falling forward, a more reclined position is advisable. It may also help to use head supports. Typically, a child who requires this amount of stability will be receiving therapy services and will already have an adapted chair to provide the necessary support. If not, the child is probably eligible for special equipment through California Children's Services, the family's insurance company, or the local regional center.

- Hips should be placed at the back of the seat.

- Feet should be flat on a footrest or the floor with knees and ankles flexed at a 90-degree angle.

- Shoulders and arms should be forward.

Suggestions for adaptation:

- If a child is leaning more to one side than the other, additional stability can be provided by placing a rolled towel or beanbags at the child's sides.

- Use Dycem on the chair seat to help prevent the child from slipping forward.

- Use a hip strap for additional stability and security.

Lying on the stomach. When placing children with increased muscle tone on their stomachs, place a towel roll or small bolster under the chest to provide additional support and stability. This technique allows children to explore while using their elbows for support and stability.

Suggestions for adaptation:

- Place large beanbags to children's sides to prevent them from rolling.

- Try placing children on a wedge as an alternative position. Wedges can be commercially purchased or made from either foam or wood.

Lying on the side. Side lying can afford a comfortable position for some children. The following are important points to consider when placing a child in this position:

- Children should lie on a soft, comfortable surface such as a foam mat.

- The back should be straight against a stable surface.

- Both arms should be forward.

- The top leg should be bent.

Suggestion for adaptation:

- Use beanbags to help children experience more stability in the side position. A large beanbag can be placed over the bottom leg in such a way that the majority of the beans are on the sides of the leg without too much pressure on the top of the leg. Homemade beanbags—a large cloth bag and pinto beans—are best. The width and length of bag can be made to fit your specifications.

Lying on the back. Lying on the back is not usually encouraged for children with high muscle tone because it encourages them to push back if they are not well positioned. However, it does offer a positioning option. The following strategies can be of help:

- Lay a child's head on a beanbag or pillow so that the child's neck is encouraged to flex forward. This will help prevent the child from pushing back.

- Place a bolster, wedge, or large pillow close to the hips so that the hips and knees are bent. Use beanbags to help hold the legs in place.

- Place rolled-up towels or beanbags under the shoulder to encourage a child to bring the arms forward.

Positioning and handling children with high muscle tone almost always requires consultation with their parents or physical or occupational therapists. Caregivers should protect themselves and the children they are caring for by asking for help.

Appendix 8-C

Determining If a Child Is Well-Positioned and Ready for Play

Observing children's positions

Awareness of children's positions is extremely important because children with physical disabilities may fatigue, slip into awkward positions, or experience discomfort more quickly and easily than other children.

The following questions will help caregivers further determine if children are well-positioned:

- Are children positioned in ways that allow for success?

- Are positions secure and stable?

- Has a child in care remained in one position for more than 15 or 20 minutes?

- Can children comfortably use their hands and reach for toys?

- Are children positioned alongside their peers?

Helpful hints for better positioning

- Use Dycem or other nonslip material to help the child maintain position.

- Use beanbags to gain stability and help hold the child in place.

- Use adaptive chairs as recommended by parents, the occupational therapist, or the physical therapist.

- Use adaptive standers as recommended by parents and/or therapists.

- Use bolsters, towels, or wedges to help give children the support they need as recommended by parents and/or therapists.

- Adjust time allotted to specific activities according to the child's cues, comfort level, and needs.

Appendix 8-D

Addresses of Distributors and Manufacturers of Products Useful in the Care of Children with Disabilities

J. A. Preston Corporation
60 Page Road
Clifton, NJ 07012
Telephone: (800) 631-7277

This company distributes equipment for special education needs, including feeding chairs.

Fred Sammons, Inc.
P.O. Box 3697, Dept. 728
Grand Rapids, MI 49501-3697
Telephone: (800) 323-5547

This company distributes a variety of therapy and rehabilitation equipment, including spoons, cups, and foam for built-up handles. The antislip product Dycem can also be purchased through this company.

Tupperware Home Parties
P.O. Box 2353
Orlando, FL 32802
Telephone: (800) 858-7221

Tupperware sells a plastic cup with a wide base.

Chapter 9

Nuts and Bolts: Administrative Issues in Serving Children with Exceptional Care Needs and Their Families

By Barbara Coccodrilli Carlson, Abby J. Cohen, and Kathy Heftman

Introduction

Caregiving has evolved into a highly organized profession with a complex overlay of
governmental rules and regulations serving
as safeguards for children, families, and care
providers. The purpose of this chapter is to
alert child care providers to specific administrative issues to be
considered when providing care to children with disabilities or
other exceptional care needs. The chapter covers licensing,
insurance and liability rates, contracts, discrimination, confi-

*Jus est ars boni et
aequi. (Law is the
technique of justice.)*

— Celsus

dentiality, and philosophies and policies that apply to programs for children with disabilities. A list of resources that address administrative issues is included in this chapter.

Setting the Stage

Imagine a situation in which a child with a disability is enrolled in a child care program. The following example will highlight issues and responses commonly encountered in the care of children with disabilities.

John Lowe has called you to inquire whether his daughter, Maria, age two and one-half, can enroll in your center. John tells you over the phone that Maria has epilepsy and is developmentally delayed. You set up an appointment with John to bring Maria in to visit your facility. Following are questions you might want to have answers to prior to meeting Maria and her father.

Are my facility and program subject to the provisions of the Americans with Disabilities Act? Yes, whether Maria is accepted or not. The Americans with Disabilities Act (ADA), signed into law July 26, 1990, guarantees equal opportunity in public accommodations to individuals with disabilities. Child care centers and family day care facilities located in homes are specifically defined as "public accommodations" in the regulations implementing the act.

Under the ADA, administrators of child care programs may not deny persons with disabilities (children or parents) opportunities to participate in the services offered. Programs operated by religious organizations and located in their facilities are exempt from ADA requirements, but state law (the Unruh Civil Rights Act) prohibits religious organizations in California that operate child care programs from discriminating. (Comparisons of California law to the ADA may be found in Appendix 9-A.) Whether administrators of programs will need to modify physical barriers—widen a doorway, for example—or adjust an existing practice, such as feeding an older child, in order to give all children an equal opportunity to benefit from services is determined on a case-by-case basis.

ABOUT THE AUTHORS

Barbara Coccodrilli Carlson is the Early Childhood Program director for the Miriam and Peter Haas Fund. She formerly coordinated the Integrated Early Childhood Programs Project for the New York State Council on Children and Families. She is an attorney and has worked as both an early childhood special education teacher and a "generic" child care teacher. She is the proud parent of two young children, one having special needs. At the time this chapter was originally written, Barbara was a staff attorney at the Child Care Law Center in San Francisco. Barbara has served on the executive commit-tees of the High Risk Infant Interagency Council of San Francisco, the Epilepsy Society of San Francisco, and the Developmental Disabilities Council of San Francisco.

Abby J. Cohen is the managing attorney at the Child Care Law Center. She has been with the Law Center since 1983 and has counseled providers, made presentations, and written extensively on child care issues. Since 1991 her work has centered on the Americans with Disabilities Act and its impact on child care.

Kathy Heftman has been the paralegal at the Child Care Law Center since January, 1990. She provides information and materials to those in the child care community who call the Center for information about requirements of the Americans with Disabilities Act.

Will state licensing law allow my program to accept Maria? In California, child care centers and family child care facilities in homes are licensed by the Community Care Licensing Division of the California Department of Social Services. There are no specific regulations relating to the care of children with disabilities in family day care homes. As a general rule, child care licensing regulations do not prohibit operators of programs from accepting children with disabilities. State regulations that apply to child care facilities do specify that medical assessments include identification of each enrolling child's special problems and needs (Section 101220(b)(3) of Title 22 of the *California Code of Regulations*).

The Community Care Licensing Division does provide a medical assessment form to child care centers that asks the child's physician to make a determination as to whether the child is able to "participate" in a child care program. There is, however, no corresponding regulation that would prohibit a program's operators from accepting a child even if the physician makes a negative determination regarding the child's potential for participation (see the *Community Care Licensing Manual* of the Department of Social Services, Section 101220, "Medical Assessments").

Section 101319(c) of the manual, "Admission Policies," provides that "the licensee shall be allowed to accept children who are physically handicapped, mentally disordered, or developmentally disabled, provided that the center is able to meet the individual needs of each child." Child care providers should be aware that this is a hazy standard at best and will probably be changed in the near future to comply with the ADA.

Providers should be aware also that much of the law governing licensing and its regulations are being reviewed for compliance with the ADA. In the meantime, some interpretations of policies have been developed and are offered as recommendations based on the Licensing Division's interpretation of existing regulations. These interpretations and recommendations are subject to change, possible litigation, and judicial interpretation.

Will state licensing provisions require me to obtain a fire clearance for Maria? State licensing law is clear that child care centers and large family child care homes must have a fire clearance for nonambulatory children, those unable to leave a building unassisted in an emergency (see the *Community Care Licensing Manual,* sections 101152(n)(1) and 101161). Operators of small child care facilities located in homes are specifically exempt from requirements to obtain fire clearances (see California *Health and Safety Code* Section 1597.45(d)). Children who depend on mechanical aids such as crutches, walkers, and wheelchairs are always defined as nonambulatory under licensing regulations, and the facilities they use will always require a fire clearance. This blanket definition may come under scrutiny because of the passage of the ADA. It is clear, however, that if Maria *can* leave the building unassisted under emergency conditions, a fire clearance will not be needed.

Providers should be aware that licensing evaluators may have differing interpretations of the need for fire clearances for facilities that house children with disabilities. In some instances child care providers have been informed that they need a special license for children with epilepsy. Although such a requirement has been found to be a misinterpretation of regulations—there is only one license required—licensing authorities may require a fire clearance if a child who has epilepsy is considered nonambulatory because of a high number of seizures per day. This requirement applies to large family day care programs (those with more than six children) and child care centers.

Caregivers have the right to disagree with an evaluator. They should do their homework first, however, and ask the evaluator to point to specific regulations that back up his or her point of view. Be polite but firm. If the evaluator is referring to regulations you are unfamiliar with, ask to see the regulations. If you are not satisfied, don't hesitate to ask to speak with the supervisor or the district manager of the licensing agency. Your local child care resource and referral agency and the Child Care Law Center are additional resources that may prove helpful. (See the list of agency resources at the end of this chapter.)

Will I have to write and follow an Individualized Educational Plan for Maria? An Individualized Educational Plan (IEP) is a required legal document that identifies the educational services needed

and the goals and objectives set for children eligible for special education. Licensing law does not require an IEP for children with disabilities who are enrolled in child care programs. Caregivers may participate in a program plan with other professionals, but this participation is not required in order to accept Maria or any other child with special-care needs.

If my facility is licensed as an infant center only, can I accept a child like Maria who is more than two years of age? Yes. Licensing law allows a child whose developmental needs require continuation in an infant care center to remain there up to a maximum age of three years (*Community Care Licensing Manual,* Section 101361). Because Maria's father indicates that Maria is developmentally delayed, it is likely she will qualify for this exception.

Can I share information about Maria's special needs with my staff or other agency personnel? Yes, but only with her father's permission. As a general rule, a caregiver or caregiving entity should obtain a written release before disseminating any personal information. Absent such "consent," the individual who is the subject of the released information may be able to sue you or press criminal charges against you. This is particularly true in the case of medical, psychological, and social information. And in California, *each* disclosure of HIV status *must* be made pursuant to individual, written consent from the affected person or that person's guardian.

Clearly, the best policy is to collect relevant information from family members regarding a child's particular needs and then determine, with the family's consent, who else might need the information. If the facility's director determines that the classroom staff need medical information on Maria, either the child's guardian can give this information to the staff directly or the director can obtain written permission for each person who will receive the information regarding Maria's medical status.

Will my insurance policy be canceled or my rates raised if I accept Maria? Probably not. Most providers polled who serve children with disabilities have indicated that they have not had their policies canceled or their rates raised, though accepting children with special-care needs has made some insurers nervous. No guaranteed protections from cancellation or nonrenewal exist, but most program administrators report that they have not experienced cancellation or nonrenewal.

Keep in mind, however, that insurers may raise premiums if it can be demonstrated that acceptance of children with special-care needs increases the insurer's underwriting risk. The Child Care Law Center has information and handouts available on insurance and liability issues and the ADA. A specific discussion of liability insurance and the ADA is found in Appendix 9-B.

Important Note: If a policy application or statement specifically calls for disclosure of the enrollment of children with special medical or developmental needs, it is important to notify the insurer if the operators of the program accept Maria after the insurance takes effect. Failure to notify the insurer of such enrollment when the policy requires it may result in refusal by the insurer to pay claims under the policy. The policy may also refer to certain "assumptions" on the part of the insurer. Any change in circumstances bearing on these "assumptions" must also be reported to the insurer.

Do I need a special type of contract to care for Maria? It is important to cover all special circumstances when entering into a contract for child care services with *all* parents. Caregivers should decide what their

needs and concerns are, as well as those of the child and family, and should make sure that the contract addresses these needs. The financial terms of child care services, the limits on hours and services, other program policies, and the responsibilities that caregivers assume for a particular child should be addressed in each contract. For example, program administrators might want to spell out whose responsibility it is to transport Maria to the physical therapist. For general information regarding contracts between parents and providers and to obtain sample forms, see "Child Care Contracts: Information For Providers," which may be obtained from the Child Care Law Center, 22 Second Street, 5th Floor, San Francisco, CA 94105, (415) 495-5498.

How might I be liable if I accept Maria? Caregivers might ask, "Can I be sued if I accept Maria and she or one of the other children gets hurt?" The best advice regarding liability is, first, to prevent injury by complying with applicable laws and regulations and by maintaining a safe program and, second, to buy appropriate insurance. An operator of a child care program may owe a "higher duty" of care and supervision to a child who has a disability or is otherwise vulnerable than that operator would owe to other children in the program. If a child's vulnerability to injury is known to the program's operator, that operator will have a responsibility to take special precautions for that child. Even if unaware of a child's special need or vulnerability, the program's operator could nonetheless be liable if that child is injured or is injured more severely than a person without the vulnerability would be injured.

Therefore, it is essential that information is obtained in writing from all parents or legal guardians identifying any special care needs their child may have. In the case of

Maria, a form providing such information should be filled out and signed by her father. This requirement should be noted in the parent's handbook and in the child care service contract.

Can I be sued if I don't accept Maria? Maybe, depending on Maria's needs for special accommodations and your ability to provide them. Under the ADA, child care programs may not discriminate against persons with disabilities but must consider if accommodations can be made. The act outlines a process of analysis that operators of programs must engage in to determine whether a child can be served. The Child Care Law Center's publications on the ADA and child care issues describe this process in some detail. Program operators can be sued if they either (1) fail to engage in the analysis required by the law and simply refuse to serve a child based on assumptions or stereotypes; or (2) refuse to make certain accommodations that, according to the ADA, are reasonable for the program's operators to make. Operators should be able to document their compliance with the process required by the ADA for each child with a disability who seeks accommodations in their programs. (Appendix 9-C offers a brief overview of the responsibilities of operators of private programs. Appendix 9-D includes a flowchart of this process of analysis.)

Will I be reimbursed at a higher rate from the California Department of Education if I accept Maria? Yes. If the program has a current contract with the Department, state law provides an adjusted reimbursement rate for children with exceptional needs (1.2 times the regular rate) and for children with severe handicapping conditions (1.5 times the regular rate). (See California *Education Code,* sections 8265.5 and 8208, and the Department's Child

Development Division Policy Memorandum #90-04 (9/90).) Children with exceptional needs who would be considered eligible for special rates are those who have been determined eligible for special education services by an individualized education program team. Children with severe disabilities are those who require care in programs in which staff is trained in serving children with the following disabilities: autism, blindness, deafness, severe orthopedic impairments, serious emotional disturbances, or severe mental retardation.

These increased reimbursement rates are available to eligible children in "mainstreamed" settings. To pay this higher rate for Maria, the Department would require either a copy of Maria's Individual Education Plan, her Individual Program Plan developed by the Regional Center, documentation of services provided by another public or private agency or medical facility that specializes in services to children with handicapping conditions, or a service plan provided by such an agency. It is a good idea for a program's operator to talk to a consultant in the Department's Child Development Division who is familiar with such programs to determine the appropriate reimbursement level and the documentation required for each child with special care needs who is under consideration for enrollment.

Summary

We have seen that there may be additional administrative steps required in order to care for children like Maria. However, with assistance, support, and persistence from a willing provider, more children with disabilities are gaining access to child care programs in California. Increased opportunities for children with disabilities present new administrative challenges to providers. The need in the decade of the 1990s is for child care leaders to collaborate with advocates for children with disabilities to facilitate interpretations of regulations that promote the inclusion of these children.

This chapter is intended to assist in the development and implementation of policies that favor the inclusion of children with disabilities in child care programs. There are special administrative challenges, as this chapter has described, in caring for children with exceptional needs. A thorough understanding of the ways in which these challenges can be met is essential to the successful placement and care of these children.

KEY POINTS

1. Operators of all licensed child care centers and family child care homes in California may enroll children who have disabilities or other special-care needs.

2. A fire clearance for nonambulatory children must be obtained by operators of large family child care homes and centers. A fire clearance is not required for small family child care facilities.

3. Operators are not required to develop or follow an Individualized Education Plan for any child they enroll.

4. Licensing provisions allow a child whose developmental needs require continuation in an infant care center to remain there up to a maximum age of three years.

5. Information about any child may be shared only with the written permission of the child's parent or guardian for each disclosure.

6. Insurers should be notified when a child with disabilities is enrolled if the operator's policy application, statement, or policy "assumptions" call for disclosure.

7. Operators should write all agreements that address special circumstances or services into contracts with parents.

8. Operators should request—in writing—that all parents inform them of any special needs their children may have.

9. The California Department of Education will reimburse current child care contractors at a higher rate for children with exceptional needs and children with severe disabilities.

10. Operators of child care centers and family child care facilities are subject to the provisions of the Americans with Disabilities Act, unless they are operated by religious organizations, which are exempt from the public accommodations provisions of the ADA. However, religious programs in California must comply with the Unruh Civil Rights Act.

Resources

All Kids Count. The Arc, National Headquarters, 500 East Border, Suite 300, Arlington, TX 76010, (817) 261-6003, (817) 277-0553 TDD, 1993.

This book is designed to inform child care providers about the law and to familiarize them with the importance and value of including all children in regular child care settings.

The Americans with Disabilities Act and Its Implications for School Districts. Concord, N.H.: Parent Information Center. (P.O. Box 1422, Concord, NH 03302-1422, telephone (603) 224-7005, V/TDD.)

The Americans with Disabilities Act: Its Implications for Parent Training and Information Programs. Concord, N.H.: Parent Information Center. (P.O. Box 1422, Concord, NH 03302-1422, telephone (603) 224-7005, V/TDD.)

The Americans with Disabilities Act: Questions and Answers. Washington, D.C.: Public Access Section/Distribution Center, Civil Rights Division, U.S. Department of Justice, September, 1992. (P.O. Box 66738, Washington, D.C. 20035-6738.)

This booklet is designed to provide answers to some of the most often asked questions about the Americans with Disabilities Act.

Caring for Children with HIV or AIDS in Child Care. San Francisco: Child Care Law Center, revised 1994.

The second volume in the center's ADA series, this publication is a detailed guide to the legal responsibilities of child care providers to admit and care for children with HIV or AIDS. The guide includes sections on admitting and accommodating children with HIV/AIDS under the Americans with Disabilities Act, universal infection control precautions, confidentiality, and background information on the transmissibility of the virus.

Caring for Children with Special Needs: The Americans with Disabilities Act and Child Care. San Francisco: Child Care Law Center, 1991.

The first volume in the Child Care Law Center's upcoming ADA series, this comprehensive publication addresses the new issues of interest to and responsibilities of child care providers around the country stemming from passage of the ADA. Contents include a step-by-step guide to a provider's responsibilities under the act, a discussion of the increased costs associated with caring for a child with special needs, and a review of the types of accommodations a child might need.

Child Care and the ADA: Highlights for Parents. San Francisco: Child Care Law Center, 1994.

This guide, intended for parents who use child care services, highlights the ADA's requirements, with specific attention to the concerns parents may have about how inclusion will affect their children. It is also available in Spanish.

Child Care and the ADA: Highlights for Parents of Children with Disabilities. San Francisco: Child Care Law Center, 1994.

Written for parents of children with disabilities who intend to use or are currently using child care, this guide reviews families' rights and responsibilities under the ADA. It covers such topics as how the ADA differs from Section 504 and IDEA, who decides whether the response of the child care program is adequate, and how parents can help the child care program meet the needs of children with disabilities. It is also available in Spanish.

Confidentiality and Collaboration: Information Sharing in Interagency Efforts. Denver: Education Commission of the States, 1992. (ECS Distribution Center, 707 17th Street, Suite 2700, Denver, CO 80202-2427, telephone (303) 299-3692.)

HIV and AIDS: Employment Issues in Child Care. San Francisco: Child Care Law Center, 1993.

This third volume in the center's ADA series is a detailed guide to the legal responsibilities of operators of child care programs who hire and work with staff who have HIV or AIDS. Included are sections on the application and hiring process under the Americans with Disabilities Act, universal infection control precautions and the OSHA regulations, training of staff and parents, the hepatitis B vaccine requirement, and confidentiality issues.

Legal Guide for Child Care Resource and Referral Agencies. San Francisco: Child Care Law Center, 1991.

This guide covers regulatory issues, liability, confidentiality of information, privacy, and tax issues. It includes useful sections on legal issues that affect providers, such as employment policies, contracts, zoning, liability, and the reporting of child abuse.

Agency resources

California Child Care Resource and Referral Network, 111 New Montgomery Street, 7th Floor, San Francisco, CA 94105, telephone (415) 882-0234; 626 N. Coronado Terrace, Rm. 219, Los Angeles, CA 90026, (213) 413-7071.

This nonprofit public benefit corporation represents 71 child care resource and referral agencies located in 57 counties throughout California. In addition to helping parents find child care, resource and referral agencies provide technical assistance to new and existing child care providers. The California Child Care Resource and Referral Network can refer you to the resource and referral agency in your community which, in turn, can recommend programs in the community that care for children with special needs.

Child Care Law Center, 22 Second Street, 5th Floor, San Francisco, CA 94105, telephone (415) 495-5498.

The Child Care Law Center is a nonprofit legal services organization dedicated to improving and expanding child care services. The center provides expert assistance to legal services attorneys, child care advocates, child care providers, parents, and policy makers and assists them in overcoming the legal impediments to accessible, affordable, high-quality child care services. The center provides services and materials that include advice and counseling, consultation and referral, litigation, publications, training support and materials, advocacy support, and representation. The staff of the center are recognized national experts in the area of child care for children with special needs.

Community Care Licensing Division, California Department of Social Services, 744 P Street, Mail Stop 19-50, Sacramento, CA 95814, telephone (916) 324-4031.

This is the agency responsible for licensing California child care centers and family day care homes. The Sacramento office can put you in touch with your local licensing office as well as the child care ombudsman for your region. The Child Care Ombudsman Program of the Community Care Licensing Division is designed to provide information to parents and the general public on child care licensing standards and regulations.

National Council of Independent Living, 2111 Wilson Boulevard, Suite 405, Arlington, VA 22201.

The council serves independent living centers.

Pacific Disability Business Technical Assistance Center (DBTAC), 440 Grand Avenue, Suite 500, Oakland, CA 94610, telephone (415) 465-7884.

This center is authorized by the National Institute of Disability and Rehabilitation Research to provide information, materials, and technical assistance to individuals and entities that are covered by the Americans with Disabilities Act.

Parent Information Center, P.O. Box 1422, Concord, NH 03302-1422, telephone (603) 224-7005.

This center serves the parents of children with disabilities and adults with disabilities.

Public Counsel, 601 South Ardmore Avenue, Los Angeles, CA 90005, telephone (213) 385-2977.

Public Counsel is the largest *pro bono* law office in the nation. It is the Southern California affiliate of the Lawyers' Committee for Civil Rights Under Law and is the public interest law firm of the Los Angeles County and Beverly Hills bar associations. The firm helps indigent children, youth, adults, families and eligible community organizations in a number of areas. Public Counsel's activities are far-ranging and affect a wide spectrum of people who live at or below the poverty level. The firm provides advice and *pro bono* representation to care providers who serve low-income families and nonprofit child care centers in the areas of licensing, zoning, insurance, and landlord-tenant issues. It helps local governments develop ordinances and policies related to child care and makes presentations on legal issues of concern to the child care community.

Appendix 9-A

California's Laws Prohibiting Discrimination Against Persons with Disabilities: Expanding the Requirements of the ADA

(© 1993 Child Care Law Center, 22 Second St., 5th Floor, San Francisco, CA 94105, telephone (415) 495-5498, fax (415) 495-6734. mgdl2:state.ada 2/3/94)

In 1990, the Americans with Disabilities Act (ADA) was signed into law, making it one of the most comprehensive civil rights laws ever enacted. The ADA establishes protections for people with both physical and mental disabilities against discrimination in employment, public accommodations (including child care programs), state and local public services, telecommunications, and public transportation. It also provides protections for people who are *regarded as having a disability*, who have a *record of disabilities*, and who are *associated with people with disabilities*. Moreover, the ADA not only requires that people in these protected groups be afforded protections from discriminatory actions, such as denial of services or employment, the ADA also requires employers and service providers to take steps to reasonably accommodate the special needs of individuals with disabilities in order to afford them equal opportunity.

The ADA is not the only law that prohibits discrimination against people with disabilities. Other federal, state, and local laws also prohibit discrimination against people with disabilities, and the protections afforded by some of these laws differ from the protections afforded by the ADA. While the enactment of the ADA has contributed to greater uniformity among these laws, some inconsistencies still persist. The best rule of thumb to assess your legal responsibility in situations where a state law differs from the ADA in the amount of protection afforded to a person with a disability is to apply whichever law offers the most protections for people with disabilities in any given situation. In some cases, state law may offer more protections than the ADA.

Prior to the enactment of the ADA, some federal, state, and local laws prohibited discrimination on the basis of disability, but they were not nearly as comprehensive in their protections as the ADA. In

California, state laws protected only people with physical disabilities (and not those with mental disabilities) and did not provide protections for the other three ADA-protected classes (those persons *regarded as, with a record of,* or *associated with*). On the other hand, the protections afforded by California's antidiscrimination laws apply to a larger pool of employers and service providers than the ADA does. Significantly, with recent legislative amendments, California's laws have been enhanced to meet or exceed the protections afforded by the ADA (with some exceptions). It is important, therefore, for California employers and service providers to become familiar, not only with the requirements of the ADA, but also with state laws where they differ from ADA requirements.

Public accommodations

Discrimination against people with disabilities in public accommodations under California law is governed primarily by the Unruh act. While this law formerly protected only people with physical disabilities, it was amended in January, 1993, to protect people with physical and mental disabilities, as well as those who are *regarded as* disabled, and those with a *record* of disability. Significantly, it does not expressly indicate protections for people who are *associated with* people with disabilities, but it is safe to assume that the latter class of people is also protected, because the new amendments clearly state that, "a violation of the right of any individual under the Americans with Disabilities Act of 1990 shall also constitute a violation of this section."

The ADA prohibits discrimination by a public accommodation (including a child care program) of any size, as does the Unruh act. But, where the ADA exempts religious organizations under certain conditions (such as church-operated child care programs) from its public accommodations requirements, Unruh has a much more narrow religious exemption. Under state law, religious organizations may discriminate on the basis of religion, but only if it is necessary for the free exercise of religious beliefs and practices. Religious organizations may not discriminate against people with disabilities through the public accommodations they offer. As far as people with disabilities are concerned, religious organizations are treated no differently under state law than any other organization offering a public accommodation. This means that, while church-operated child care programs in California are not required to comply with the ADA, they are required to comply with essentially the same requirements under state law.

The ADA's requirements for reasonable accommodations encompass not only equipment, services, policies, and practices that might be necessary in order to ensure full participation by people with disabilities in the services and programs offered by public accommodations; the act also requires removal of architectural barriers when this can be done without undue difficulty or expense. Most child care programs will be covered by the ADA and will be required to comply with this barrier removal provision. But church-operated child care programs are not covered by the ADA, and must look to state law.

State law seems to depart somewhat from the ADA in this respect. While, on the one hand, Unruh states expressly that it is intended to meet or exceed the protections offered by the ADA, on the other hand, it just as clearly states that it does not require public accommodations to make any structural alterations, modifications, or improvements that the State Architect does not require. This seems to mean that, where the ADA does require removal of architectural barriers, state law does also. But where programs are exempt from the ADA barrier removal requirement, Unruh does not impose this responsibility on otherwise ADA-exempt programs (such as church-operated child care programs).

Under California's Uniform Building Code, child care programs that have the capacity to care for more than 20 children are required to make architectural modifications to conform with the building code accessibility specification. This rule will apply to church-operated as well as to secular programs. Church-operated programs that have a capacity of 20 children or fewer, however, appear to be exempted under state or federal law from making architectural changes to their facilities, although these programs will still be required to make other types of reasonable accommodations.

The following chart summarizes some of the main differences between state and federal laws that prohibit disability-based discrimination in public accommodations as these laws apply to differing circumstances.

Circumstance	ADA	State Law—Unruh
size of program	all	all
associated with	protected	probably protected
programs operated by religious organizations	exempted	covered
architectural barrier removal— religious programs	exempted	21-child-plus capacity
architectural barrier removal— secular programs	required	implicit requirement

Employment

Employment discrimination against people with disabilities under California law is addressed primarily by the Fair Employment and Housing Act (FEHA). Like the Unruh Act, this recently amended law indicates the legislative intent to provide the same or broader protections under this law as are provided by the ADA.

One of the most important differences between the FEHA and the ADA is the number of employers who are prohibited from discriminating against people with disabilities. Prior to July, 1994, the ADA prohibited only those employers with 25 or more employees from discriminating against people with disabilities. But since July, 1994, it has been illegal under the ADA for employers with 15 or more employees to discriminate against people with disabilities.

FEHA, on the other hand, prohibits an employer with five or more employees (full-time or part-time) from discriminating against people with physical disabilities. While FEHA also provides protections for people with mental disabilities, the state protections conform more precisely to the ADA protections. FEHA has prohibited discrimination against people with mental disabilities by employers with 15 or more employees since July, 1994.

Smaller employers covered by state law, but not by the ADA (those who employ 5 to 24 workers) have most of the same legal obligations towards employing and accommodating people with physical disabilities as larger employers do under the ADA, including the requirement to remove structural or architectural barriers whenever it can be done without much difficulty or expense.

FEHA also provides protections to people who are regarded as having, or having had, a disability but does not protect those associated with people with disabilities. Unlike the Unruh Act, FEHA is intended to be construed narrowly, and, therefore, it is unlikely that people associated with people with disabilities will be protected from discrimination by smaller employers under state law.

Some smaller employers are exempt from California's FEHA. In contrast to the Unruh act, FEHA allows for a broad exemption for religious organizations. Religious organizations that employ fewer than 25 employees, therefore, are not prohibited from discriminating in employment on the basis of disability. The ADA, on the other hand, does not exempt religious organizations from its anti-discriminatory employment provisions. So, under the ADA, religious organizations that employ 25 or more workers may not discriminate on the basis of disability. Unlike religious organizations, other nonprofit organizations are not exempt from FEHA provisions.

The following chart summarizes some of the main differences between state and federal laws that prohibit discrimination in employment against persons with disabilities as these laws apply in differing circumstances:

Circumstance	ADA	FEHA/State Law
size of employer		
after July, 1992 disabilities and 25 with	25 or more employees	5 or more with physical mental disabilities
after July, 1994	15 or more employees	5 or more with physical disabilities and 15 or more with mental disabilities
associated with	protected	not protected
architectural barrier removal	required	required
religious organizations	covered	exempted

Appendix 9-B

Liability Insurance, Child Care and the ADA: Between a Rock and a Hard Place?

(© 1993 Child Care Law Center, 22 Second St., 5th Floor, San Francisco, CA 94105, telephone (415) 495-5498, fax (415) 495-6734. mgdl2:state.ada 2/3/94)

Background

The Americans with Disabilities Act (ADA) presents a new opportunity for child care providers in both family day care settings and in child care centers to offer their services on a nondiscriminatory basis to children with disabilities. The ADA requires that individuals with disabilities be served in the most integrated setting appropriate to their needs. Many child care programs are eager to comply with the ADA but express concern that once they begin serving children with disabilities and inform their insurance companies, they may have difficulty obtaining or maintaining appropriate liability insurance or keeping the cost reasonable.

The concerns of providers are based on experience. During the child care insurance crisis which followed the McMartin case, subpoenaed documents from the insurance companies revealed that many of them would not underwrite providers who served special-needs children. Other companies would place additional, often quite onerous, requirements on the providers or would arbitrarily increase premiums. These increases were not described as being made on an individualized basis; the mere notification by the provider that they were serving a child with a disability—regardless of the nature of the disability—would result in increased premiums. In states that require liability insurance as a condition of licensure or receipt of governmental subsidies, the lack of available, affordable insurance could have particularly serious consequences. However, as described below, there may be some strategies available to providers that will allow them to offer their much-needed services to children with disabilities while at the same time maintaining essential, affordable liability insurance.

What the ADA says

The ADA makes very clear that public accommodations, including child care programs, cannot refuse to serve a person with a disability because an insurance company bases its coverage or rates on the absence of persons with disabilities. This requirement was intended to address a frequently offered reason for denial of services by operators of public accommodations. The material explaining the ADA (the preamble), however, requires that underwriting and classification of risks must be based on sound actuarial principles or must be related to actual or reasonably anticipated experience. The law clearly states that the classification of risks is not to be used as a subterfuge to evade the purposes of the ADA.

While advocates sought to require the insurers to provide the applicant with the actuarial data if requested, the Department of Justice did not adopt this requirement as a regulation. Consequently, while there may be a legal basis for challenging an insurance company's decisions to refuse to insure; to refuse to continue insuring; to limit the amount, kind, or extent of coverage; or to raise rates; the process by which this challenge could be mounted—namely a lawsuit against the insurance company—remains difficult and expensive.

How can providers respond? Advocacy strategies

It is important that care providers bring to public attention refusals to insure or unwarranted premium increases by insurance companies based on the enrollment of children with disabilities. This includes contacting, as appropriate, family day care associations, resource and referral agencies, the Child Care Law Center, disability advocacy groups, the media, state insurance commissioners, and members of Congress. In order for advocacy efforts on this issue to be effective, it will be essential to know that providers are being affected. Additionally, if particular companies seem to be the culprits, it may be possible to establish a pattern of discrimination that would be useful in the legal strategies described below. If providers commonly are not successful in either obtaining actuarial data to back up insurance company decisions or find the data obtained does not support the company's claim, this information could form the basis for demanding that the state insurance commissioner (insurance or department) take action. If large numbers of providers are denied liability insurance because they serve children with disabilities or if they find their premiums dramatically increased, it will be much more likely that public opinion can be mobilized to assist providers. It is hoped that such advocacy would ensure that providers would not continue to be put between a rock and a hard place.

How can providers respond? Legal strategies

Filing lawsuits under the ADA. If liability insurance is canceled, not offered, limited, or is unduly expensive because a child care program is serving a child with disabilities, program operators should make a formal request of the insurance company to offer actuarial data to back up its decision. If the response is unsatisfactory (and operators may need an expert consultation to determine this), the ADA would allow the argument that the insurance company's classification of risk is being used as a subterfuge to avoid the purposes of the ADA. Proving that an insurer's actions are an attempt to avoid insuring child care programs that care for disabled children, and not just a reflection of actuarial risks, may be a very difficult case to make. But a pattern by an insurance company of repeatedly canceling policies or raising rates to exceedingly high levels may help to demonstrate ADA violations, particularly if the company's actions do not seem to correlate with

the extent of the disability in question. Under the ADA, it may be impossible for either the family of the child with the disability or the provider to file a complaint with the Department of Justice or to file a private lawsuit. The provider should have the right to sue as "an entity or person associated with a disabled person," one of the protected classes under the ADA. More likely than not, the burden of bringing a lawsuit against an insurance company may fall on the provider because the family may be unwilling or unable to file a lawsuit, given the expense involved and the fact that the ADA requires the child to be served regardless of the availability of insurance. (However, it is also true that most parents of children who are disabled have as much interest as any parent in having their child's provider insured.) At this point, lawsuits filed by either providers or families against insurance companies remain untested and the results unknown.

Filing lawsuits under state laws. Some state laws prohibiting discrimination against the disabled and/or prohibiting unfair business practices may provide an avenue for redressing insurance problems. For example, in California, the Unruh Act prohibits businesses and public accommodations from discriminating against people with disabilities, but, unlike the ADA, the right to sue under this law belongs exclusively to the person who has the disability, and not to one who is "associated with" a disabled person. On the other hand, almost anyone may sue a business for unfair business practices under California law. The California *Business and Professions Code* (Section 17204), will probably allow a provider who cares for children with disabilities to sue an insurance company if the provider believes that an insurance company violated the Unruh Act by canceling the provider's liability insurance. Again, this type of lawsuit has yet to be tested in the courts.

Promoting legislation. Work to develop legislation and regulation that is favorable to child care providers. Demand public hearings by state insurance commissions or departments to examine the problem of insurance availability and propose legislative and regulatory or administrative strategies to aid providers. One possibility would be to seek state legislation that would forbid companies that offer liability insurance from engaging in unjustified discrimination against people with disabilities *and* providers of public accommodations that serve people with disabilities. Insist that real "teeth" are built into the legislation so that providers can rely to a greater degree on the state to enforce these requirements rather than being forced to challenge discrimination through private lawsuits.

Resources

Child Care Law Center
  22 Second Street, 5th Floor
  San Francisco, CA 94105
  Service hours: Tuesdays and Thursdays, 9 a.m.
  to noon, telephone (415) 495-5498,
  fax (415) 495-6734

Chuck Quackenbush, Insurance Commissioner
  State of California
  Telephone (213) 897-8921
  San Francisco Office, telephone (415) 904-5410
  Consumer Information and Complaints, telephone (800) 927-4357

Appendix 9-C

Implications of the Americans with Disabilities Act on Child Care Facilities

(© 1993 Child Care Law Center, 22 Second St., 5th Floor, San Francisco, CA 94105, telephone (415) 495-5498, fax (415) 495-6734. mgdl2:state.ada 2/3/94)

The Americans with Disabilities Act (ADA) was signed into law on July 26, 1990. The ADA extends civil rights protections to individuals with disabilities. The law contains a section protecting employment rights, a section requiring nondiscrimination on the part of local and state governments, a section requiring nondiscrimination in public accommodations, a section requiring improvements in telecommunications, and a subsection of the public accommodations section requiring nondiscrimination in public transportation.

Under the ADA, individuals are disabled if (1) they have a physical or mental impairment that substantially limits one or more of their major life activities; (2) they have a history of such impairment; or (3) they are regarded as having such an impairment, meaning people treat the person as disabled whether they are or not. Individuals with such diseases as AIDS and tuberculosis are included in the definition; acute diseases such as chicken pox would not be considered a disabling condition. The ADA, unlike many other disability laws, includes mental disabilities. Individuals are also protected if they are "associated" with a person with the disability, e.g., a child care provider.

Implications for child care programs under the public accommodations provisions

Child care centers and family day care homes are specifically included as public accommodations. This antidiscrimination section took effect on January 26, 1992. However, child care programs operated by religious organizations are exempt from ADA requirements.

Eligibility for services

A child care program may not use eligibility requirements that exclude or segregate individuals with disabilities unless such exclusion or segregation is necessary for the operation of the business (a very high standard to meet) or necessitated by safety considerations, and even then must be based on actual risks and not generalizations or stereotypes. A child care program may exclude individuals with disabilities if they pose a direct threat to others that cannot be mitigated by modifications in policies, practices, or procedures or by the provision of auxiliary aids. The services must be offered in the most integrated setting appropriate to the needs of the individual.

Modifications in policies, practices and procedures

An operator of a child care program must make reasonable modifications in policies, practices, and procedures in order to accommodate individuals with disabilities. However, a modification is not required if it would fundamentally alter the service or operation of the child care program.

Auxiliary aids and services

An operator of a child care program must provide auxiliary aids and services when they are necessary to ensure effective communication with individuals with hearing, vision, or speech impairments. Auxiliary aids include interpreters, tapes, large print materials, and so forth. Aids that would result in an "undue burden" (significant difficulty or expense) or would "fundamentally alter" the nature of the services rendered are not required. However, if an aid or service would not result in either of these it would have to be provided.

Removal of barriers in existing facilities

Physical barriers to entering and using facilities must be removed when such removal is "readily achievable — or easily accomplishable and able to be carried out without much difficulty or expense." This is determined on a case-by-case basis in light of the resources available and safety considerations. The removal of barriers might involve the rearrangement of tables or play areas, the installation of access ramps, the installation of grab bars in toilet stalls, and so on. Even if a barrier cannot be removed, the law provides that alternative means must be taken to make the services accessible.

New construction

All newly constructed child care facilities occupied after January 26, 1993, for which the last application for a building permit or permit extension is certified complete after January 26, 1992, are required to be accessible to individuals with disabilities.

Alterations

Since January 26, 1992, alterations to child care facilities must provide accessibility to the maximum extent feasible. Alterations made to a "primary function area," must provide an accessible path of travel to the altered area and to bathrooms to the extent that the added accessibility costs are not disproportionate to the overall cost of the original alteration (i.e., do not exceed 20 percent).

ADA and the liability insurance issue

ADA regulations make it clear that a child care program cannot refuse to serve an individual with a disability because its insurance company conditions coverage or rates on the basis of a program that does not include persons with disabilities. However, the regulations do not contain measures that would prohibit insurers from canceling policies or raising premium rates on this basis. California child care programs may be able to prevent insurance increases or cancellations if these are based on generalizations or stereotypes rather than actual risks under the Unruh Civil Rights Act. However, this has not yet been tested in the courts.

Fees for services

Child care providers have often charged higher fees for special needs children than for other children. Under the ADA, the cost of taking measures to comply with the ADA cannot be charged only to the family of the child with the special needs. It must be spread out among all the families or taken as a tax credit or deduction. It appears that a family may be charged directly for measures that exceed those necessary for compliance with the ADA or for measures that could not ordinarily be undertaken because they were not readily achievable or would create an undue burden, assuming the additional charges are agreed to by the family.

The ADA's effect on landlord-tenant relationships

Under the ADA, landlords and tenants are both responsible for meeting the requirements of the ADA. Who is responsible for what will be determined through lease or contract arrangements. The ADA's effect will become an important consideration for child care program operators in signing new leases or in considering whether to renew current leases. Caregivers are also advised to review their current leases for the allocation of responsibility in compliance with federal law. If the operators of programs are forced to shoulder all the responsibility, they must ensure that they have both the resources and the legal authority to undertake alterations in common areas as well as in the areas they are leasing.

Transportation

Regular transportation services provided by child care programs are also subject to ADA's requirements. Barriers in existing vehicles must be removed in cases in which such removal is readily achievable.

Preemption

The ADA does not preempt state or local laws that provide equal or greater protections to people who are disabled. Federal, state, and local laws can give disabled individuals an array of legal options to pursue if they are discriminated against.

Remedies

Both private individuals and the U.S. Department of Justice can enforce the public accommodations provisions of the ADA. Private plaintiffs can obtain injunctive relief and attorney's fees. There are no money damages available. If the U.S. attorney general files the lawsuit, she or he can obtain injunctive relief, fines up to $50,000 for the first violation and up to $100,000 for subsequent violations, and compensatory damages if requested by the Department of Justice. Good faith efforts are taken into account.

Resources

For additional information about the ADA, contact the U.S. Department of Justice hotline (between 11 a.m. and 5 p.m. EST weekdays) at (202) 514-0301 (voice) or (202) 514-0381 (TDD) or the Child Care Law Center on Tuesdays and Thursdays from 9 a.m. until noon at (415) 495-5498.

Appendix 9-D

Determining Admissibility to Care
Under the Americans with Disabilities Act

(© 1993 Child Care Law Center, 22 Second St., 5th Floor, San Francisco, CA 94105, telephone (415) 495-5498, fax (415) 495-6734. mgdl2:state.ada 2/3/94)

ADA goal:

To *reasonably accommodate* individuals with disabilities in order to *integrate* them into the program to the extent feasible, given *each individual's* limitations

ADA principles:

- INDIVIDUALITY. The limitations and needs of *each* individual
- REASONABLENESS of the accommodation to the *program* and to the *individual*
- INTEGRATION of the individual *with others* in the program

Types of accommodations:

- AUXILIARY AIDS AND SERVICES. Special equipment and services to ensure effective communication
- CHANGES IN POLICIES, PRACTICES, AND PROCEDURES
- REMOVAL OF BARRIERS: architectural, arrangement of furniture and equipment, vehicular

Reasons to deny care:

- ACCOMMODATION IS UNREASONABLE, and there are no reasonable alternatives.
    - For **auxiliary aids and services,** if accommodations pose an *UNDUE BURDEN* (will result in a significant difficulty or expense to the program), care may be denied.
    - For **auxiliary aids and services,** or **changes in policies, practices, or procedures,** if accommodations *FUNDAMENTALLY ALTER* the nature of the program, care may be denied.
    - For **removal of barriers**, if accommodations are *NOT READILY ACHIEVABLE* (cannot be done without much difficulty or expense to the program), care may be denied.
- DIRECT THREAT

    The individual's condition will pose or does pose a significant threat to the health or safety of other children or staff in the program, and there are no reasonable means of removing the threat.

Determining Admissibility to Care
Under the ADA, Title III: "Public Accommodations"

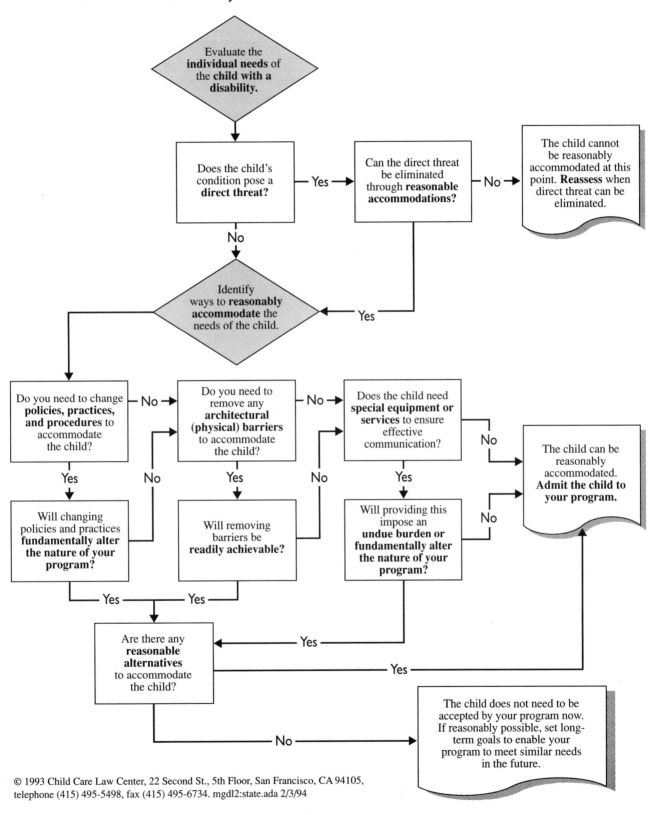

© 1993 Child Care Law Center, 22 Second St., 5th Floor, San Francisco, CA 94105, telephone (415) 495-5498, fax (415) 495-6734. mgdl2:state.ada 2/3/94

Publications Available from the Department of Education

This publication is one of more than 600 that are available from the California Department of Education. Some of the more recent publications or those most widely used are the following:

Item no.	Title (Date of publication)	Price
1204	Adult Education Handbook for California (1995 Edition)	11.50
0883	The Ages of Infancy: Caring for Young, Mobile, and Older Infants (videocassette and guide) (1990)	65.00*
1079	Beyond Retention: A Study of Retention Rates, Practices, and Successful Alternatives in California (1993)	4.25
1219	California Private School Directory, 1995-96 (1996)	17.50
1086	California Public Education: A Decade After *A Nation at Risk* (1993)	4.75
1207	California Public School Directory (1995)	17.50
1273	California Special Education Programs: A Composite of Laws (1996)	no charge
1143	Children's Choices: A Cookbook for Family Child Care Providers (1995)	11.95
1179	Continuation Education in California Public Schools (1995)	7.25
0978	Course Models for the History–Social Science Framework, Grade Five—United States History and Geography: Making a New Nation (1991)	9.50
1034	Course Models for the History–Social Science Framework, Grade Six—World History and Geography: Ancient Civilizations (1993)	9.50
1132	Course Models for the History–Social Science Framework, Grade Seven—World History and Geography: Medieval and Early Modern Times (1994)	12.75
1247	Course Models for the History–Social Science Framework, Grade Ten—World History, Culture, and Geography: The Modern World (1995)	17.50
1180	Course Models for the History–Social Science Framework, Grade Twelve—Principles of American Democracy (1994)	15.25
1093	Differentiating the Core Curriculum and Instruction to Provide Advanced Learning Opportunities (1994)	6.50
1045	Discoveries of Infancy: Cognitive Development and Learning (videocassette and guide) (1992)	65.00*
1056	Essential Connections: Ten Keys to Culturally Sensitive Care (videocassette and guide) (1993)	65.00*
1124	Exemplary Program Standards for Child Development Programs Serving Preschool and School-Age Children (Spanish) (1994)	6.00
0751	First Moves: Welcoming a Child to a New Caregiving Setting (videocassette and guide) (1988)	65.00*
0839	Flexible, Fearful, or Feisty: The Different Temperaments of Infants and Toddlers (videocassette and guide) (1990)	65.00*
0809	Getting in Tune: Creating Nurturing Relationships with Infants and Toddlers (videocassette and guide) (1990)	65.00*
1083	Handbook for Teaching Vietnamese-Speaking Students (1994)	5.50†
0737	Here They Come: Ready or Not—Report of the School Readiness Task Force (summary report) (1988)	4.50
0712	History–Social Science Framework for California Public Schools (1988)	7.75
1154	Home Economics Education Career Path Guide and Model Curriculum Standards (1994)	17.00
1140	I Can Learn: A Handbook for Parents, Teachers, and Students (1994)	8.00
1178	Independent Study Operations Manual, 1993 Revised Edition with 1994 Updates (1994)	30.00
1055	Infant/Toddler Caregiving: A Guide to Cognitive Development and Learning (1995)	12.50‡
1057	Infant/Toddler Caregiving: A Guide to Culturally Sensitive Care (1995)	12.50‡
1024	It's Elementary! Elementary Grades Task Force Report (1992)	7.00
0869	It's Not Just Routine: Feeding, Diapering, and Napping Infants and Toddlers (videocassette and guide) (1990)	65.00*
1104	Just Kids: A Practical Guide for Working with Children Prenatally Substance-Exposed (1994)	8.25
1227	Keeping Kids Healthy: Preventing and Managing Communicable Disease in Child Care (1995)	14.00
1155	Kids' Time: A School-Age Care Program Guide (1994)	10.50
1266	Literature for the Visual and Performing Arts, Kindergarten Through Grade Twelve (1996)	9.50
1216	Martin Luther King, Jr., 1929–1968 (1995)	7.00
1183	Meeting the Challenge: A History of Adult Education in California—From the Beginnings to the 1990s (1995)	12.50
1144	Moral, Civic, and Ethical Education Handbook (1995)	9.50
1113	On Alert! Gang Prevention: School In-service Guidelines (1994)	6.50
1137	Organizing a Successful Parent Center: A Guide and Resource (1994)	4.25
0753	Respectfully Yours: Magda Gerber's Approach to Professional Infant/Toddler Care (videocassette and guide) (1988)	65.00*
1191	Safe Schools: A Planning Guide for Action (1995 Edition)	10.75

* Videocassette also available in Chinese (Cantonese) and Spanish at the same price.

† Also available at the same price for students who speak Cantonese, Japanese, Korean, Pilipino, and Portuguese.

‡ Other Infant/Toddler Caregiving guides also available at the same price: Creating Partnerships with Parents (item no. 0878); Language Development and Communication (0880); Routines (0877); Setting Up Environments (0879); and Social-Emotional Growth and Socialization (0876).

Prices are subject to change. Please call 1-800-995-4099 for current prices and shipping charges.

Item no.	Title (Date of publication)	Price
1127	Sampler of History–Social Science Assessment—Elementary, A (Preliminary edition) (1994)	$8.25
1192	Sampler of History–Social Science Assessment: Winter 1994-1995 Addendum, A (1995)	8.25
1125	Sampler of Science Assessment—Elementary, A (Preliminary edition) (1994)	9.00
1246	School Attendance Review Boards Handbook: Operations and Resources (1995)	6.50
0870	Science Framework for California Public Schools (1990)	8.00
1040	Second to None: A Vision of the New California High School (1992)	6.50
0752	Space to Grow: Creating a Child Care Environment for Infants and Toddlers (videocassette and guide) (1988)	65.00*
1134	Teachers' Catalog of Grants, Fellowships, and Awards (1994)	5.50
1044	Together in Care: Meeting the Intimacy Needs of Infants and Toddlers in Groups (videocassette and guide) (1992)	65.00*
1261	Visual and Performing Arts Framework for California Public Schools, Kindergarten Through Grade Twelve (1996)	14.00
1185	Volunteer Programs in California Public Schools (1994)	10.00

* Videocassette also available in Chinese (Cantonese) and Spanish at the same price.

- -

Order Form

Date _____

To: California Department of Education
Bureau of Publications, Sales Unit
P.O. Box 271
Sacramento, CA 95812-0271

Name _____

Address _____

_____
City   State   ZIP code

O Please send me a free copy of the current *Educational Resources Catalog.*

Item number	Title of publication	Number of copies	Price per copy	Total
1256	Project EXCEPTIONAL: A Guide for Training and Recruiting Child Care Providers to Serve Young Children with Disabilities			$

Make checks payable to: California Department of Education

Note: Mail orders must be accompanied by a check, a purchase order, or a VISA or MasterCard credit card number, including expiration date. Purchase orders without checks are accepted from educational institutions, businesses, and governmental agencies. Telephone orders will be accepted toll-free (1-800-995-4099) for credit card purchases. Stated prices are subject to change. Please order carefully; include correct item number and quantity for each publication ordered. *All sales are final.*

Total number of copies [ ]

Total cost of items $ _____

California residents: Please add sales tax. _____

Shipping and handling charges (See chart.) _____

TOTAL AMOUNT $ _____

Shipping and Handling Charges					
Total number of copies	Add	Total number of copies	Add	Total number of copies	Add
1–9	$ 4.95	40–49	$17.95	80–199	$35.95
10–19	7.95	50–59	21.95	200–300	47.95
20–29	10.95	60–69	26.95	300–449	59.95
30–39	13.95	70–79	32.95	450+ call for information	

O Payment enclosed

O VISA   O MasterCard

Card number: _____

Expiration date: _____

Signature: _____
(Must be signed for credit card sale)

96-77586

93-05 003-0101-95 300 5-96 2,500

Prices are subject to change. Please call 1-800-995-4099 for current prices and shipping charges.